ABSOLUTE BEGINNER'S GUIDE

TO

Creating Web Pages,

Second Edition

Todd Stauffer

201 West 103rd Street,
Indianapolis, Indiana 46290

D1275273

Absolute Beginner's Guide to Creating Web Pages, Second Edition

International Standard Book Number: 0-7897-2895-8

Library of Congress Catalog Card Number: 2002113847

Printed in the United States of America

First Printing: November 2002

05   04   03   4   3

Trademarks

Warning and Disclaimer

Associate Publisher
Greg Wiegand

Executive Editor
Candace Hall

Acquisitions Editor
Candace Hall

Development Editor
Sean Medlock

Managing Editor
Thomas Hayes

Project Editor
Tricia Liebig

Copy Editors
Candice Hightower
Sossity Smith

Indexer
Mandie Frank

Proofreaders
Juli Cook
Kellie Cotner

Technical Editor
Lindy Humphreys

Team Coordinator
Cindy Teeters

Interior Designer
Anne Jones

Cover Designer
Anne Jones

Page Layout
Michelle Mitchell

Contents at a Glance

Table of Contents

About the Author

Todd Stauffer is the author or co-author of more than 25 computing books, including *HTML Web Publishing 6-in-1*, *HTML by Example* with Ann Navarro, and *Creating Your Own AOL Web Page* with Andy Shafran. Stauffer has written for a number of magazines, including *Publish* magazine, *Silicon Alley Reporter*, *Working Woman*, and *MacAddict*.

Todd has worked as an advertising writer, technical writer, and magazine editor, all in consumer-oriented computing. Outside of computing, he's also a humor columnist and a travel/automotive writer. You can reach him via his Web site, at `http://www.mac-upgrade.com`.

Acknowledgments

I'd like to thank Todd Green and Dean Miller, who gave me the opportunity to write this book, helped develop the outline, managed submissions, and acted as understanding taskmasters throughout the process. Thanks also to Tricia Liebig, Sean Medlock, and Lindy Humphreys for their hard work on the manuscript.

Sections of this book are updated and adapted from my earlier work, *HTML Web Publishing 6-in-1*, published in 1997 by Que. I'd like to thank the editorial team who worked on that book, including Jane Brownlow, Mark Cierzniak, Kate Givens, and Henry Wolin. The material from that book that survives in this one (a lot has changed in Web publishing, but not everything) was developed and managed by those great folks.

As always, thanks to Neil Salkind and the entire staff of the Studio B agency for keeping me clothed and fed and to Donna Ladd for keeping me going strong.

We Want to Hear from You!

As the reader of this book, you are our most important critic and commentator. We value your opinion and want to know what we're doing right, what we could do better, what areas you'd like to see us publish in, and any other words of wisdom you're willing to pass our way.

As an associate publisher for Que, I welcome your comments. You can email or write me directly to let me know what you did or didn't like about this book—as well as what we can do to make our books better.

Please note that I cannot help you with technical problems related to the topic of this book. We do have a User Services group, however, where I will forward specific technical questions related to the book.

When you write, please be sure to include this book's title and author as well as your name, email address, and phone number. I will carefully review your comments and share them with the author and editors who worked on the book.

Email: `feedback@quepublishing.com`

Mail: Greg Wiegand
       Que
       201 West 103rd Street
       Indianapolis, IN 46290 USA

For more information about this book or another Que title, visit our Web site at www.quepublishing.com. Type the ISBN (excluding hyphens) or the title of a book in the Search field to find the book's page.

INTRODUCTION

The Internet has come a long way. In fact, even if you're only a few months past 10 years old, you've seen the Internet and the World Wide Web grow up to affect nearly every aspect of global culture—education, commerce, politics, and entertainment. It's been a fast change and one that affects most of us either personally, professionally or both.

One of the results has been the need for Web publishing skills for many knowledge workers, educators, and professionals. Hobbyists, club members, and parents can benefit as well from knowing a little something about Web publishing. In fact, Web publishing may one day be the "typing" of the future—nearly anyone with a secondary education will need a firm grasp on the basics.

For now, it's an important bullet point on many résumés as well as the key to many plum assignments, both paid and unpaid. If you're ready to put together and manage your own Web site, then it's time to get a book on the subject and start learning. The *Absolute Beginner's Guide to Creating Web Pages* is the perfect place to start.

Is This The Book for You?

You can divide the study of Web publishing into two approaches—those that focus on the underlying *code-level* technologies and those that teach the broad strokes of Web publishing via graphical Web editors. This book is a friendly guide to the first of these approaches, showing you how to dig into the HTML and XHTML standards to build Web pages, manage Web sites, and augment them with further levels of complexity—style sheets and scripting among them. At the end of this book, you'll understand many of the more complex issues involved in Web publishing, even if you don't have a single Web page to your name.

Let me stress, however, that this book is not for everyone. The *Absolute Beginner's Guide to Creating Web Pages* is designed to take you from basic computer literacy—you understand how to create files and type in Windows, the Macintosh OS, or a variant of Unix—and help you build, manage, and maintain your first Web pages and Web sites. You'll do this by building, chapter by chapter, an understanding of the authoring codes (for creating Web pages), the graphical and multimedia technologies, and eventually the scripting and programming basics necessary for a fully interactive and interesting Web site.

If you're interested in Web publishing skills for use in your company, organization, or education, you should find this book a great place to start. All the principles are outlined, terms are defined, and fundamentals are explained. And that's done without the "cutesy" approach that some other beginner series can devolve into.

But I also want to be honest about the approach. If your goal is a "Web Page in a day," this book isn't for you. Likewise, if you plan to begin your foray into Web publishing using a particular graphical tool, such as Macromedia Dreamweaver, I'd suggest a book that specifically discusses that tool.

I believe that the approach in the *Absolute Beginner's Guide to Creating Web Pages* is the best one, because it's still very important to understand the underlying code of today's Web pages to truly soak up a new skill. Although graphical tools can help, anyone who wants to really understand Web pages and put together entire Web sites should consider the code-level approach that is found in these pages. Fortunately, learning XHTML, style sheets, and the like really isn't all that tough—in my opinion, a pricey Web editor can sometimes just get in your way!

How This Book Is Organized

This book is very much a tutorial. It moves linearly from an introduction and overview of the basic Web publishing concepts, through the fundamentals of creating a Web page, and on to more complex topics. Here's a breakdown:

Part I: Creating Web Pages—In this first section you're introduced to the concepts and terms you'll see throughout the book, including the Internet, the Web, HTML, XHTML, style sheets, JavaScript, and many more. Chapter 2, "A Crash-Course in Web Design," offers a primer on Web design fundamentals and Chapter 3, "What You Need to Get Started," covers the tools you'll need before setting out on your Web authoring adventure (text editors and applications to manipulate graphics). This section ends in Chapter 4, "Creating Your First Page," with the creation of a sample Web page and a template for future pages.

Part II: Design and Conquer—In this second section you learn most of the basics of creating Web pages using XHTML. You begin with basic text and paragraph formatting, including headings, text styles, and special types of paragraph blocks, including bulleted and numbered lists. Chapter 6, "Visual Stimulus—Adding Graphics," introduces you to Web images, including how to add them to pages and what file formats you can use. Chapter 7, "Building Hypertext Links," is all about creating hyperlinks—the technology at the heart of the Web—including links that point to external Web pages and those that point to parts of the current document. Chapter 8, "Basic Tables," introduces you to XHTML tables, which can be used, as discussed in Chapter 9, "Advanced Table Elements and Table Design," for formatting entire pages. Chapter 10, "Get Splashy: Style Sheets, Fonts, and Special Characters," discusses style sheets: the "modern" way to change the appearance of text, alter margins, and otherwise control the look of your Web pages. Chapter 11, "Advanced Web Images and Imagemaps," finishes out the section with an in-depth look at Web images, including how to optimize them for use in your pages.

Part III: Building Your Site—Part III moves on to some of the Web-building technologies that can be applied to an entire Web site—a collection of individual pages that work together. Chapter 12, "Creating Sites with HTML Frames," begins with XHTML Frames, which enable you to split a Web browser window into different frames so that more than one Web page can be displayed at once. Frames are a great way to quickly create an "interface" for viewing many different Web documents. Chapter 13, "Adding Multimedia and Java Content," discusses multimedia content—

movies, animations, and audio—along with Java technology, which actually enables you to place small computer programs on a Web page with which your users can interact. Chapter 14, "Site-Wide Styles: Design, Accessibility, and Internationalization," finishes this section with a look at how you can use the style sheet specifications to select and alter the look of all the documents that comprise your Web site.

Part IV: Interacting with Your Users—In this section you learn some of the technologies you can use on the Web to receive input from your users and respond to that input. Chapter 15, "Adding HTML Forms," begins with a primer on XHTML forms, which enable you to add entry boxes, checkboxes, menus, and other controls to your Web documents. Chapter 16, "CGIs and Data Gathering," introduces you to CGI programming, which is often used in conjunction with XHTML forms to respond to user input via forms. Chapter 17, "Forums, Chats, and Other Add-Ons," focuses on enhancements for your Web server—specifically, scripts and other programs you can use to add page counters, interactive forums, and chat rooms.

On the Web

When you are finished reading this book, you can find several additional chapters online to take you even further by teaching you about more advanced subjects. You can find the chapters by navigating to the Que Web site, http://www.quepublishing.com/, and going to this book's Web page, which you can get to by typing the ISBN (0789728958) into the Search field. You'll find a link to download the chapter files when you get to the book page.

"Introduction to JavaScript" and "JavaScript and User Input" pick up where the book leaves off, discussing how to use JavaScript to provide lots of good interactive options for users visiting your Web sites. "Adding Dynamic HTML Elements" covers some topics that are often called "dynamic HTML" or DHTML, because they combine JavaScript and style sheets to make the appearance of Web pages seem to change in response to choices that the user makes.

A couple more chapters focus on software and services you can use to extend your Web publishing experience. "Graphical Editors" covers some popular graphical Web-authoring packages, such as Macromedia Dreamweaver and Microsoft FrontPage. "Web Publishing Services" takes a look at some different Web server solutions, including free Web servers and companies that offer e-commerce solutions.

Conventions Used in This Book

As you're reading you'll notice that a few different elements are used within the body of the text to break things up and to offer some additional information. Those items include

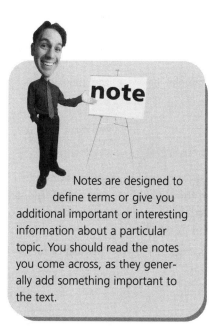

note

Notes are designed to define terms or give you additional important or interesting information about a particular topic. You should read the notes you come across, as they generally add something important to the text.

tip

A tip is usually a suggestion or shortcut that's along the same lines as the body text, but a little off topic. If you find the tip useful, you can make use of it in your Web authoring; otherwise, it should be safe to ignore.

Pay close attention when you see the Stop sign, because this alerts you to potential problems that might cause hours of wasted effort if you don't heed the warning and read how to handle it.

You'll also find sidebars in some chapters that go off on an interesting tangent, generally to simply offer more information than you really *need* on a given topic. If you want to ignore sidebars, you should be able to without trouble.

As you read the text, you'll come across some typographic conventions as well. When certain elements and attributes, particularly those that are special parts of the XHTML specification, are mentioned in the text, they'll appear in a `different font`, from the regular body text. Items that you're meant to type, on the other hand, will often appear in **bold**. And code listings that require more than one line will be:

```
separated from the text.
And will often appear in small chunks between the paragraphs
that explain that code.
```

For More Information

To ask a question, report an error, or for more information on the this book, visit `http://www.mac-upgrade.com/abgwp/` on the Web. There you'll find updates from me, Q&As (if I receive any questions), and links to my email address and online forums for asking questions or making comments.

Thank you for considering this book and I wish you the best of luck—and skill—in your Web publishing projects!

PART

i

CREATING WEB PAGES

- The basics of how the Web works, including the protocols and acronyms you see throughout this book

- The present and future of HTML and XHTML, including exactly what you need to learn

- The fact that HTML isn't as difficult as programming and, in fact, is surprisingly easy to learn

- Although HTML isn't programming, Web publishing does offer other levels of complexity, which are discussed here and in later sections of this book

1

THE FUNDAMENTALS OF WEB PUBLISHING

The Internet has quickly become so completely integrated into our lives that there's no assessing the full nature of its value. Along with email and other technologies, the World Wide Web is a huge part of the Internet phenomenon. However, those Web pages don't get there by themselves. Knowing something about Web publishing is important for most anyone, particularly those of us with something to create, discuss, share, or sell. If you've ever thought that you'd like to create a Web page, build a Web site, or just know a little something about how this all works, you're ready to learn more about Web publishing.

How the Web Works

The World Wide Web isn't a particular place on the Internet, nor is it a particular computer or something that you can "log into." Instead, the best way to describe the Web is as a *service* on the Internet. Using certain protocols, computers that are designated as *Web server* computers—because they're connected to the Internet and run Web server software—can respond to requests from *client* computers running *Web browser* software.

Every computer on the Internet has an address. When a request comes into a Web server computer from a particular address, it responds by sending the requested file back to that address. When the browser application receives that file, it reacts accordingly, generally by displaying the file as a Web page, image, or multimedia element within the browser's own window. In other cases, the browser might recognize that it can't handle the file, so it hands it off to a *helper* application or saves the file in a designated place on the client computer's hard disk.

During a typical Web surfing session, this back-and-forth communication happens repeatedly for each page—not only do the words need to be downloaded, but so does every image and multimedia feed (sounds, digital movies, and so on). This is possible because both computers are connected to the Internet. They both recognize a protocol for transmitting and receiving commands, and the client computer can recognize the language that's used to re-create and display the Web page in the Web browser application. So, we're dealing with three different protocols or languages here.

The first of these protocols is the Transmission Control Protocol/Internet Protocol, or TCP/IP. This is how computers are connected to one another on the Internet. Each computer is given an address, which is then used to identify the computer and enable it to send commands and data from one place to another. If you have a computer that you plan to use on the Internet, you need to establish a TCP/IP connection for that computer, whether it's via a telephone modem, cable modem, DSL

> **note**
>
> It's easy to confuse the Internet and the Web, but they *are* different. The Internet is the global network of wires, servers, and protocols that enables millions of computers to communicate with one another. The Web is a *service* that's made available over the Internet. It's just one means of accessing information and communicating via the Internet, along with email, Internet chat, file transfer, and others.

connection, or some other means, such as a corporate or institutional network-based connection.

After you have that TCP/IP connection up and running, launch a Web browser application, which uses the Hypertext Transfer Protocol (HTTP) to trade commands and communication. Then, the Web server sends Hypertext Markup Language (HTML) documents to your Web browser, which displays them to you. Let's look at these protocols—HTTP and HTML—more closely.

What Is HTTP?

The Hypertext Transfer Protocol (HTTP) is the underlying protocol that makes it possible for Web browsers and Web servers to communicate. A fairly simple protocol, it isn't terribly interesting to most Web designers because it's used exclusively by the Web browser and Web server computers to communicate. So, you don't necessarily need to know the intimate details of how HTTP works in order to be a Web author. But the basics don't hurt.

The Web browser requests a connection, via an HTTP command, with the Web server computer. If the Web server computer is able to grant the request, the Web browser then requests particular files that it believes are available on that Web server computer. If the files are available, the Web server computer sends them to the Web browser, which can then display the files if it's capable of doing so.

> **note**
>
> All a computer needs to be a *Web server* is an Internet connection and Web server software. In fact, such software is built into most modern operating systems—Windows, the MacOs, and Unix all offer Web servers, sometimes as simpler "Web Sharing" solutions. The Web server sits on the Internet, waiting for *Web browser* applications (Netscape, Internet Explorer, and their ilk) to contact them and ask for documents. The server then responds by sending the document to the address specified by the Web browser.

Note that HTTP isn't the only protocol that's in use on the Internet. There are also protocols designed for transferring files (File Transport Protocol, or FTP) or transferring email messages (Post Office Protocol, Simple Mail Transport Protocol), among others. In fact, there are even variations on HTTP, such as Secure HTTP (SHTTP), which uses an encrypted, or coded, communication between the Web browser and server to transmit and receive secure information, such as Web commerce information and credit card numbers.

But the protocol tends to work behind the scenes. Indeed, the only place where you really need to worry about the protocol you're using is when you're creating hyperlinks, as discussed a little later in this section. (You also dig a little deeper into HTTP when you're creating HTML forms, discussed in Chapters 15, "Adding HTML Forms" and 16, "CGIs and Data Gathering.")

What Is HTML?

The Hypertext Markup Language (HTML) is a series of standard codes and conventions designed to create pages and emphasize text for display in programs such as those found in Web browsers. Using HTML, you can create a Web page that includes formatted text and commands that cause the Web browser to load and display images or other multimedia elements (movies, sounds, and animations) on that page.

HTML's name gives you a hint as to what it is—it's a *markup language*, which distinguishes it, primarily, from a programming language. In general terms, HTML is a set of instructions that tells a Web browser how certain text and images should be displayed on the page. In most cases, this is done using commands that dictate the organization of a document. For example, an HTML document might include a command, like the following, that tells the browser that certain text is to be regarded as a heading in the document:

`<h1>Welcome to My Page</h1>`

note

Although newer versions of HTTP are under development, the most common version is HTTP 1.1, which differs from the original in that it enables a connection between a browser and server to stay open longer, resulting in slightly better performance.

A Web page is defined as a single HTML document, regardless of its length. When viewing a single Web page in your browser, you may not have to scroll the page at all, or you may have to scroll through many screens' worth. In either case, you're viewing just one Web page.

The `<h1>` and `</h1>` surrounding the heading text are called *tags*, and they make up the `<h1>` *element*, which tells a Web browser that the text between the tags is a "level one" heading. The browser then knows to treat this text differently than regular paragraph text, or text that is supposed to be a bulleted list.

Likewise, an HTML document can include a command that tells the Web browser to load an image file and place it on the page:

`<img src="image.jpg" />`

This code tells the Web browser to load an image called `image.jpg` and place it on the Web page.

Even the images and multimedia you see on a Web page are part of the markup of HTML. Whereas in a Word document images are embedded as part of the document, an HTML document points to the location of image files, which must be individually available alongside it. Every HTML document is nothing more than a plain text document and no images or multimedia are a part of that HTML document.

So, when a Web browser reads an HTML document, it also reads instructions for loading and positioning any images or multimedia files that you've decided to include. Among those instructions, an HTML document almost invariably includes instructions for creating a *hyperlink*—a link to other HTML documents.

Hypertext and Hyperlinks

One of the keys to HTML—and, by extension, a key to the way the Web works—is its support of *hypertext* links. Using special commands in HTML, a Web author can change certain text to make it "clickable." When the user clicks hypertext, as shown in Figure 1.1, that user's Web browser generally responds by loading a new Web page. (I say "generally" because sometimes clicking hypertext will cause a helper application such as RealAudio or Telnet to appear, or it may cause a file to be downloaded to your hard disk.)

FIGURE 1.1

Hypertext links usually appear on a Web page in a different color and underlined.

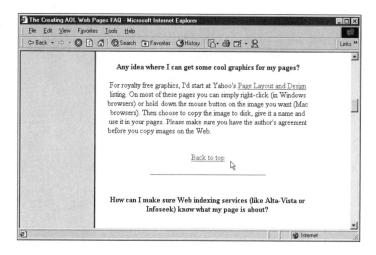

However, not all links are necessarily text—images can also be clickable. In that case, it's more appropriate to call the link a *hyperlink* instead of hypertext, but it's not terribly important. The terms are basically interchangeable.

What's more important is recognizing what a big part hyperlinks play in Web publishing and the World Wide Web. Nearly every page on the Web is in some way linked to every other page. On a smaller scale, hyperlinks make it important for you to consider the organization of your site. They also make it possible for your Web page to take part in a larger world of related pages.

note

How is it possible to link to all these pages? Using HTML markup, you simply create a link that points the Web browser to another address on the Web. Every page on the Web (and most other Internet resources) has a special address that uniquely identifies it, enabling the Web browser to specifically request that page. Those addresses are called Uniform Resource Locators (URLs).

This book is much easier to read if you say "URL" like the name "Earl" instead of "You-are-ell."

Uniform Resource Locators

Most Internet services have some sort of addressing scheme so you can find a particular resource easily. For each service, the format of these addresses tends to be a bit different.

For example, you would send an email message to my America Online account using the address `tstauffer@aol.com` in an email application. On the other hand, to access the AOL public FTP site (where you might download the AOL software application), you would enter the following address in your FTP application: `ftp.aol.com`.

Web browsers are capable of accessing many different types of Internet services, and the Web is about accessing individual documents. So, the URL is a combination of addresses, such as `ftp.aol.com`, and some additional elements that allow you to specify the type of Internet service and the particular document you'd like to retrieve. That way, URLs can be used to access, by address, most any document or service that's accessible via a Web browser. An URL follows the format:

```
protocol://internet_address/path/filename.ext
```

or
```
protocol:internet_address
```

Here's an example of an URL to access a Web document:
```
http://www.microsoft.com/windows/index.html
```

Look at this address carefully. According to the format for an URL, `http://` is the protocol and `www.microsoft.com` is the address of Microsoft's Web server computer. That's followed by a slash (/) to suggest that a path statement is coming next.

The path statement tells you that you're looking at the document `index.html`, located in the directory windows.

The two basic advantages to URLs are:

■ First, they enable you to indicate explicitly the type of Internet service involved. HTTP, for example, indicates the Hypertext Transfer Protocol. However, a URL could easily include a different protocol. You'll look at this part of the URL in a moment.

■ Second, the URL system of addressing gives every single document, program, and file on the Internet its own unique address.

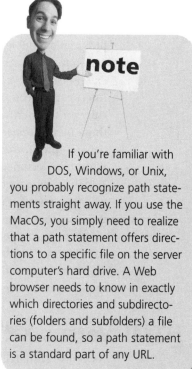

note

If you're familiar with DOS, Windows, or Unix, you probably recognize path statements straight away. If you use the MacOs, you simply need to realize that a path statement offers directions to a specific file on the server computer's hard drive. A Web browser needs to know in exactly which directories and subdirectories (folders and subfolders) a file can be found, so a path statement is a standard part of any URL.

The Different Protocols for URLs

HTTP is the protocol most often used by Web browsers to access HTML pages. Table 1.1 shows some of the other protocols that can be part of an URL.

TABLE 1.1   Possible Protocols for a URL

Protocol	Enables Access to...
`http://`	HTTP (Web) servers
`https://`	Some secure HTTP (Web) servers
`file://`	HTML documents on your hard drive
`ftp://`	FTP servers and files
`gopher://`	Gopher menus and documents
`news://`	A Usenet newsgroup server
`news:`	A particular Usenet newsgroup
`mailto:`	An email message addressed to a particular email address
`telnet:`	A Remote Telnet (login) server

By entering one of these protocols, followed by an Internet server address and a path statement, you can access nearly any document, directory, file, or program available on the Internet or on your own hard drive. As you can see in Table 1.1, URLs extend beyond Web servers to other types of Internet protocols. FTP servers are used specifically for transferring files (as opposed to viewing those files). Gopher servers were the (largely defunct) precursors of Web servers that made plain-text documents available for retrieval. A Telnet server is used for remote login connections, where you enter a username and password, and then use command-line syntax to accomplish things on the server computer. Most Web browsers can display FTP site listings and Gopher menus, and some can send email messages, but most require a helper application for Telnet access.

The `mailto:`, `news:`, and `telnet:` protocols have slightly different requirements for creating an URL. `mailto:` is followed by a simple email address, `news:` is followed by just the newsgroup name, and `telnet:` is followed by just a server address (no path statement).

HTML Versus XHTML

As you've seen, HTML is a markup language designed to combine text, multimedia, and hyperlinks to create a Web page. HTML is also a moving target, though, because several different versions have been introduced since it first appeared in the early 1990s. Although each version has built upon the last, and most Web browsers are designed to be "backward-compatible" with previous versions, it's important to know something about current and future versions of HTML.

Who Sets HTML Standards?

The World Wide Web Consortium (http://www.w3.org) is responsible for creating the specifications that other companies adhere to (for the most part) when creating such things as Web browser applications and devices for viewing Web pages. The W3C is an industry group, founded by Tim Berners-Lee, that includes most of the major players in the corporate world of Web development (such as Microsoft, Netscape, AOL, and AT&T).

One of the tasks the W3C undertakes is maintaining the HTML specification. Because technology is always changing, the W3C constantly works on new versions of the HTML standard. Every so often, it publishes *working drafts* that attempt to codify the advances in technology and capabilities of HTML and the Web, while keeping in mind the needs of the majority of Web browsers and users. (For instance, the W3C might reject or alter an element that one of the browser companies invents because it only works in visual Web browsers, leaving out users of text-based browsers or browsers for the visually impaired.)

After a working draft has been published and is bandied about by peers and the public for a while, it becomes final and is published as the official *recommendation*. Then, Web browsers and authoring tools implement the parts of the *recommendation* that they haven't already (by the time the specification is official, most companies have rolled in the majority of the new elements discussed at the recommendation stage) and then release new versions of their products. While browser companies aren't forced to follow the specification set by the W3C, failing to do so means the pages created by Web authors may be incompatible in different browser versions. So, most of the browser companies attempt to keep up with the standards.

The HTML specification has gone through this updating process many times, through various versions, from an HTML 1.0 standard to the most recent HTML 4.01 standard (finished in 1999). Since then, HTML development has been focused on making HTML's core elements compatible with XML (eXtensible Markup Language), a newer standard that is designed to be a foundation for many other markup languages. XML can be used to create and define markup languages that are specific to certain applications, industries, and so on. Because of the power of XML, one of the W3C's recent goals has been to *recast*, or rewrite, HTML in XML so that the standards are compatible. At the same time, it's done everything it could to keep the new HTML as similar to the old HTML as possible, so as not to introduce too many compatibility problems.

Why a New Standard?

The result of this recasting of HTML is called XHTML. While it may seem that changing the name to XHTML would mean it's a really big deal, the truth is the current version, XHTML 1.0, is only slightly different than its predecessor, HTML 4.01. XHTML does have a few differences, but mostly it's just a bit more strict than HTML has been in the past, requiring that authors be more diligent in the way they implement their Web pages. Overall, though, it's easy enough to grasp.

Why the new standard? Essentially, as more Web browsers support XML, XHTML will become only one module of many different XML-based markup languages that can be understood and displayed by browsers and other applications. That makes it possible, for example, to create a math-specific markup language to display complex mathematical formulae in pages that are rendered by XML-compliant applications.

Strict adherence to the XHTML standard will also make the future a bit easier to cope with. Already many different types of devices and applications are used to access the Web, from phones and handheld computers to devices used by the physically challenged. XHTML is designed to take all those browsers into account. The better your code conforms to the standard, the better it will render in a variety of circumstances.

Which Should You Use?

It may seem obvious that you should use the latest standard, XHTML 1.0, but it actually isn't *quite* that simple. The problem is, even within the XHTML 1.0 standard, there are two basic approaches: a *strict* approach and a *transitional* approach. While using strict XHTML would seem ideal, doing so can have an unintended drawback—it can fail to work in older Web browser applications. Although the vast majority of computer users upgrade their Web browsers fairly regularly, there are still quite a few older computers out there, with older browsers that may not recognize all the changes XHTML requires.

So, you have to decide if you'll work with strict XHTML or transitional XHTML. In fact, you have to declare one or the other within your Web document, as discussed in Chapter 4, "Creating Your First Page." Throughout this book, you'll focus on the strict XHTML commands and settings. However, under some circumstances I'll also show you the transitional options, when they differ. That way, you can opt to use a transitional approach to XHTML, which simply includes more of the older commands and properties, while knowing the difference between the two.

Neither the strict approach nor the transitional approach is right or wrong. Eventually (we're talking years), the strict approach will be more completely supported by Web browsers and recommended more stringently, so that non-graphical Web browsers and other devices can access your data. For the immediate future, however, using the transitional elements and properties is perfectly acceptable.

HTML Is Not Programming

You might be a little intimidated by all these acronyms, abbreviations, and specifications-speak. Don't be. Heck, I had to look most of that stuff up as I was writing this, just to make sure I was up-to-date! In most cases, HTML and XHTML concepts are surprisingly simple after you have the basic sense of the way the markup works.

It may be comforting to keep repeating to yourself that HTML isn't anywhere near as complex as programming. Whereas *programming* is the process of creating scripts or applications using complicated computer languages such as C++ or Java, creating Web pages is generally referred to as *authoring*. That's because most of what you're doing is simply entering text, and then adding codes in and around that text to organize it on the page. From there, you add elements that cause images or multimedia to appear on the page, or elements that make the page look better. That's what a good portion of this book deals with and it's all you need to know to put together informative, organized Web pages.

Beyond basic XHTML markup, two other Web publishing concepts are discussed in this book. The first concept is *style sheets*, which make Web pages look pretty (or at least different), with a variety of sizes, fonts, colors, and so on. The second concept is *scripting*, which actually *is* programming, but on a smaller scale and used in tandem with XHTML markup and style sheets.

Markup Fundamentals

While scripting and style sheets can get a little involved, the markup itself is pretty straightforward. Essentially, you type text on a page, and then you add elements to the page to organize it. HTML and XHTML have only two basic types of elements—empty elements and non-empty elements.

Empty elements do something on their own—they add a line to the page, add an image to the page, or cause a multimedia file to be loaded and displayed. One example is a simple element that's used to create a horizontal line on the page:

```
<hr />
```

Non-empty elements, also called *containers*, are used to do something to the text that they surround. For example, if you wanted to strongly emphasize certain text on the page, you could do so with strong tags surrounding the text:

```
This is a <strong>very</strong> important
point.
```

Notice the slash. In both HTML and XHTML, the slash is used to indicate the closing tag of a non-empty element, such as the strong element. In XHTML, it's also important to put that closing slash in an empty element, such as the horizontal rule tag shown earlier. In older HTML implementations, the trailing slash wasn't necessary.

note

The trailing slash in an empty element is often added with a space for readability, such as **<hr />**. The space isn't required, though, so **<hr/>** would be valid, as well.

HTML and XHTML must be much more complicated than this, right? Otherwise, it's tough to justify the other hundreds of pages in this book. Well, they *are* a bit more complicated, but not so much in theory as in practice. A good deal of getting to know HTML or XHTML is understanding the element *attributes*, which are simply used to fine-tune the way a particular element appears or acts on the page. For example, consider the basic tag for placing an image on the Web page:

`<img src="image.jpg" />`

The `<img />` portion of the tag is really the complete image element, although it wouldn't be of much use without the `src` (source) attribute that tells the image element what file to locate. Beyond that attribute are others, such as the `alt` (alternative text) attribute that offers text that can be displayed when the image can't be, or the `align` (alignment) attribute that can be used to align the image, as in the following:

`<img src="image.jpg" alt="Welcome to the site" align="top">`

Now you see how elements can get more complicated—they tend to offer a lot of options.

If you're familiar with previous versions of HTML, these lines of code may look slightly different from what you've seen. The examples in this book conform to the syntax guidelines for XHTML coding, which include the following:

■ XML is case-sensitive, so all elements should be lowercase, such as `<p>`, `</p>`, and `<br />`.

■ All elements must have closing tags or trailing slashes, even if they are empty elements, such as `<hr />`.

■ All attributes must have quotes around them, such as `<img src="file.jpg" align="left">`.

Even if you aren't used to the HTML of the past, know that XHTML is easy to read and learn, thanks to these new conventions.

Decorating with Style Sheets

Basic markup elements are the first level of complexity in HTML and XHTML. The second level of complexity, particularly with XHTML, comes from the need to use and understand style sheets. *Style sheets* are how Web pages get some of their personality and, well, style. You'll use style sheets to change the fonts, colors, sizes, and placement and positioning of text and other elements on the Web page.

This is an important distinction. When you're using typical XHTML markup to create a Web page, you're not really altering or determining the exact *appearance* of the text—at least, not in terms of the font faces, sizes, and other such attributes. Instead, XHTML markup is used to categorize and arrange text.

In the past, HTML and HTML extensions (elements supported by browsers, but not endorsed by the W3C) have made it possible to directly alter the appearance of text or other items on the page, using elements such as the <font> element or attributes such as color and various others. Although many such pages (including some I've developed) continue to use those conventions, the transition to XHTML requires that these elements be avoided in favor of style sheets.

When using style sheets, instead of directly altering text or other items on the page, portions of the page are labeled and then compared against a style sheet that the Web browser can use to style the page. The Web browser can also opt *not* to style the page, as in the case of the more limited browsers built into mobile phones and handheld computers. In that case, the style sheets separate the XHTML code from the styling of the page, making it possible for more devices to access the page and organize it correctly, while using as much of the style information as it can.

For instance, a text-only browser built into a mobile phone may be able to display certain text as a heading and other text as a hyperlink, but may not be able to specify Arial as the font family and 14-point as the font size. When you place those style-specific commands in a style sheet, the text-only browser is free to ignore them, while still displaying the page and its organizational elements.

Adding Scripts to the Mix

The third level of complexity for the Web author is scripting. Today's browsers support standard scripting languages, which enable you to do quite a bit to make your Web page less static and more exciting and interactive to the user. The possibilities range from something as simple as a *rollover* effect (when the user points at text in the browser window, it changes the color, size, or some other attribute of the text, as shown in Figure 1.2) to complex applications that can be accessed via a Web browser.

note

Up to Chapter 10, "Get Splashy: Style Sheets, Fonts, and Special Characters," we'll be discussing primarily organizational XHTML markup. In Chapter 10, you'll see how style sheets fit into the mix, as well as more discussion on the difference between style sheets, which are recommended, and direct style markup, which isn't.

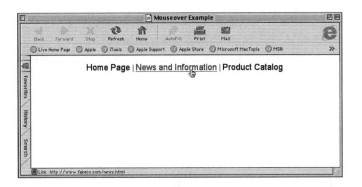

Scripting is indeed programming, but you'll find
that it isn't terribly difficult to grasp, particularly
when you understand the fundamental concepts
behind programming logic. The scripting language JavaScript (and its relatives ECMAScript
and JScript) is a straightforward scripting language that enables you to get started quickly
with useful scripts.

Scripting also works with both XHTML and style
sheets to add interactivity to your pages, bringing
things together in Dynamic HTML or DHTML.
Although XHTML has replaced DHTML as everyone's favorite Web-related acronym, you'll see
that creating dynamic pages can be useful and
entertaining as well.

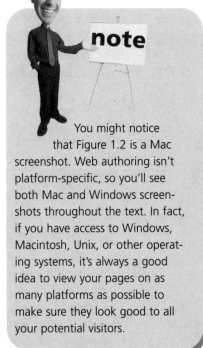

note

You might notice
that Figure 1.2 is a Mac
screenshot. Web authoring isn't
platform-specific, so you'll see
both Mac and Windows screen-
shots throughout the text. In fact,
if you have access to Windows,
Macintosh, Unix, or other operating systems, it's always a good
idea to view your pages on as
many platforms as possible to
make sure they look good to all
your potential visitors.

Summary

This chapter covered a bit of the background that
you need to understand before jumping into Web
publishing. It started with a brief history of the
Internet, and then it discussed the World Wide
Web, including its protocols, its languages, and its
addressing scheme, the URL. HTML and XHTML were defined and discussed, and
you learned that XHTML is the future of Web development and will be the specification taught in this book. XHTML comes in both strict and transitional varieties, with
the transitional version allowing older elements and compatibility with older

browsers. Throughout this book, the emphasis will be on strict XHTML, but transitional elements and markup will be discussed, too.

The chapter concluded with a discussion of the different levels of complexity involved in Web publishing, from the relatively simple—creating and organizing Web pages—to the somewhat more complex—styling the pages and adding scripts and other dynamic elements.

In Chapter 2, "A Crash-Course in Web Design," you'll be introduced to the fundamentals of Web design, including how to organize your page, how to plan pages and sites that work well, and how to use XHTML standards to their fullest to build robust and compatible sites.

2

A CRASH-COURSE IN WEB DESIGN

Chapter 1, "The Fundamentals of Web Publishing," hinted at some of the issues we'll discuss in this chapter, particularly style sheets and their role in HTML markup. There's a definite tug-of-war in the world of Web design, where two different approaches—a visual approach and an organizational approach—have clashed with earlier HTML specifications. XHTML clarifies this considerably, separating organizational and visual design and making it a little easier to develop Web pages that look good while communicating effectively in a wide variety of applications. What that approach means to you, and why you might care, is what you'll read about in this chapter.

The Fundamentals of Page Design

Planning for the Web takes a number of forms, from planning individual pages to planning an entire site made up of pages that you've decided to group together on the Web. Let's begin with a look at the individual page—how a page should look, and how to avoid some common mistakes as you're beginning to create pages. In this section, we'll look at some fundamental tenets of page design for the Web:

- The theory behind XHTML and style sheets
- Organizing the page according to the logic of HTML and XHTML
- Separating content on the page from the design of the page
- The use of images, multimedia, and interactivity to further your Web design goals

At the end of this section, we'll take a look at some sample Web pages and consider their design advantages.

Web Design Theory

HTML was created to help disseminate scientific and academic information over what started off as a government and higher-education project—the Internet. Over time, HTML became the language of many different Web-based tasks, including education, entertainment, and commerce. HTML wasn't really conceived for those tasks, however, particularly when it came to creating highly visual pages. So, developers of Web browsers, such as Netscape and Internet Explorer, added their own non-standard HTML-like commands and cleverly tweaked the HTML specification to create some tricky and attractive-looking pages.

While that was okay with Web designers and Web browser developers, it didn't always sit right with the W3C, which is in charge of maintaining and codifying the Web's standards. Perhaps even more importantly, it didn't fit well with XML, the next generation of markup languages that the entire computing world has shown an interest in.

In the past few years, HTML has been recast as XHTML and returned to its roots of organizing and disseminating information instead of beautifying it. Making pages look good is left to a technology called *style sheets*, as was touched on in Chapter 1. In other words, XHTML once again separates the organization of the page from its appearance, as HTML did originally. So what does this mean for Web authors?

In a nutshell, it means you'll want to consider the *function* of your Web design before you consider its *form*. While it may seem appropriate to figure out what the page will look like before wondering what it will say, that's a notion you'll need to alter slightly. XHTML's primary focus is organizing and communicating information, so that's the best way to approach learning and using XHTML.

However, that's not to say that pages can't be attractive and entertaining. They can be both of those things. But XHTML offers methods that are more correct for accomplishing those entertaining, attractive pages. These methods will also make your page accessible to browsers designed for the physically challenged, non-graphical browsers for handheld devices or mobile phones, or even browsers designed to access the Web using audio only, such as phone-based browsers. With a well-organized, XHTML-compliant page, you should be able to do all of this in a way that's satisfying to your designer's eye.

Organizing Your Page

It's difficult to separate your overall Web site from each individual page—you'll need to consider your Web site's organization before you can finish each page and make it part of the whole. We'll discuss some of that in upcoming sections.

Having said that, there are some basics you should consider for each page you create. Web pages can vary dramatically in the way they organize material, from a basic page with paragraphs and headings to a more complex page that uses a newsletter-style approach. Of course, some pages may have no discernible organization, which is to be avoided whenever possible.

Here are some quick tips:

- **Keep it simple**—While plenty of exciting Web technologies are available—images, sounds, video, and animation—you should only use them if they further the goals of your page's content.

- **Create content-driven designs**—Your page should be primarily designed to focus your user's attention on the content and communicate that content as quickly as possible. This means using subheads, emphasized text, and hyperlinks to help your reader quickly understand the information you're trying to present.

- **Chunk-ify**—Using headings, bulleted lists, and other markup elements, you can take a long page of text and break it into chunks of information that are easier for your visitor to digest. Adding images and dividing lines also make the page easier to read.

- **Balance page length**—Another issue when designing a page is knowing when to quit and move on to another page. Web pages that scroll on forever will often lose the reader's attention, and the page may end up taking a long time to download. On the other hand, pages that are too short can also be annoying to the readers because they have to keep clicking to the next page to keep reading.

To summarize, it's important to remember that your visitors are likely looking for useful pages that offer them important or entertaining information. At the same time, most people don't enjoy reading long passages on a computer screen, so you'll want to break things up along organizational lines with headings, emphasized text, images, and other such elements (see Figure 2.1). Finally, remember that not all your visitors are even using a visual browser. If you stick to conventional organization and XHTML recommendations, you can create an appealing page that always works well on handheld computers and assistive browsers.

FIGURE 2.1

On the left, a solid page of text; on the right, a page broken up with headings and lists.

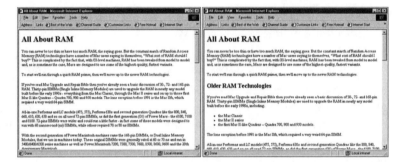

Before you begin creating pages within your site, you should consider how best to present your material. One way to do that is to consider how traditional publications, such as books, newspapers, and magazines, organize information. For instance, this book attempts to keep your interest by organizing pages logically, using subheadings within topics, and breaking things up with images. You can do the same things with a Web site, with the added advantages of hyperlinks and multimedia.

A newsletter or newspaper uses headings, subheads, and sidebars to communicate information, as well as images that are positioned with text wrapping around them. Again, you can accomplish a similar look using XHTML to organize the page for best viewing (see Figure 2.2). Quite a few Web sites use the newsletter approach, including most daily newspapers. For instance, the New York Times (http://www.nytimes.com/) uses such an approach, with hyperlinks that lead you deeper into each story.

FIGURE 2.2

With the newsletter approach, using XHTML table elements, the page is broken up into columns and rows.

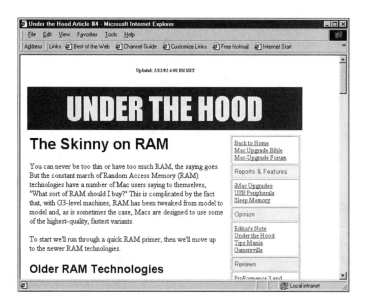

You can even model your Web site after a mail-order catalog. If you're selling products or real estate, you might want to create pages that include pictures, descriptions, prices, and so on. Like a mail-order catalog, you'll want all the pages to be consistent, attractive, and easy for the reader to use. You can do this with a combination of basic XHTML elements, images, and an attention to detail.

Images and Multimedia

Beyond the basics of dividing your pages into chunks of information, you can also use images and multimedia on the Web. While these items shouldn't be used indiscriminately, they can make your Web site much more interesting and useful to the reader.

You'll use two basic types of images—those you create yourself, and existing photos. Images you create yourself can be anything from logos and banner images to charts, graphs, or cartoons that you use to get your point across. Photos can be taken with a digital camera, captured from videotape or DV camcorders, or scanned with a

note

When you *export* an image, you're simply saving it in a new file format. While most Web browsers can't display native Excel charts, they can display images saved in the GIF and JPEG file formats. So, you'll export your chart as a compatible image, using a special command in the application (often it's **File**, **Export**).

scanner. Whatever the approach, images can go a long way toward keeping your readers interested while communicating key information quickly.

USA Today offers a lesson to Web authors—why write out something that can be communicated effectively in a table or chart? If you have such information, you can often create a chart or graph in a program such as Excel, and then export it as a Web-compatible image.

Then, add the image to your Web page and you've instantly made things a bit easier to understand and a touch more convenient for the reader, who can take in the information more quickly. (Figure 2.3 shows a Web page that uses a graphic to communicate information.)

Images are great for catalog sites, classifieds, and even press releases that you create for your company or organization. In fact, the only way you can go wrong is to either use images that don't communicate the right information or use too many images on one page. Avoid extraneous images, which can slow down your page's download in the visitor's Web browser, and you'll be on the right track.

note

There's another problem with some multimedia, which will be expanded on in Chapter 13, "Adding Multimedia and Java Content." To view many multimedia elements, your reader will need additional software. If your reader doesn't have that software, they'll have to go through the additional step of downloading it.

FIGURE 2.3

Using an image can improve a page's appearance and readability by breaking up the text a bit.

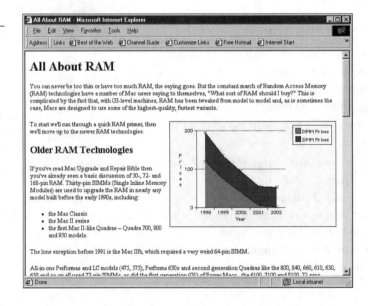

With multimedia, the possibilities are even more exciting, but the problems are manifold. While adding a video, audio clip, or animated short to your page may be fun and entertaining, most multimedia still takes a long time to reach the user's browser.

That means you should only use multimedia when it's absolutely necessary to communicate something useful, or when you make it available as an option. You can allow users with high-bandwidth connections to view the multimedia, without slowing down those using modems or other lower-bandwidth Internet connections.

As you'll see in Chapter 13, there are quite a few decisions you need to make when it comes to using multimedia in your pages, but it's definitely an interesting and exciting option for Web authors. At the same time, multimedia can be a huge stumbling block for slower Web connections, so it's something to be added with care.

Bandwidth refers to the amount of data that can be retrieved or sent via a particular Internet connection at one time. High-bandwidth connections are available in many businesses and homes via DSL, cable modems, and other technologies. However, it's still a growing market, with the majority of users using dial-up modems or other slower connections.

Interactivity and Scripting

You'll find that your Web pages can be used to interact with the user, creating a two-way dialog instead of simply publishing items and making them available for passive consumption. Web pages can be used to receive feedback from users, accept purchase orders, and even enable users to communicate with one another. One way to manage all this is to use XHTML form elements that add menus, buttons, and switches to your Web page. These form elements are similar to parts of other applications you'll find on your computer (dialog boxes for settings, for instance), but can be used on a Web page to accept input of some kind from your visitors (see Figure 2.4).

You can also use a combination of interactive elements (such as menus, buttons, or other application-like selectors) to enable users to navigate your Web site. This adds a level of complexity to your Web authoring, but it can make your Web site easier to use. You can even use some special commands that react to the user pointing at a particular part of the page, for instance, making the page almost seem alive with activity.

FIGURE 2.4

Form elements
are used to inter-
act with the
user.

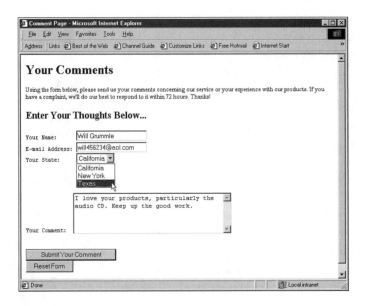

FIGURE 2.4

Form elements are used to interact with the user.

However, the extent of interactivity you choose still hinges on the basic questions of Web design. Do the buttons, menus, and active elements communicate additional information? Do they help the user navigate the page (or Web site) more effectively? And do they add more to the experience than they detract? If they don't, a simpler page design may be the better answer.

What Good Pages Look Like

So what does a good Web page look like? Some of my favorite pages are simple in their presentation, with a focus on the content instead of on images or multimedia. This focus makes it possible for a page to be viewed on any number of Web browsers and other items.

For a representative of this category, you need to look no further than the W3C itself, where the HTML and related specifications are debated and codified. Although the site can be dense with information, it's broken up with boxes, headings, hyperlinks, and paragraphs (see Figure 2.5).

Most Web sites aren't designed to communicate material that's quite as heavy (and, well, dense) as the Web publishing standards, so you'll likely encounter sites that are a bit more lively. CINet's sites tend to do a good job of this, offering straightforward navigation and very clean presentation of story headlines, summaries, and date-lines. Just by glancing at the site, you get a good idea of what material is available and how it's organized. Figure 2.6 shows `http://www.news.com/`, the main technology news site at CINet.

FIGURE 2.5

The W3C's site offers some insight into text-heavy, well-organized pages. (The page shown is http://www.w3.org/MarkUp/.)

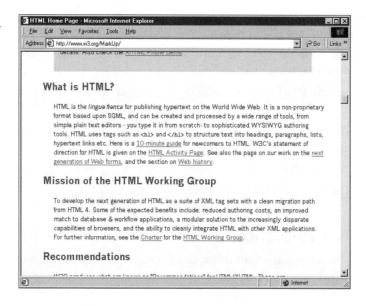

FIGURE 2.6

Note that ClNet's news page does have images, but they're used somewhat sparsely to enhance the text, not overwhelm it.

Planning a Site

You've now seen some of the elements that define a good Web page. But in most cases, what you'll create as a Web author won't be a single page, but an entire site. If that's the case, you'll want to do a little planning before you get too deep into the creative process. How you implement your Web site will affect a number of things, including how you design individual pages, how you save those pages on a Web server, and even how the pages are decorated and beautified—particularly if you rely on style sheets for your site.

In this section, let's look at some of the considerations you need to make when planning your site:

■ Thinking about the audience for your Web site and how that will affect the design

■ Your options for designing and implementing Web sites

■ The elements and ideas that make a good site

Considering Your Audience

Perhaps the most important factor in site design is considering your audience, not only for the topics you'll be covering, but also for the technology and capabilities they're likely to have. You should also consider how voluntary their participation in your site is, and how much they'll put up with before deciding to leave.

Most Internet ventures—such as Webzines, catalogs, and online applications—need to be incredibly well designed, not only visually, but from a site-wide organizational point of view. That's because the audience for these sites is not necessarily a captive one—a user may opt to leave your site very quickly, for any number of reasons. The way to convince your users to stay on your site (aside from compelling content or wonderful prices) is with a straightforward design that doesn't get in the way. You should also do everything you can to make the user comfortable, while doing nothing that makes them wait, confuses them, or irritates them.

Sound like a tall order? Generally, you can satisfy these things by considering a few basic criteria:

■ **Organize your site**—Make it easy for your visitors to find the information they're seeking. For example, if you want users to contact you via the Web, postal mail, or phone, you should have a link that clearly states Contact Information, Address and Phone Info, or something similar. If you put this important information in a section called Other Info or About Our Organization, it may be a bit tougher for the user to find. How you organize your site can dictate other things, such as how difficult it is to use and update.

■ **Focus on navigation**—Hand-in-hand with site organization is site navigation. Put more simply, you need to create hyperlinks to other pages on your

Web site that make sense to the user, and ideally that are always in the same place. Navigation should also be simple to grasp and easy on the eyes.

■ **Stay within technical boundaries**—Don't require your users to have a particular multimedia technology for basic navigation or information gathering. For instance, if you require all your visitors to view a Macromedia Flash animation to see important information on your site, you're cutting out a large chunk of your audience, particularly if your site isn't specifically targeted at high-tech issues or applications. Although a site devoted to movie trailers might require QuickTime, you shouldn't require it on your astronomy discussion site without good reason and/or alternatives.

■ **Remember your target and goals**—If you're aiming your site at a particular group or demographic, you should consider their level of computing expertise and the technology they're likely to use. The more general-interest your site is, the less complicated and more clearly designed it should be. If you're creating a site for Internet gaming, it's probably okay to design the site with bells, whistles, and links everywhere. If you're creating a site about strategy board games, however, you may want a simpler site for newer Internet users who may not have the latest technology.

One of the best sites when it comes to usability, organization, and universal usefulness is Yahoo!. It's a low-requirements site that still offers good organization along with some bells and whistles (see Figure 2.7).

FIGURE 2.7

Yahoo!'s pages organize a great deal of content and are targeted at all sorts of browsers.

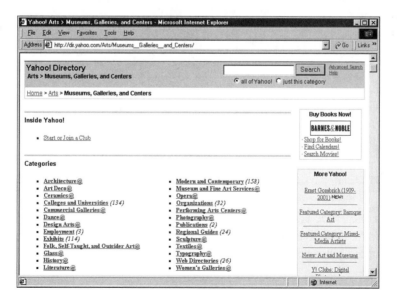

Organizing the Site

Once you have a sense of your audience, the next consideration is how to organize your site. How you do this is up to you, but we can discuss some general guidelines.

For a simple site, the organization will probably be clear. If you have, say, five different pages, you can probably store all of them in the main directory on your Web server, and you can place hyperlinks to each of them on each of the other pages on your site. Let's say you have a real-estate site that includes five pages: the index page, a page of homes for sale, a page about the area, a page about mortgage rates at local banks, and a page about you, the agent. Such a site is easy to organize because you can include links to every one of those pages at the top of all the other pages (see Figure 2.8).

FIGURE 2.8

With this simple approach to organizing your site, you can link to every page.

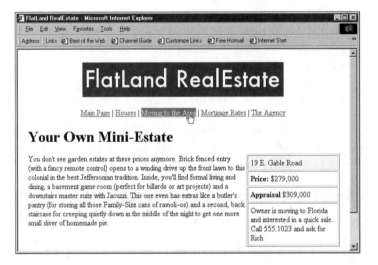

But what if that same page had links to individual pages that discussed each house? There might be 10–15 houses available at a given time, so you couldn't possibly put a link to each house at the top of every page. Instead, links to those houses might only show up a special index page for linking to the house pages.

Now you've made the organization a bit more complex, as it's beginning to look like the chart shown in Figure 2.9.

At this point, you'll need to start making decisions. On one hand, each of the individual house-description pages could have links to all the other house-description pages—but that will become tedious to update. Or, each of the house-description pages could have direct hyperlinks to the contact and mortgage information pages—although that might be confusing to the user.

FIGURE 2.9

As the organiza-
tion becomes
more complex,
so can the inter-
face for users.

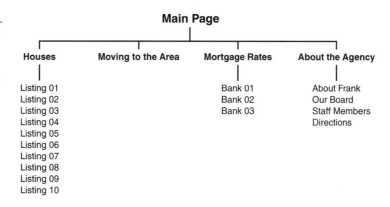

Another solution would be to take the Yahoo! approach and make the path to the current page apparent on the page itself, as shown in Figure 2.10. In fact, note that the page shown is using a hybrid approach—the current path to the page is shown, as well as convenient links at the top of the page. These options, if consistently presented on every page on the site, can make navigation as easy as can be for the user.

FIGURE 2.10

At the top are
standard links
for main sec-
tions of the site;
on the page
itself, links make
the path appar-
ent.

As the site grows even more complicated and the pyramid of pages grows, you'll have to continue to refine this approach. But this is a solid approach, used by sites as large as Yahoo! and About.com. It's worth considering on your own pages.

Design Ease and Consistency

I've harped on consistency quite a bit already, and for good reason—giving your pages a consistent look helps define them as a cohesive Web site, and a consistent approach to the site's interface makes it easy to navigate. If you don't have these things, you risk alienating the user.

Beyond the organization of your site, there are two areas where consistency pays off. First, the interface that's used to navigate the pages should be consistent. For most sites, that means having basic, text-based navigation hyperlinks that appear on every page, even if some pages also use images or multimedia for navigation.

Second, a consistent look is something that's even easier to manage when you use style sheets with your XHTML pages. Style sheets, discussed in Chapter 10, "Get Splashy: Style Sheets, Fonts, and Special Characters," and Chapter 14, "Site-Wide Styles: Design, Accessibility, and Internationalization," allow you to define the font family, text color, and many different attributes of text, paragraphs, and other elements on your page. They're a strength when it comes to consistency because you can define a single style sheet for an entire Web site. This is a simple way to choose the look of all your pages at once, while adhering to XHTML standards and making your pages available in a variety of situations and mediums. As you're creating pages and designing sites over the next few chapters, keep in mind that you'll be able to give your sites a unique look using style sheets, which are discussed in Chapter 10.

HTML Trends and Issues

I've mentioned that one of the reasons for creating XHTML was to enable compliant Web sites to better support a disparate audience of Web browsing applications and devices. That's one of the trends that XHTML development has been moving toward. Combined with broader support for style sheets in Web browsers, the newer standards make it easy for Web sites to communicate with many different types of devices, and look good on them, too. That includes assistive browsers, handheld computers, and even browsers designed to speak content aloud and accept voice commands from the user.

Beyond simply adhering to these standards, you'll find that making your Web pages broadly available will require you to take advantage of all the tools at your disposal. In a sense, creating accessible and widely useful Web sites is a mindset, because it means taking advantage of some additional attributes and doing a little extra work to support browsers other than Internet Explorer and Netscape. Let's take a quick look at some of these issues.

Accessibility

The latest XHTML standards give you a number of ways to offer support for Web browsers that assist site-impaired and other special-needs users. For instance, an image element can include alternative text that can be displayed instead of the image. (This is discussed further in Chapter 6, "Visual Stimulus—Adding Graphics.") This text can be used on non-graphical browsers to explain what the images show. In certain cases, you can even create a hyperlink to a longer, text-only description of the image that might be useful for blind visitors with Web browsers that speak text aloud or make text available in Braille.

Other elements offer assistive features as well. For instance, the elements used to create HTML forms pages—those that enable you to choose from menu items, radio buttons, and entry boxes—now offer increased assistive features. This makes it easier for visitors with assistive browsers to use your sites.

The most important factor in making your pages available to a wide audience, however, is to design them as simply and logically as possible. That means using headings, paragraphs, bulleted lists, and other elements with more emphasis on the content of the page than on its look. For instance, even pages that use simple XHTML table elements for design purposes can be difficult to interpret on non-graphical Web browsers. A more simply organized page, using headings and paragraph text, can be viewed on a variety of Web-enabled devices.

Internationalization

XHTML offers some elements and attributes that make it a little easier to publish flexible pages for a worldwide audience. For instance, a number of elements can accept the `lang` attribute, which enables you to specify the language being used for a particular element. This language attribute can be reinterpreted by the browser, or displayed differently if desired. This attribute, along with the `<q>` element (which can be used to display quoted text in different international formats), is discussed in Chapter 5, "Formatting Your Text."

Another aspect of internationalization is the use of automatic translation software to make your page readable in other languages. In general, this software is most effective on the simplest pages. If you'd like others to be able to translate and read your pages, you should endeavor to use the clearest language possible. Stick to the simplest words and grammar, and avoid colloquialisms, metaphors, and cliches. (For instance, "He's a bear on the ballfield" won't translate out of English all that well, while "He is a good player" will.) You might even offer special simplified pages for the cleanest international translations, if you feel it's appropriate. Some sites that offer these translation capabilities include

- **Google.com**—See `http://www.google.com/help/faq_translation.html` for details.
- **AltaVista.com**—Offers the BabelFish service at `http://babelfish.altavista.com/`.
- **FreeTranslation.com**—Another site that will translate nearly any page is at `http://www.freetranslation.com/default.htm?tab=web`.

Browser Compatibility

Finally, browser compatibility has been a constant challenge and sometimes a source of frustration. Different browsers will sometimes interpret commands differently, or may offer their own elements in place of those that are part of the XHTML standard. While this problem has gotten better as browsers have incorporated more of the official standards, sometimes you still need to add two different elements that do the same thing to support different browsers. You should also make a habit of testing your pages in different browsers to see the differences. Using style sheets and other tricks can eliminate some of the problems, but it's an issue to keep an eye on. It'll be discussed throughout the book.

Summary

In this chapter you were introduced to the basic principles of Web page and site design, including some of the fundamental tenets. The simpler your page and the simpler the system for navigating your Web site, the more accessible your Web site will be to readers. This includes organizing each individual page, organizing entire sites, and considering how your design approach can affect all your users, including those who are using non-graphical browsers or who want to translate your page into spoken text, Braille, or another written language. You also saw some examples of good sites and got some suggestions for other sites to emulate.

In the next chapter, you'll be introduced to the tools you need to create Web documents, and you'll see how to publish those documents on the Web.

IN THIS CHAPTER

- Different types of editors for creating Web pages
- Tools for graphics, animation, and scripting
- How Web server space works
- Obtaining Web server space and uploading files to that space

3

WHAT YOU NEED TO GET STARTED

Web publishing doesn't require expensive or complicated tools. In fact, you'll find that you can get away with using just a simple text editor, like those that come with Windows, Unix, or the MacOs. In addition, you can find useful downloadable shareware applications to help you with HTML, graphic images, and multimedia. Beyond the basic tools, you also need to look into Internet services if you plan to make your Web pages available on the Internet.

The Basic Tools

As discussed in Chapter 1, "The Fundamentals of Web Publishing," HTML documents are nothing more than plain-text documents with markup commands that instruct a Web browser to arrange and format text in certain ways. Other commands are used to add images, hypertext, and multimedia to the page, but those commands are still plain-text commands that are interpreted by the Web browser.

The plain-text nature of HTML documents means that all you really need to hand-code HTML is a text editor application. It can be something as simple and friendly as Windows Notepad (see Figure 3.1) or the Mac's SimpleText editor. You have similar choices in other operating systems—vi or emacs in any Unix and Unix-like OS, and TextEdit in MacOs X.

FIGURE 3.1

HTML pages can be edited in simple text editors such as Windows Notepad.

The main issue to remember is that your documents need to be saved as plain-text or ASCII documents, so your text editing application must be capable of saving such documents (as opposed to, say, Microsoft Word format or Rich Text Format). You can use a word processing application to create your HTML documents, as long as you save the documents as plain-text.

If you do opt to use a word processor (which I don't really recommend), note that many of them have the specific option of saving files as HTML documents. Generally, you *don't* want to do that because the word processor translates the page, as typed, into HTML, adding markup to maintain the appearance of the document in your word processor. In other words, it ignores the HTML markup that you've entered yourself and adds markup so that the page appears with the tags intact when displayed in a browser (see Figure 3.2).

ASCII stands for *American Standard Code for Information Interchange*, a standard method for representing English letters and numbers in computing. The most universal format for text documents on computing platforms, it's the basis of many files being read by different sorts of computers, such as HTML documents.

FIGURE 3.2

If you use a word processor for your pages, save them as text, not as HTML. Otherwise, your element tags appear when the page is viewed in a Web browser.

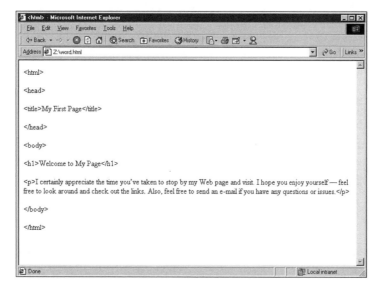

Instead, you should save the document as plain-text, text, or ASCII text, but with the filename extension .htm or .html (more on that later).

Ideally, though, you'd use either a text editor—which can be very basic or rather specialized—or an HTML editor that enables you to edit the HTML *source code* (the text and markup) directly. Let's look at each possibility.

Text Editors

As noted, you can opt to use the simple text editors included with your operating system. In Microsoft Windows, it's Notepad; in the MacOs it's SimpleText or TextEdit. Unix and Linux systems offer a number of text editors, from basic to sophisticated.

If you'd like to move up to the next level, however, you'll find that a good programmer's text editor may be helpful in creating and organizing your HTML code. Popular editors for Microsoft Windows include TextPad (www.textpad.com), UltraEdit (www.ultraedit.com, shown in Figure 3.3) and EditPlus (www.editplus.com),

note

Where do you find these programs? Throughout the next few sections, you'll see the Web sites associated with the individual editors that are recommended. But if you'd like to do a little surfing on your own, try www.download.com/, which offers links to the vast majority of shareware, freeware, and demonstration applications available for all the different computing platforms.

among many others. The Macintosh has fewer text editors, although BBEdit and BBEdit Lite (www.barebones.com) are very highly regarded, for both MacOs 9 and MacOs X. (MacOs X also includes Unix-style text editors via its Terminal application.)

FIGURE 3.3

In UltraEdit you can manage multiple text files, see HTML codes in special colors, and access a quick reference panel of HTML elements.

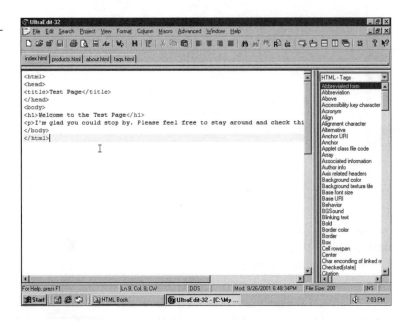

Most text editors you come across are designed to work well for HTML authoring, as well as other types of markup and programming. You'll find that some of them automatically recognize markup as such, turning them into different colors for easy viewing. Others may offer a toolbar button for displaying an HTML document in a Web browser (to test how it looks and whether hyperlinks are working correctly), a spell-checking feature, or other interesting options. Experiment a bit to find a text editor that really works well for you.

HTML Editors

The other type of editor you might consider downloading or purchasing is one that's specifically designed for HTML documents. These editors come in two basic flavors—*source code editors* and *WYSIWYG editors*. WYSIWYG, which stands for "What You See Is What You Get," means you're editing the Web page as it will look in a Web browser. In this case, you're not marking up text and adding HTML commands and elements, but rather typing text, importing images, and moving items around on the page, much as you'd do in a word processing or desktop publishing program.

Because *Absolute Beginner's Guide to Creating Web Pages* focuses on editing XHTML source code (the raw text and markup elements), WYSIWYG editors are not discussed in the book itself, but you can go onlineto find "Graphical Editors," a chapter that will introduce you to some of the more popular graphical editors, such as Dreamweaver and FrontPage. (See the Introduction of this book for details.) You'll find that a WYSIWYG editor is a great tool to have on hand for prototyping and editing Web sites. That said, it's important to learn the raw XHTML first, particularly if you aspire to do Web publishing professionally, because no WYSIWYG editor is perfect. They can't always adhere to the latest standards, they aren't all capable of more complex tasks (such as scripting or interactive elements), and sometimes you need to "dig into the code" to get them to work exactly as you'd like them to. If you want to go beyond a text editor, you might look into one that's specifically designed to help you edit HTML source code. For Microsoft Windows, some recommended editors include HotDog Professional and HotDog PageWiz (www.sausagetools.com), HandyHTML (www.silveragesoftware.com), and CoffeeCup HTML Editor (www.coffeecup.com). For Macintosh, popular options include PageSpinner (www.optima-system.com) and WebDesign (www.ragesw.com). The latter is shown in Figure 3.4.

FIGURE 3.4

WebDesign is a Mac HTML editor that makes it easy to edit HTML source code.

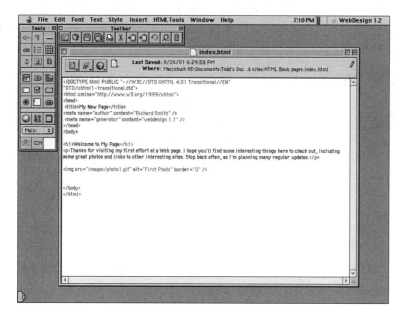

If you need to watch out for anything with HTML editors, it's that they're up-to-date and support the level of HTML (or XHTML) that you want to use for your authoring. For the purposes of this book, you should use an editor that supports HTML 4.01 Transitional or XHTML 1.0 Transitional, if it's an option. (If you're trying to create strict documents, you can use XHTML 1.0 Strict if the editor supports it). Older HTML editors may support an older standard, or may recommend elements or markup that don't conform to the newer standard. You can probably still use them; just be aware of the differences.

Other Tools You'll Want

Beyond editors to help you create your HTML documents, the Web author's arsenal isn't complete without some other tools. In particular, you definitely need a good image editing application on hand to help you convert and tweak the images that you plan to use on your Web pages. As you dig deeper into Web authoring, you may also find you'd like to work with other applications that enable you to create animated content and multimedia content, as well as other tools that simply make being a Web author easier.

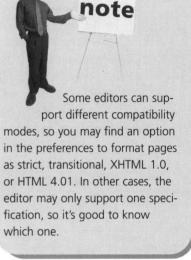

Some editors can support different compatibility modes, so you may find an option in the preferences to format pages as strict, transitional, XHTML 1.0, or HTML 4.01. In other cases, the editor may only support one specification, so it's good to know which one.

Graphics Editors

If you plan to put images on your Web pages—and I bet you do—you need a decent application for translating, cropping, resizing, and otherwise tweaking your images. Of course, your options include some wonderful and expensive commercial applications, such as Adobe Photoshop and Macromedia Fireworks. If you don't have such applications, however, you might opt instead for downloadable shareware options. Two of the most popular for Microsoft Windows are Paint Shop Pro (www.jasc.com/) and LView Pro (www.lview.com/). For Macintosh, the standard-bearer is GraphicConverter (www.lemkesoft.com/). For Linux and other open source operating systems, it's the Gnu Image Manipulation Program or GIMP (www.gimp.org).

Whichever graphics application you opt to use, you want to be able to perform at least a few basic tasks:

- Creating images using shapes and text.
- Cropping and resizing images.
- Changing the number of colors used to render the image.
- Saving images in JPEG, GIF, or PNG formats.
- Working with the special features of the various graphics file formats, such as transparent GIFs and progressive JPEGs.

These things are discussed in much more detail in Chapters 6, "Visual Stimulus—Adding Graphics," and 11, "Advanced Web Images and Imagemaps." For now, bear in mind that you might want to shop around (either on the Web or in the computer store) for a graphics editing application.

Animation Tools

Web animation comes in a few different forms. One way to animate images on a Web page is to use the animated GIF specification, which is less interactive (it doesn't respond to user input such as mouse clicks) but common for animated images such as online advertisements.

You'll find a few animated GIF applications available as freeware or shareware, although some animation tools—particularly those designed for creating Web advertisements—tend to be a bit more expensive than shareware image-editing applications. Try Ulead GIF Animator (www.ulead.com) and Animagic GIF Animator (www.rtlsoft.com/animagic/index.html) for Microsoft Windows. For Macintosh, try GifBuilder (homepage.mac.com/piguet/gif.html) or VSE Animation Maker (vse-online.com/animation-maker/index.html).

Up one step from animated GIFs are Macromedia Flash animations. Flash is very popular, in part because it allows for interactivity. Viewers of a Flash animation can click controls to make choices within the animation, altering what they see next. This is popular with car manufacturers, Web application businesses, and many others who want to show products or ideas in a multimedia presentation.

Aside from Macromedia's own Flash application (www.macromedia.com/flash/), which retails for several hundred dollars, other Flash tools include CoffeeCup Firestarter (www.coffeecup.com/) for Microsoft Windows and ez-Motion (www.beatware.com/) for Macintosh. Chapter 13, "Adding Multimedia and Java Content," discusses Flash in more detail.

Multimedia Tools

Editors and image applications are the basic tools in the Web author's arsenal, but you may want to go beyond those basics if your focus is on multimedia content. You may find yourself creating movies using QuickTime, Windows Media, or other multimedia formats. Or, you may find yourself creating and editing sound files for your Web site—anything from basic background sounds using the MIDI standard (for computer-synthesized playback of songs) to the MP3 standard for CD-like recorded audio playback.

If that's the case, you want to shop around for applications that enable you to create and edit such media. Before venturing too far afield, however, be aware that such tools may come bundled with Microsoft Windows and the Macintosh OS, depending on the version of the operating system with which you're working. Microsoft Windows Me and later versions include Windows Movie Maker, which enables you to edit video recorded on a *DV-compatible* camcorder. You can then turn that video into Windows Media or a similar format that can be displayed via the Web. Similarly, many Macintosh models include iMovie, which offers simple editing of DV video and exporting to the QuickTime movie format. QuickTime Pro is available for both Windows and Macintosh users, offering some simple tools for editing and translating movie files into QuickTime format for display on the Web.

Likewise, many different applications are available for editing and translating sound files into one of many Web-compatible sound formats. Such applications include Sound Forge XP (www.sonicfoundry.com) for Microsoft Windows and

note

DV stands for *Digital Video*, a file format for video images that are recorded using DV-compatible camcorders (often on MiniDV cassettes). The video is easy to edit using a computer application such as Movie Maker or Apple's iMovie. DV is quickly becoming a popular competitor for VHS camcorders.

Sound Studio (www.felttip.com/) for Macintosh. iTunes, included with most Macs, is also capable of creating MP3 and other sound files, and the QuickTime Pro player can be used to translate between different sound formats.

Scripting Resources

Some of the Web editors discussed earlier can also be helpful with popular scripting languages such as JavaScript and JScript. At the same time, you may want to seek out utility applications that can help you with JavaScript, or even cut-and-paste JavaScripts that you can use when creating your pages. A few such applications for Microsoft Windows are iCoder (www.eport.webhoster.co.uk/iCoder/), JavaScript Tools (www.sausagetools.com/), and JavaScript Developer (www.liquidsoftware.cjb.net/).

Finding a Web Server

Before you can display your HTML pages on the Web, you need access to a Web server. This may already be taken care of for you, especially if you are creating pages and posting them within your organization or corporation. When you want to update the site, you just need to know how and where to send your HTML and related files, or you might need to know how to copy them over the network to your Web server.

Otherwise, if you're working within a smaller organization or on your own, you need to make some arrangements for obtaining Web server space and figuring out how to get your files online.

What Is a Web Server?

A Web server is simply a computer that runs software designed to send out HTML pages and other file formats (such as multimedia files). The server should have a relatively high-speed connection to the Internet (faster than typical modem connections, for example) and should be powerful enough to deal with a number of simultaneous connections.

Generally, Web server software requires a fairly robust operating system (like Unix, Linux, Windows NT/2000, or MacOs X). However, software is available for other versions of Microsoft Windows, and earlier Macintosh OS versions are popular for smaller (and reasonably worry-free) Web sites.

Dealing with an ISP

For any sort of connection to the Internet, you probably need to work with an Internet service provider (ISP). ISPs offer dial-up and special high-speed connections to the Internet, as well as Web servers and other types of Internet servers for your use.

For the typical smaller Web site, you want a *hosted* account, sometimes called a *shared hosting* account. This simply means that you share space on one of the ISP's Web server computers with others who have hosted accounts. Generally, this gives you an URL that begins with the name of the ISP's host computer, but points to a special directory for your HTML pages. For example:

`http://www.isp.com/username/index.html.`

tip

You can access lists of ISPs around the country (and the world) at `thelist.com` or `www.yahoo.com/Business_and_Economy/Companies/Internet_Services/Web_Presence_Providers/`. You might also check with your current ISP for Web deals, because many popular online services offer free or cheap Web space.

For this type of service, prices range from free (particularly if you already use other services from that ISP) to $25 or so, depending on the amount of storage space you have and how many megabytes of downloaded *traffic* your site is allowed to handle. The more traffic, the more expensive your site is.

At the next level, you might decide that you'd prefer to have your own *domain name*. This means your Web site is accessible at an URL similar to `http://www.yoursitename.com`, such as `http://www.fakecorp.com`. Clearly, this is desirable for organizations and businesses, although you may opt to register a domain name for your own personal or avocational use as well.

In general, ISPs help you register a domain name when you're establishing new service, but that isn't completely necessary. You can register domain names on your own via a number of different services, such as Register.com (`www.register.com/`) and Network Solutions (`www.networksolutions.com/`). Prices for domain registration can vary, although most name brand services charge $25–$35 per year for a domain name.

After you have a domain name registered, your ISP can set up a Domain Name Service (DNS) record that tells other DNS servers around the world to point to a particular server computer whenever that domain name is requested. So, `www.fakecorp.com` points to the server that the ISP has provided for your Web pages, and others are able to access your pages easily.

note

Domain names always have domain name extensions, such as `.com`, `.net`, and `.org`, which are used to differentiate otherwise identically named sites. For instance, `w3.com` and `w3.org` are two different Web sites. The number of domain name extensions has multiplied recently, with possibilities such as `.biz` and `.info`.

DO YOU ALREADY HAVE SERVER SPACE?

If you use an ISP for your Internet access, there's a decent chance that you already have Web server space available to you. Most of the major national and international ISPs (such as ATT WorldNet, America Online, and Prodigy.net) offer free Web space with most of their account types.

If your ISP offers free space, all you need to do is find out how much space you get and how to take advantage of it. You may also want to look into any options your ISP offers for registering domain names. In most cases, having your own domain name associated with the Web server space costs extra. "Web Publishing Services," which is a chapter available online, has more information on free and commercial Web server options. (See the Introduction for details on how to download this chapter.)

What Software Does Your Server Run?

For HTML documents, images, and most multimedia feeds, the software that your ISP uses for its Web server computers is largely irrelevant. However, when you get into more advanced tasks—or when you decide you want to take advantage of interactivity options and add-ons—the type of software your ISP uses can become much more important. So, these are a few questions you might consider asking a customer service representative at your ISP (or a prospective one):

- *Can I run CGI scripts? If so, which languages?* Although most basic Web sites don't deal in CGI scripts, you may need them if you want to add interactivity to your site in the guise of HTML forms, bulletin-board forum software, or database access. Note that in some cases a particular language version may be required (such as Perl 5 instead of Perl 4), so knowing the version numbers can be helpful. (See Chapters 16, "CGIs and Data Gathering," and 17, "Forums, Chats, and Other Add-Ons," for more information.)

- *Which extensions and server side includes are available?* Depending on the Web server software and any extensions that are installed, you may be able to add special commands to your HTML documents that make it possible to display the current time, hit counter, and quite a few other options that are specific to particular Web server applications (see Chapter 17).

- *How are statistics reported?* With some ISPs, you may be able to access a special URL that shows you how many people have visited your Web site, along with other information from them (such as which pages referred them to

note

You'll often find that your favorite domain names are already registered. On many of the registration service sites, you can perform a *WhoIs* lookup to see whether a domain name is registered, and to whom. Paying for a domain name that you really want, particularly if someone is "squatting" the address and not using it is still common (although perhaps not as glamorous).

Perl is a scripting language that's commonly used for programs that are stored on Web servers and used to interact with Web browsers.

your site). In other cases, statistics are stored in a special file that you need to download to your computer and then process with a statistical analysis program (generally available as a free download).

Asking these questions—particularly when you're a bit more familiar with the answers you want to hear—may help you decide on an ISP to use for your Web serving. See Chapter 17 for more details.

Accessing Your Web Server Space

After you've decided on an ISP, you're ready to create your HTML pages and upload them to the server. To do all this correctly, though, you probably need to ask a few questions:

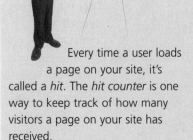

Every time a user loads a page on your site, it's called a *hit*. The *hit counter* is one way to keep track of how many visitors a page on your site has received.

With most Web server programs, the default page that is first loaded is named `index.html` or `index.htm`. So that's the name you use for the first page you'd like to present to users when they access your Web site.

- *What is my site's default URL?* This should be the ISP's host address and a directory for your username. For example, if your username is jsmith, the default URL for your site might be `www.fakeco.net/jsmith/`, `members.fakeco.net/jsmith/`, or something similar. Different ISPs organize this in different ways, so you need to make sure you get this right.

- *How do I upload files to my site's directory?* You should get instructions for accessing your Web site's directory on the Web server using an FTP application. This is discussed in more detail in the section "Updating Your Web Site," later in this chapter.

- *What limitations are there on the names I can give my files?* The Web server's operating system may not be instantly obvious to you. If this is the case, you want to ask if there is a certain filename length or a certain format for naming files that you need to follow.

- *Can I create subdirectories within my main Web site directory?* Most Web servers give you this ability, but some don't.

With those questions answered, you are able to upload and access your Web pages easily.

Organizing a Web Site's Files

You may recall from Chapter 1 that a URL is composed of a protocol, a server address, and a path to a particular document. All of those components are important. When you're creating and organizing your Web site's files, however, the most important is the path statement. If you have a system for how you store files when you're creating them on your computer (*locally*), you'll have less trouble later when you store your files on a Web server computer.

Although a Web site can be arranged in a number of different ways, you should keep in mind some rules of thumb. For the most part, you should organize your Web site files to make it easy to update your pages in the future. If you have to move all your files around every time you change something on a single page, you are also forced to change all the hypertext links on many other pages—and that can be incredibly time-consuming. Early on in the process, you should consider how your site's files will be organized. This is true even if you're only planning one page or a few pages. Organizing the images and multimedia feeds that go along with those pages is still important.

Types of File Organization

These are different types of organization for Web sites:

- *Single-directory sites:* Smaller sites, with just a few HTML pages and images, can often get by with a single directory on the Web server. All your graphics and HTML pages go in this one directory. One of the biggest advantages of this system is that links to local files and graphics require no special path statements. The disadvantage is that this sort of system can be unwieldy as your site grows, making it more difficult to update in the future.

- *Directories by function:* One way to organize more complicated sites is to put each section of related Web pages in the same directory. For example, in your main directory you might only store the index page and its associated graphics. For a business site you'd have subdirectories for sections called About, Products, Support, and so on. In each of these subdirectories, you'd include all the related HTML files and the image files for those pages.

■ *Directory by file type:* Some people prefer to create subdirectories according to the type of file, as opposed to the content of the page. Your main directory may have only the index page of your site. Other subdirectories might be called Images, Pages, Downloads, and so on. The main advantage of organizing this way is that files generally have to be replaced only once. If you use a graphic on a number of different pages, for example, you can replace it once in the Images subdirectory and all the HTML pages that access the graphic use the new one.

■ *Hybrid:* The best way to organize a large site is to use a hybrid of the two preceding methods. Creating separate subdirectories for nonrecurring items (such as individual Web pages in each category) while creating other subdirectories for items used multiple times (such as graphics) enables you to get at all the files in an efficient way. A hybrid file organization is shown in Figure 3.5.

FIGURE 3.5

In this hybrid site (displayed in Windows Explorer), different functions are organized into different folders, but a single image folder is also used for all images.

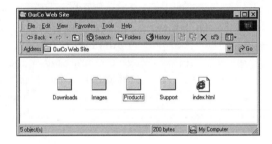

The other thing to remember when determining how you're going to organize your Web directories is that the directories themselves become part of the URL when you create them and store files using them on the Web server. So, if you go with the hybrid approach, your URLs might make more sense to the user. For example:

`www.fakecorp.com/products/mousetrap.html`

This is as opposed to a straight "functional" organization, which would result in an URL like this:

`www.fakecorp.com/webpages/mousetrap.html`

In this case, the products directory tells the user what he will see and how the Web site is organized.

Creating the Hierarchy

Once you've selected a system, the next step is to create local folders that mirror the directories you're using on your Web server. If you create a folder called images where you plan to store image files, you'll need that folder in the same *relative* location on your local hard disk and on the Web server computer.

For each Web site, create a folder somewhere on your computer. The name of it isn't important, since it will be the equivalent to the nameless root directory (/) on your Web server. For instance, if you're creating a new personal site, start by naming a folder mysite. That's where your main index.html page will be stored. Inside that folder, add other subfolders that you plan to use as part of your organizational hierarchy, such as images or products, depending on the approach you're taking. Remember that these folders need to be the same names you plan to use for subdirectories on your Web server. In fact, a good rule of thumb is to use all lowercase letters for them, in both places, just to avoid any problems with case-sensitive servers.

note

In some operating systems they're called *folders*, and in others they're called *directories*. It's just two names for items that are functionally equivalent. You'll often hear *folders* used when referring to local hard disks (particularly in Windows and MacOs) and *directories* used when referring to the server computer (which is often running Unix or a Unix-like OS).

This organizational structure will do two things for you. First, it keeps you from accidentally placing files in the wrong directories when you're uploading them to your Web site. Second, it makes it easier to create *relative URLs*, which is a topic you'll dig into in Chapter 7, "Building Hypertext Links."

Naming Your Files

You've already seen that file extensions are an important part of all the filenames you use for your Web site. Because other Web browsers may rely on a file's extension to know what sort of document or file it is, you need to include the appropriate extensions with all your Web site files.

Your Web site almost always begins with a file called `index.html` or `index.htm`. Most Web server software programs load this page automatically if the URL of your site is accessed without a specific path and file reference. For example, typing `www.fakecorp.com/` will probably result in the page `www.fakecorp.com/index.html` being loaded into your browser. Your Web site's first page (whether it's a "front door" page or the first page of your site) should be designed with this in mind.

The thing to consider when naming your files is how you plan to organize your site. If you're using a single-directory organization, your filenames should be as unique as possible, and graphics and other files should probably have names that relate to their associated Web pages. For instance:

```
about_company.html

about_header.jpg

about_ceo_photo.jpg
```

These names help you determine which files are associated with which HTML pages when you go to update those files. If you have more structure to your site (for instance, if you've created an `about` directory on the Web server), names such as `company.html` might be more appropriate because the ultimate URL path you're creating would be `about/company.html`.

Updating Your Web Site

If you organize your site well, updating it is simply a matter of replacing an outdated file with a new file using the same filename.

You need to check with your company's system administrator or your ISP's technical staff to figure out exactly how you update files. (When you sign up for service, most ISPs will tell you how to do this or provide you with documentation that explains the process.) With an ISP, you can usually use an FTP program to put new files in your directory organization on the Web site, as shown in Figure 3.6. (Some HTML editors include the built-in ability to upload pages via FTP.) The process is simple:

1. Your Web space provider requires you to enter a username and password to gain access to the Web server. In most cases, you point your FTP program to the Web server itself (for example, `www.isp.com`), although sometimes you'll log into a computer with an address that starts with `ftp`. If your Web site has its own domain name, you might need to sign into that, such as `www.fakecorp.com` or `ftp.fakecorp.com`.

FIGURE 3.6

An FTP client program is being used to transfer Web site files from my local hard drive (bottom) to the Web server computer (top).

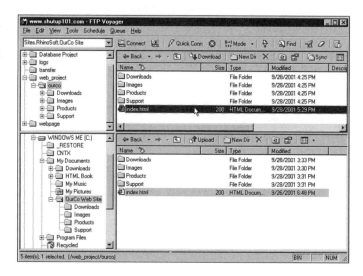

2. If the server recognizes your username and password, you'll be connected to the server. Most likely, you'll be in your personal Web site's main directory. (If not, you need to use the cd command or otherwise change directories in your FTP program.)

3. You can add files using the put command in your FTP program. If you're uploading new files, remember to place them in the same relative locations that you used on your local hard disk. (Put the image files in the image directory on the server, and so on.) You may need to create the directories on the server the first time you log in.

4. To replace an existing file, you use the put command again, this time uploading the replacement file with the same name as the file you want to replace (including the upper- or lowercase letters). This will overwrite the file, so consider whether you want a backup of the older file before you replace it. You won't be able to recover the older version unless you've created a backup of it.

As you can see in Figure 3.6, it's a good idea to maintain a folder or directory on your own hard drive that is as identical as possible to the Web site and its directory structure. That way FTP updates are easy, as is testing to ensure that your filenames and local hyperlinks have been built correctly.

Summary

In this chapter, you took a look at some of the tools that you need—and some others you might simply want—to create Web pages. You also got some suggestions for other tools, including those that help with images, animation, and multimedia files. Next, the chapter discussed obtaining Web server space from an ISP, including some of the important questions you need to ask. The chapter ended with a discussion of how your Web site's files and directories should be organized, and how you go about updating your Web site as you create and edit HTML and other Web files.

In Chapter 4, "Creating Your First Page," you'll create your first Web page, as well as a template that includes the main structural elements that you'll need on every XHTML document you create.

IN THIS CHAPTER

- Creating an HTML template
- Structuring Web documents properly
- Typing text into paragraphs
- Saving, testing, and validating the page

4

CREATING YOUR FIRST PAGE

In this chapter, you begin creating HTML documents by piecing together the required skeleton of XHTML elements into a basic template. After you've created that template, you move on to the basics of entering text for your page. After that, you learn how to save your document, test it by viewing it in a browser window, and validate it to make sure your code adheres to set standards.

Build Your HTML Template

As you saw in Chapter 3, "What You Need to Get Started," all you need to create HTML documents is a basic text editor. HTML pages, although they include the `.htm` or `.html` file extensions, are simply ASCII text files. Any program that generates ASCII text files works fine as an HTML editor—even a word processor such as WordPerfect or Microsoft Word, as long as you save correctly.

After you have that program, you're ready to create a basic template for your HTML documents. This is the skeleton of the HTML page that you use for building content-filled pages, using the markup elements discussed later in the book. The skeleton includes the *document* elements, which are simply the markup elements that define the file you're creating as a Web page.

Add Document Elements

The firstXHTML elements you learn about are the document elements. These are the tags that are required for every HTML document you create. They define the different parts of the document.

Like a magazine article, an HTML document has two distinct parts—a head and a body. The head of the HTML document is where you enter the title of the page.

To create the head portion of your HTML document, type the following into your text editor:

```
<head>
</head>
```

note

Don't let me confuse you by switching back and forth between *XHTML* and *HTML*. When I'm referring directly to the elements, I'll call them *XHTML elements*, because that's the specific standard we're going to adhere to throughout this book. When I'm referring generically to HTML as a concept or to Web documents and applications, I'll call them *HTML documents* or *HTML editors*.

This section tells the Web browser what special information should be made available about this page, and what it should call the document in the title bar of the browser window.

Now that you've got a head, you need a body, right? The body is where you do most of your work; entering text, headlines, graphics, and all your other Web goodies. To add the body element, start after the `</head>` tag and enter the following:

```
<body>
</body>
```

Between these two tags, you enter the rest of the text and graphics for your Web page.

Now, wrapped around the `<head>` and `<body>` elements, you'll add an element that's designed to tell that world that it's dealing with an HTML document: the `<html>` element. Above the first `<head>` tag, enter this:

```
<html>
```

After the `</body>` tag, type the following:

```
</html>
```

Even though your document is saved in plain ASCII text, a Web browser will know that the page is really supposed to be an HTML document.

But wait... this isn't just any old HTML document. It's an XHTML document! Because you're using XHTML, you need to be a little more specific with that first `<html>` tag:

```
<html xmlns="http://www.w3.org/1999/xhtml">
```

This attribute for the `<html>` element is `xmlns`, and it stands for *XML namespace*. It's required for XHTML-compatible documents, particularly those that strictly conform to the XHTML 1.0 standard.

So, the end result of all these elements would look like

```
<html xmlns="http://www.w3.org/1999/xhtml">
<head>
</head>
<body>
</body>
</html>
```

Now you have a nearly complete Web document, at least as far as your Web browser is concerned.

The DTD

Before any HTML document—and particularly one adhering to the XHTML standard—is truly complete, you need to add something called the DTD, or *document type definition*, to the top of the page. It's a dirty little secret that most of today's Web browser applications will read a page that doesn't have a DTD and display it without problems. However, this definition will become more and more important in the future. What is it? It's a quick element at the top of the page that enables everyone to know which languages and standards you're using for that page. As XML becomes more important on the Web, and as a wider variety of applications and devices are used to access the Web, this definition will become a requirement.

You should put a DTD at the top of every HTML document you create. Fortunately, they're simple to add. All you have to do is pick the right one.

If you're working with a page that already exists, or that has been generated by a typical WYSIWYG HTML editor, you probably want to update it with the following DTD:

```
<!DOCTYPE html
    PUBLIC "\//W3C//DTD XHTML 1.0 Transitional//EN"
    "DTD/xhtml1-transitional.dtd">
```

This is the XHTML Transitional DTD, which simply tells the Web browser that you're using the XHTML 1.0 Transitional specification for your pages. The PUBLIC attribute is followed by the specific DTD name, including the language used, which is English (EN). Note that even if you're using another language for the text on your page, the language of XHTML is always EN.

The next line of the DOCTYPE is the URL of that particular DTD file that's maintained by the W3C. This line is optional, but there's no harm in including it.

As you'll see in later chapters, the XHTML Transitional DTD enables you to use elements that directly affect the look and feel (fonts, colors, and so on) of text on the page. As noted in Chapter 1, "The Web Publishing Fundamentals," HTML isn't really designed to do this, so the XHTML Strict DTD doesn't support such codes.

Specifically, the XHTML Transitional DTD causes a Web browser to run in a backward-compatibility mode. This enables a number of non-standard elements, such as those created by the browser companies instead of the W3C, to *render*, or display in the browser, without generating errors. The other option is to have the browser run in strict mode, which requires the XHMTL Strict DTD:

```
<!DOCTYPE html
    PUBLIC "\//W3C//DTD XHTML 1.0
Strict//EN"
    "DTD/xhtml1-strict.dtd">
```

You use this definition if you don't plan to use any browser-specific codes, and you plan to use style sheets to change the appearance of elements on your page. For most of the pages you create using this book, the XHTML Strict DTD should work well.

note

Why use one or the other? As you work through the book, you'll see that using the XHTML Strict DTD will require you to use style sheets to change the appearance and layout of the text on your page, while the XHTML elements will only be used for organizing the page. With the XHTML Transitional DTD in force, you can use some special HTML elements and attributes to change the appearance of text, lists, tables, and other elements. The XHTML Transitional DTD is simply a little more lax about allowing older elements, which is why I recommend adding it to existing HTML documents that you're updating.

Also note that you don't need to space the DOCTYPE element (which is the only element in XHTML that can be uppercase), as shown in the prior examples. You can place the attributes for the DOCTYPE element on the same line if desired, as in the following:

```
<!DOCTYPE html PUBLIC "\//W3C//DTD XHTML 1.0 Strict//EN" "DTD/
xhtml1-strict.dtd">
```

The comment Element

One other element needs to be discussed before you put together your template. The comment element is a bit different from other elements. It contains text, but it doesn't have an opening or closing tag. Instead, the text for your comment is enclosed in a single tag that begins with <!-- and ends with -->. The text inside the tag is ignored by the Web browser.

Hiding the text enables you to create a private message to remind you of something, or to help those who view the raw HTML document to understand what you're doing. That's why it's called the comment element. For example:

```
<!--This is a comment that won't display in
a browser-->
```

Generally, you use the comment element for your own benefit—perhaps to mark a point in a particular HTML document where you need to remember to update some text, or to explain a particularly confusing part of your page to others who may need to update it in the future. Because it's fairly easy for anyone to view your raw HTML document, you might also use the comment element to create a copyright message or give information about yourself.

tip

It might seem like a good idea to place comment tags around other HTML elements you'd like to hide temporarily, but it's better to delete obsolete links and elements when you don't want to use them. Some browsers may inadvertently display certain elements even if they are hidden using the comment element.

Create an HTML Template

Now it's time to take what you know and create a template. By saving this template as a text file, you have a quick way to create new HTML files. Simply load the template and select File, Save As to save it as your new Web page.

1. Start by entering the following in a blank text file:

```
<!DOCTYPE html PUBLIC "\//W3C//DTD XHTML 1.0 Strict//EN"
"DTD/xhtml1-strict.dtd">
<html xmlns="http://www.w3.org/1999/xhtml">
<head>
<title>Enter Title Here</title>
<!--Designed By Lucy Smith-->
<!--Last updated 10/12-->
</head>
<body>

</body>
</html>
```

2. Next, save this as an ASCII text file called `template.html` (or `template.htm` if you're using DOS or an early version of Windows).

Now, whenever you're ready to create a new HTML document, simply load `template.html` into your text editor and select File, Save As to rename it to something more meaningful, such as `index.html` or `products.html`. You can then alter the page by adding text, links, and other markup elements.

The Document Head

As the name implies, the *head section* of any HTML document precedes the main information (or the body). The head section is defined by the `<head>` element, which is a container element. Text contained between these `<head>` and `</head>` tags tells the browser application general information about the file and is not displayed as part of the document text itself.

The `<head>` element can hold a number of other elements, including the following:

- `<title>`—The document's name
- `<base>`—The original URL of the document
- `<meta>`—Additional information about the page

Only the `<title>` element is required. The rest are optional and often do not appear in basic HTML documents. However, it's important to know how all these elements work because they can help you produce a richer, more sophisticated Web site.

Your Web Page's Title

The `<title>` element is used to give your page a name. Most graphical Web browsers display the title in the browser window's title bar. Likewise, the title is often used when the page is saved using a Web browser's bookmark or Favorites feature. The title is not the name of the file itself (such as `index.html`) but instead a few descriptive words, such as Customer Support Page or FakeCorp's Site Map.

The title element should be added inside the `<head>` element, as follows:

```
<head>
<title>FakeCorp's Bargain Page</title>
</head>
```

You should make your title informative, but keep it relatively short. A long title can look odd at the top of a browser window and may be truncated when added to a visitor's bookmark or Favorites list. Your page's title may also be used in search engines and other places as a link to your page, so it's worth some consideration. Here are some simple suggestions to help you create a better title:

- *Avoid generic titles*—Say exactly what your site does, what the page is about, and why it's interesting. Remember that any page title might be used as a bookmark or entry in a search engine such as Google or AlltheWeb.com.

- *Avoid catchy slogans*—Remember that your title should indicate the nature of the service or the purpose of the page. Just giving a company's name or motto doesn't always help, particularly if the title of many or all of your pages is the same. Instead, work your organization's name into an informative title, such as FakeCorp's Customer Support or About FakeCorp's Executive Team.

- *Use no more than 60 characters*—The XHTML specification does not limit the length of the `<title>` element. However, before you give your Web pages endlessly descriptive names, keep in mind that the space where the title is displayed (either the viewer's title bar or window label) is limited. Keep your title short.

The `<base>` Element

File paths and URLs can get a little complicated, and they tend to be a stumbling block for new Web page designers. The `<base>` element can be used to make this process a bit more palatable. Essentially, the `<base>` element is used to set the root level of all a page's relative URLs. It's a bit involved, so we'll save the specifics for Chapter 7, "Building Hypertext Links." It's mentioned here because it goes in the head of your document.

The `<meta>` Element

The `<meta>` element is used to add *metadata*, which simply means data about data. In this case, the element is used to add information about your Web page that other people or computers can use. One very common use for the `<meta>` element is to provide keywords and a description of your content to Web search engines such as Yahoo! and Excite. This makes your page easier to find for people who have similar interests.

When *search robots* encounter your page, they'll look for two fairly common `<meta>` elements:

```
<meta name="description" content="Products
offered by FakeCorp">

<meta name="keywords" content="hair, perm,
highlights, comb, dryer">
```

The first `<meta>` element in the preceding example is used by robots to describe your site in its listing in a Web directory. For the `content` attribute, descriptions should be between 50 and 200 words, depending on the search robot (shorter is probably best). Another example might be as follows:

```
<meta name="description" content="Virtual
writer's group
¬for New York, including job listings, tips,
advice and
¬discussion.">
```

note

Often called *bots*, search robots are small programs designed to comb the Web for interesting pages to catalog. Some of them are designed to read and store the description and keywords you enter for your page.

The other `<meta>` element is for keywords that you want the search robot to associate with your site. If a user enters these keywords at a major search engine, it's more likely to present your page as one of the results. The following is an example, using the New York writers' group page from the preceding example:

```
<meta name="keywords" content="writers,
writer, free-lance,
¬ for hire, articles, submissions,
postings, want ads">
```

These aren't the only uses for the `<meta>` element; just some very common ones. The `<meta>` element must include the `content` attribute and either the `name` or `http-equiv` attribute, but never both. In fact, the `name` attribute accepts generic values,

tip

`<meta>` can be used with the `http-equiv` attribute to automatically load new Web pages, as discussed in Chapter 7.

which may or may not be useful to a browser. For instance, you could add your name and a copyright for your page:

```
<META name="author" content="Rich Guy">

<META name="copyright" content="&copy; 2002 FakeCorp, Inc.">
```

In general, it's used to convey hidden information to the Web browser (when used with `name`) or to access HTTP server properties (when used with `http-equiv`).

The Body Section

The body section of all HTML documents is defined by the `<body>` container element. It has an opening tag, `<body>`, to show where the body starts, and a closing tag, `</body>`, to indicate where the body ends. Inside the body is where you'll put everything that your visitors will actually see in the browser window—text, hyperlinks, headings, images, form elements, tables, and all other XHTML markup.

The sample XHTML in Listing 4.1 shows where the body fits into the overall Web page structure. Note that it's embedded inside the `<html>` and `</html>` opening and closing tags, which means it's a substructure of `<html>` itself. Almost everything else in your document is contained in the body and thus fits inside the `<body>` and `</body>` tags.

LISTING 4.1   Sample HTML Body Element

```
<!DOCTYPE html PUBLIC "\//W3C//DTD XHTML 1.0 Strict//EN" "DTD/
xhtml1-strict.dtd">
<html xmlns="http://www.w3.org/1999/xhtml">
<head>
<title>FakeCorp Web Deals</title>
</head>
<body>
<h1>FakeCorp's Web Deals</h1>
...actual content of page
</body>
</html>
```

Figure 4.1 shows Listing 4.1 as displayed in a Web browser (including some Web content that appears inside the `<body>` element, but isn't shown in the listing).

FIGURE 4.1

Text, headings, and pretty much everything else you see on a page goes between the <body> and </body> tags in your HTML document.

FIGURE 4.1

Text, headings, and pretty much everything else you see on a page goes between the <body> and </body> tags in your HTML document.

WELL-FORMED CODE

As you'll see in this chapter and throughout the book, an important part of the process of creating XHTML-compatible documents is using well-formed code. The term well-formed means that the documents you author conform to some basic rules that are part of the basic XHTML standard. If you've worked with HTML in the past, you might notice that things are getting a bit more strict under XHTML.

For instance, well-formed XHTML tags are all lowercase (<body> instead of <BODY>), and they should all have closing tags. In the past, some container elements, such as the paragraph element, would let you get away with using only one of the tags. For empty elements, you close the tag by adding a slash (/) before the final bracket (>).

Other rules apply, as you'll see in later chapters. For instance, older HTML specifications allowed for empty attributes, such as NOSHADE, but XHTML requires an attribute to have a value, such as noshade="noshade".

Entering Paragraph Text

Most of the text you type between the <body> and </body> tags is enclosed in another important container element: the <p> (paragraph) element. This element is used to show a Web browser which text in your document constitutes a paragraph.

You might think that a paragraph element would be superfluous. In most text editors, you can simply press the Return or Enter key on your keyboard to create a new paragraph in the document. For HTML documents, though, that doesn't work. In most cases, Web browsers are designed to ignore more than one space between words, so they'll ignore any returns that you add to your HTML document while you're creating it.

To give the appearance of paragraphs, you have to use the paragraph container element. It uses the following format:

```
<p>Here is the text for my paragraph. It doesn't matter how long it is,
how many spaces are between the words or when I decide to hit the return
key. It will create a new paragraph only when I end the tag and begin with
another one.
</p>


<p> Here's the next paragraph. </p>
```

The paragraph element tells the Web browser that all the text between the `<p>` and `</p>` tags is in a single paragraph. When you start another paragraph, the Web browser drops down a line between the two paragraphs.

This is another example that has some extra spaces. Remember, spaces and returns almost never affect the way the text is displayed onscreen. In a paragraph container, the browser ignores more than one space and any returns:

```
<p>Thanks for shopping at FakeCorp.</p>
```

And:

```
<p>

Thanks

for shopping at

FakeCorp.

</p>
```

These look exactly the same when displayed in a Web browser, as shown in Figure 4.2.

note

In earlier HTML implementations, the `<p>` element could be used as an empty element. You could simply place a `<p>` tag at the beginning or end of a paragraph of text. This isn't *well-formed code*, however. It doesn't work under the XHTML Strict DTD, which requires that all container elements have a closing tag. To be on the safe side, use both tags to enclose all of your paragraphs.

FIGURE 4.2

Notice that pressing the Return key when entering text has no effect on how it's rendered.

The `<br />` Element

You've learned how to create entire paragraphs. But what if you want to specify where a particular line is going to end? Let's say you want to enter an address into a Web document, as follows:

```
<p>
Donald Johnson
12345 Main Street
Yourtown, NY 10001
</p>
```

This looks about right when you type it into your text editor. However, when it's displayed in a Web browser, it looks like the top part of Figure 4.3.

You already know what the problem is: Web browsers ignore extra spaces and returns. But if you put each of those lines within its own paragraph containers, you end up with an extra space between each line. That looks wrong too, as shown at the bottom of Figure 4.3.

The answer to this conundrum is the empty element `<br />`, which forces a line return in your Web document. (The "br" in the tag stands for "break.") Properly formatted, the address would look like this:

```
<p>
Donald Johnson<br />
12345 Main Street<br />
Yourtown, NY 10001<br />
</p>
```

note

Although some versions of Netscape's browser recognize more than one `<br />` tag and create additional line breaks, the HTML standard doesn't recognize more than one `<br />` tag in a row. One accepted way to add space in an HTML document is the `<pre>` container, as discussed in Chapter 5, "Formatting Your Text." The most appropriate way to add space on your page is via style sheets, as discussed in Chapter 10, "Get Splashy: Style Sheets, Fonts, and Special Characters."

This looks just right in a Web browser, as shown in Figure 4.4.

FIGURE 4.3

Pressing Return or Enter and using <p> containers doesn't add simple line returns in HTML documents.

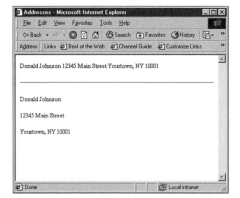

FIGURE 4.4

Here's the listing with <br /> elements at the end of each line of text.

Saving, Testing, and Validating

As you're working on a new page, it's important to go through a three-step process to make sure the page is saved properly, works well in a Web browser, and conforms to HTML standards.

Saving Your Page

If you're working from an HTML template, you've probably saved your page with a meaningful name because that's recommended immediately after you load the `template.html` document. (If not, you may have accidentally added text and markup to your `template.html` document.) If you don't have your HTML document saved with a meaningful name, select File, Save As to save the file.

When you're saving the file, remember that it should be in the same *relative* position where it will be after it's uploaded to a Web server. This can be a bit difficult to grasp at first, but it's closely related to the discussion of directories and site structure in Chapter 3, "What You Need to Get Started." If you're saving the file `products.html` in your products folder on your hard drive, it should be bound for the products directory on your Web server. Otherwise, moving files around can mess up their links to images and hyperlinks, as you'll see in Chapters 6, "Visual Stimulus—Adding Graphics," and 7, "Building Hypertext Links."

Testing Your Page

You need to use a Web browser to check on the appearance of your Web page as you create it. Almost any Web browser can load local pages from your hard drive, just as they can load HTML pages across the Web. Check the menu of your Web browser for a command such as **File**, **Open File**. Then use the Open dialog box to locate the HTML document and load it into your browser, as shown in Figure 4.5.

FIGURE 4.5

Select a file and click **Open** to load an HTML document from your hard drive and display it in the browser window.

To test an HTML document in your Web browser

1. Select **File**, **Save** to save any changes you've made to the HTML document in your text editor.

2. Switch to your Web browser application, and then choose **File**, **Open File** to open the file in your browser.

3. The document should appear in your Web browser. Check it for problems, typos, and other issues.

4. Switch back to your text editor and make any changes that are necessary, or continue working on the page. When you're done, select **File**, **Save** again.

5. If the page is already open in your Web browser, you should be able to click the **Reload** button to see the changes you just made and saved in the HTML document.

Validating the Page

Finally, after you've saved and tested your page, you're ready to validate it. Although validation isn't a requirement, it's a good idea. In essence, an automated testing application determines whether your page meets the W3C's guidelines for compatibility with HTML (or XHTML, in many cases). If your page validates, you know it completely conforms to the standard and that you don't have any *syntax errors* that could affect the display of your markup. If the page doesn't validate, either you're dealing with a typo or you've used an element that isn't valid in the HTML or XHTML specification you're testing against. Most validators will give you an error report so that you can fix the error.

So how do you test? You have a few choices. The most obvious choice is HTML Tidy, whose source code is maintained by Dave Raggett of the W3C. The code is available in numerous formats, including a validation program that runs at the Windows command line. Many other versions of the software have been written and ported, including Windows, Mac, and Unix graphical applications and editors. See `http://www.w3.org/People/Raggett/tidy/` for a list of these other versions. Note that some popular HTML editors also support HTML Tidy add-ons and plug-ins, such as support within NoteTab for Windows and BBEdit plug-ins for Macintosh.

A Web page doesn't *need* to pass a validator in order to work correctly in Web browsers. Indeed, many pages on the Web today wouldn't pass a validator. But adhering to the standards is growing more and more important, particularly with XHTML. If your page passes, it's likely to be displayed correctly in the broadest range of browsers.

The W3C also offers a validator for style sheet coding (CSS, or cascading style sheets) at `http://jigsaw.w3.org/css-validator/`.

Likewise, you can use a third-party validator application that you download to your computer. CSE HTML Validator Lite (`http://www.htmlvalidator.com/lite/`) is one such application for Windows that has the added advantage of being freeware. A Real Validator (`http://www.arealvalidator.com/`) is a Windows shareware option.

Finally, you can use a validator that checks HTML over the Web. In this case, you need to have uploaded your page to a Web server already, and you need to know the URL of the page that you want to validate. Then, you visit the validator's Web page and enter the URL. A number of such validators exist, but you only need to concern yourself with the W3C's, which is the most authoritative. You can find it at `http://validator.w3.org/`.

Summary

In this chapter you learned how to create an HTML template, including the fundamentals of the DTD and the main page elements. You then learned how to add to that basic template by filling out the head of the document, as well as typing text into paragraphs within the body of the document. Then you learned how to save, test, and validate your pages.

In Chapter 5, you'll learn the elements used for organizing and formatting text on the page, including headings, block-level elements, and lists.

PART

DESIGN AND CONQUER

5

FORMATTING YOUR TEXT

At this point, you're familiar with the HTML template, you've typed some text into paragraphs, and you've successfully saved and validated the work you've done so far. In this chapter, you learn quite a bit about styling and organizing text as you type it into the body of your HTML document.

Organize the Page

After you've placed some basic paragraphs on your page, you may be ready to break them up a bit. You can do that with two different elements discussed in this section: headings and horizontal lines. Headings are very important to a well-organized page, particularly one that offers a lot of text. Horizontal lines can be helpful, too, in defining sections of a Web document visually.

Add Headings

Heading elements are containers, and unlike many other XHTML elements, they double as paragraph elements. Ranging from level 1 to level 6, headings enable you to create different levels of emphasized headlines to organize your Web page. This is an example:

```
<h1>Level one headers are the largest for headlines</h1>
<h2>Level two is a little smaller for major subheads</h2>
<h3>Level three is again smaller, for minor subheads</h3>
<p>This is regular text.</p>
<h4>Level four is about the same size as regular text, but emphasized</h4>
<h5>Level five: again emphasized, but smaller than regular text</h5>
<h6>Level six is generally the smallest heading</h6>
```

See Figure 5.1 for the results.

FIGURE 5.1

The different levels of headings you can use.

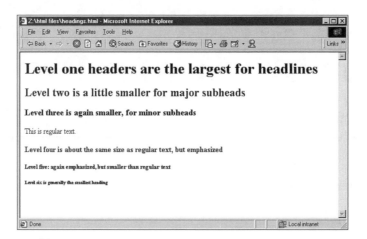

Ideally, headings should be used in descending order, and you shouldn't skip a number—that is, an `<h3>` shouldn't be the next heading to follow an `<h1>` without an `<h2>` between them. In practice, some Web authors will use a particular heading size to make text appear smaller or larger as desired. This is not well-formed code, though, because different browsers can render small headings in different ways. The better plan is to use style sheets to choose font sizes, as discussed in Chapter 10, "Get Splashy: Style Sheets, Fonts, and Special Characters."

You cannot include a heading element on the same line as regular text, even if you close the heading element and continue with unaltered text. A heading element has the same effect as a `<p>` element, in that it creates a new line after its "off" tag. Consider the following:

```
<h1>This is a heading</h1> And this is plain text.
```

This will look nearly the same in a browser as

```
<h1>This is also a heading</h1>
<p>And this is paragraph text.</p>
```

In both cases, the Web browser places the header text and text that follows on different lines, with the header text appearing larger and the plain text appearing at "normal" size. (Also note that the first example is not well-formed code. The second half of the line should be enclosed in a paragraph element.)

Horizontal Lines

Want to divide paragraphs with more than just spaces? The `<hr />` element places a line across the width of the Web browser's window. If the reader changes the size of the window, the line resizes to match. The `<hr />` element is an empty element, so it does not require a closing tag. (The "hr" stands for "horizontal rule," which simply means a horizontal line.)

A horizontal rule inserts a paragraph break before and after the rule. The `<hr />` element can be added anywhere in a document, although it always appears on its own line.

```
<hr />
<h2>Review: Burrito Factory</h2>
<p>This week we report on two great lunches at the Burrito Factory, a
wonderful little restaurant with locations on the Upper West Side and in
the West Village.</p>
```

The `<hr />` element can also accept some attributes that change its appearance, but these attributes should be used only if you're working within the confines of the XHTML Transitional DTD. These attributes are not strict XHTML. (If you do want to stay strict, you should use style sheet commands instead of these attributes, as discussed in Chapter 10.) They give you control over the weight of the line, its length, and the location of the horizontal rule within the browser's window. You can also drop the etched look of the line in favor of a solid black rule. Table 5.1 lists the `<hr />` parameters and what they do.

TABLE 5.1 Style Attributes for `<hr />`

Attribute	Description
size	Sets thickness of the horizontal line
width	Sets width in pixels or a percentage of the viewer window's width
align	Enables the line to be justified left, center, or right within the viewer window
noshade	Changes the appearance of the horizontal line to be solid black with no etched effect

You can add any of these attributes by typing them into the `<hr />` element before adding the closing bracket (`/>`). An example is

```
<hr size="4" width="50%" align="center"
noshade="noshade" />
```

Styling Your Text

When you're ready to move beyond simple paragraphs of plain text, your next step is to begin styling that text. All it takes is a little more markup, in the form of tags that you place on either side of the text you're typing onto the page. Beyond that, you need to put a little bit of thought into which type of style elements you're going to use—*physical styles* or *logical styles*.

Physical styles are those that specifically tell the browser how the text should be emphasized or changed. Boldface, for example, is a physical style. Logical styles, on the other hand, simply suggest to the browser that the marked-up text should be emphasized in some way. The elements `<em>` (for "emphasize") and `<strong>` (for "stronger emphasis") are logical elements.

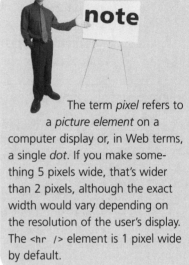

The term *pixel* refers to a *picture element* on a computer display or, in Web terms, a single *dot*. If you make something 5 pixels wide, that's wider than 2 pixels, although the exact width would vary depending on the resolution of the user's display. The `<hr />` element is 1 pixel wide by default.

It might seem that the logical elements are redundant, but they really aren't—in fact, they're preferred. That's because not all Web browsers can display particular physical styles, such as boldface. If a cellphone-based browser can't display boldface, it ignores your `<b>` element. If you use a logical element instead, however, the phone may be able to emphasize the text onscreen in another way. For instance, the `<strong>` element generally makes text appear bold in a graphical browser. In a non-graphical browser, however, the `<strong>` element could be rendered differently—perhaps underlined or highlighted. But that same non-graphical browser would probably ignore the `<b>` element.

In general, you should at least consider using a logical style before automatically typing a physical style, even though the physical styles may seem more familiar. That way, your meaning and emphasis can reach a broader community of readers and visitors.

Physical Style Elements

If you've used almost any word processor, you instantly recognize the physical style elements. Physical styles emphasize your Web page's plain text with boldface, italic, and underlining. These elements are absolute, which means that every Web browser should display these physical style elements in exactly the same manner.

Although some browsers may not be able to display logical text styles the way you expect them to be displayed, there is no way for a browser to misinterpret a physical style. Bold is bold. Italic is italic. If the browser can't display a physical style, it almost invariably ignores it.

Table 5.2 contains some descriptions of physical styles.

TABLE 5.2   Physical Styles and Their Meanings

Element	What It Does...
`<b>, </b>`	Boldface
`<i>, </i>`	Italic
`<tt>, </tt>`	Monospaced typewriter font
`<u>, </u>`	Underlined
`<big>, </big>`	Makes text bigger
`<small>, </small>`	Makes text smaller
`<sub>, </sub>`	Subscript
`<sup>, </sup>`	Superscript

Adding a physical style element to your Web page is simple. The key is selecting the text that is contained by the style tags. The contained text is what is styled in the Web browser:

1. Enter text into your HTML document.

2. Place the cursor at the beginning of the text you'd like to style. Type the opening tag for the style element you'd like to apply to this text.

3. Move the cursor to the end of the text you want to style.

4. Type the closing tag for the style you're applying to this text. This is an example of some physical style elements added to the example Web page:

```
<p><tt>Site News:</tt> We've changed around the posting schedule for
<i>new</i> restaurant reviews. They'll now be posted on
<b>Wednesdays</b>, by popular demand, so that everyone has ample
chance to get out on <u>Thursday and Friday</u> to try them
out.<sup>*</sup></p>
```

```
<p><sup>*</sup>This promise is subject to our sleeping schedule and
whether or not the restaurant is open earlier in the week!</p>
```

Figure 5.2 shows how these physical styles are rendered in a Web browser.

FIGURE 5.2

Generally browsers don't vary in how they display physical styles.

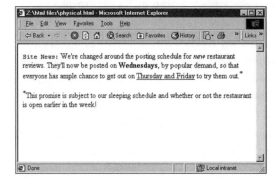

Logical Style Elements

In Chapter 4, "Creating Your First Page," you learned that the paragraph element doesn't just create space between blocks of text—it actually defines the enclosed text as an element called a "paragraph." That's an important distinction, because it means a paragraph is actually a logical element in HTML. The paragraph element doesn't define a fixed amount of line spacing in point size, or a particular margin. Instead, it leaves the exact determination of what a paragraph is (within certain limits) up to the Web browser application.

In HTML, *logical styles* work similarly. A logical style is one that can be rendered by the Web browser in any way that it chooses. Although most browsers tend to render paragraph text in a familiar way (single-spaced with a blank line between the paragraph and the next container), paragraphs could be rendered in other ways—all green text with a flush-right margin, for example—if

note

Placing markup tags right next to the text they represent is important, as in `Tuesday and <b>Thursday</b>` as opposed to `Tuesday and<b> Thursday</b>`. This ensures proper spacing in the browser. In the second example, some browsers (or other agents) may render the line with `andThursday` running together.

the browser programmer or user decided this was necessary. The same holds true for text that's surrounded by a logical style container element. The browser makes the text bold, italic, highlighted, green, spoken louder (in a text-to-speech browser), or whatever is appropriate for that particular browser application.

Each logical style element has an opening tag and a closing tag that form a container for the inserted text. Table 5.3 describes these logical styles.

TABLE 5.3 Logical Styles and Their Meanings

Element	The Enclosed Text Is…
`<em>, </em>`	Emphasis
`<strong>, </strong>`	Stronger emphasis
`<cite>, </cite>`	A citation or a reference to an outside source
`<code>, </code>`	Computer programming code
`<dfn>, </dfn>`	The primary or defining instance of the term
`<samp>, </samp>`	Sample output, often rendered in a way similar to code
`<kbd>, </kbd>`	Representing text typed at the keyboard
`<var>, </var>`	A variable or value
`<q>, </q>`	Quoted text
`<abbr>, </abbr>`	An abbreviation
`<acronym>, </acronym>`	An acronym

In a graphical browser, `<em>` usually italicizes text and `<strong>` usually makes it boldface. But in other browsers, `<em>` might do something different, such as underline the text with a solid line, while `<strong>` might cause the text to be highlighted. In a text-to-speech browser, `<em>` text might be louder than paragraph text and `<strong>` text louder than both. The basic idea is that `<strong>` is just a bit more emphatic—visually or otherwise—than `<em>`.

The other styles in Table 5.3 tend to be used for particular purposes, mostly related to scientific or technical documentation. Again, a browser designed for such documentation could be very creative in how it displays those elements. In most browsers, they'll be italicized, monospaced, or won't have special styling at all.

Listing 5.1 shows an example similar to the one shown in Figure 5.2, but it uses logical styles instead of physical ones. The results are pictured in Figure 5.3.

LISTING 5.1   Logical Styles

```
<p><em>All users</em> need to remember to log out of
their terminal accounts <strong>before leaving</strong>
the computer lab. To <dfn>log out</dfn>, type
<kbd>logout</kbd> or <kbd>exit</kbd> at the prompt.
When you see the result <samp>Thank you.
Goodbye.</samp> on screen, you'll know that it's safe
to turn off the terminal display. Please do so using
the button on the front of the display.</p>
```

The <q> element is used to place language-specific quotation marks around text within paragraphs or similar container elements. In current browsers, this usually just adds quotation marks around the text. In future browsers, it may offer curly quotes, for example. In other cases, it can be used for alternative display and/or for responses by assistive browsers, such as a change in inflection for a computer-voiced browser page. This is an example:

```
<p><q lang="en">I'm not really sure what you
mean,</q> Jack said.</p>
```

> **tip**
>
> Internet Explorer for Macintosh enables you to use a personal style sheet to view pages any way you like. Select **Web Content** in the Preferences dialog box, and then enable the **Use My Stylesheet** command. (You need to locate a stylesheet document, as discussed in Chapter 10.) Netscape and IE for Windows enable you to choose colors and fonts. Opera (http://www.opera.com), which is available for a variety of operating systems, offers extensive control over how elements appear in your browser window.

FIGURE 5.3

In a typical browser, logical styles are rendered in a way that's similar to physical styles.

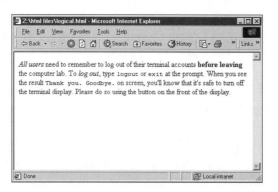

The lang attribute is optional and accepts two-letter abbreviations for different language types, such as "fr" for French and "es" for Spanish (Español).

The last two logical style elements, <abbr> and <acronym>, are a little different. In essence, they're used to provide additional information about truncated words. The Web browser may or may not opt to render this additional information for the reader, but it can be helpful. Both elements can accept two attributes: `lang` (for language) and `title`. The `title` attribute is used to hold the actual definition of the abbreviation or acronym. Theses are some examples:

```
<abbr lang="en" title="United States of America">U.S.A.</abbr>

<acronym title="situation normal all fouled up">snafu</a>

<acronym lang="fr" title="Association Canadienne pour la Recherche en
Economie de la Sante">ACRES</a>
```

Ideally, if a browser recognizes an abbreviation or acronym, that browser somehow expands the definition of the abbreviation or acronym when prompted. For example, Internet Explorer displays the definitions in a small pop-up window when it's pointed to, as shown in Figure 5.4.

FIGURE 5.4
In IE for Windows, the text is in the title attribute when you mouse over a word that's contained by `<abbr>` or `<acronym>`.

Paragraph Style Elements

Chapter 4 discussed the paragraph element, which is used for most of the text that you put on your Web pages. However, `<p>`, `</p>` isn't the only paragraph container element. Other elements can also be used in place of the paragraph element to contain blocks of text in different ways.

The `<pre>` Element

The *preformatted text* element, represented by the tags `<pre>` and `</pre>`, is a little different from the paragraph element in that it recognizes every space and hard return that you type between the tags. Unlike the paragraph element, you don't

tip

You might notice that this is an easy way to make text pop up around items that aren't actually abbreviations or acronyms, but simply words (or phrases) for which you'd like to see little pop-up windows appear (with definitions or help, for instance) when the mouse is pointing at them.

need to add `<br />` or other tags to render line returns. Between `<pre>` tags, the lines tend to look exactly like what you type. The following example is illustrated in Figure 5.5:

```
<pre>
Missed the Saturday dance,
    Heard they crowded the floor.
I couldn't bear it without you,
    I don't get around much anymore.
</pre>
```

FIGURE 5.5

With *pre* tags, your spacing and returns are honored.

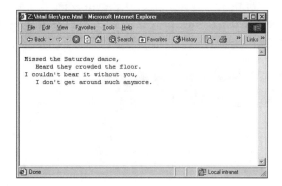

Preformatted text is excellent for items like programming code examples that you want to indent and format appropriately. The `<pre>` element also enables you to align text for table creation by padding it with spaces. However, because those tables appear in monospaced font, you may prefer to spend the extra time constructing the standard HTML tables, discussed in Chapter 8, "Table Basics."

Using `<pre>` for Tables

One use for `<pre>` is to create a primitive table. The key to making this work correctly is alignment. If you simply enter text between the two `<pre>` tags, you can use the space bar to line up each column, and what appears in the browser should be very similar to what you type. For instance:

```
<pre>
```

note

Actually, you can use style sheets to change the font of text inside a `<pre>` element, which makes it more attractive for uses like the preceding poem. However, this doesn't help much with `<pre>` tables, discussed in the next section, because such tables rely on the monospaced font to make columns line up correctly.

```
Year      Event
1965      I was born
1966      First novel completed
</pre>
```

Realize, however, that if you use XHTML elements within the `<pre>` element, you'll need to compensate for the space taken up by their tags. For instance:

```
<pre>
Year      Event
1965      I was born
<b>1966</b>      <i>First</i> novel completed
</pre>
```

Because the tags in the third line don't exist on the final page, the spacing will be correct, even though it looks misaligned when typed.

To create a simple table:

1. Open your template and enter the following (or a similar table) between the `<body>` tags. You may need to play with the spacing a bit to line everything up:

```
<h1>Average Hourly Rate, Per
Region</h1>
<pre>
Region    Handywork  Creative
Business  Advertising
NorthWest    $40         $50         $75
$100
NorthEast    $35         $45         $70
$95
SouthEast    $30         $40         $65
$90
SouthWest    $25         $35         $55
$75
</pre>
```

2. Save the HTML document, and then use the **Open File** command in your browser to proof it. Keep playing with it until it looks right.

tip

In fact, in `<pre>` tables you should probably avoid emphasis styles (both logical and physical). It is nearly impossible to align columns correctly in every browser when one row is bold and other rows (or columns) are plain text. Different browsers make bold text a fraction wider than regular text, so the row or column becomes increasingly misaligned. Even if it looks good in your browser, chances are it doesn't work in all of them.

note

Even within the `<pre>` container element, tabs are not recognized by browsers. If you're using a text editor or word processor, fight the urge to use the Tab key to align `<pre>` elements. Use the spacebar instead. (Some HTML editors add spaces when you press the **Tab** key, which would work okay.)

The `<blockquote>` Element

Historically, the `<blockquote>` container element has been used more for its physical attributes than for its logical ones. Generally, the `<blockquote>` element indents each of the margins of the paragraph it contains, making it look different from other paragraphs on the page. Although that remains the case even in XHTML, it shouldn't be your primary motive for using `<blockquote>`. The following is a listing that uses `<blockquote>` simply for its indenting qualities:

```
<h1>Site News!</h1>

<blockquote>The site is up and running, including some
<strong>introductory reviews</strong>, <em>a feature on baking at
home</em> and <tt>Quick Bites</tt> -- a column focused on getting quick,
healthy meals around town. Also, don't forget to check out the
<em>Discussion Forums</em> and please consider signing up for a
subscription to the <strong>Just In...</strong> newsletter, featuring
updates and new restaurants as soon as we post them.</blockquote>
```

Figure 5.6 shows what this looks like in a browser.

FIGURE 5.6

The `<block-quote>` element in action.

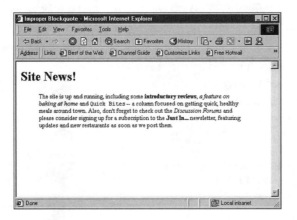

Now, although this isn't illegal by any means, it'd be better to use a paragraph element, and then rely on style sheets to change the width of the margins. According to the W3C, the `<blockquote>` element should be used for presenting quoted material, such as

```
<p>From the Gettysburg Address:</p>

<blockquote>Four score and seven years ago, our forefathers brought forth
on this continent a new nation, conceived in liberty and dedicated to the
proposition that all men are created equal.</blockquote>
```

This example is a more correct use of the `<blockquote>` element (and it's shown in Figure 5.7). That said, it's okay to use `<blockquote>` to simply indent text, as long as you realize that some browsers may (and are allowed to) interpret the paragraph slightly differently.

FIGURE 5.7

The <block-quote> element used appropriately.

For the record, the <blockquote> element renders as regular body text font, the same style featured throughout the rest of your HTML document. It doesn't recognize additional spaces and returns that you enter as you type in the HTML document. As with <p>, the text in a <blockquote> container is spaced uniformly.

The <blockquote> element can also accept the cite attribute, which enables you to include the URL for a particular quotation. You can use this to show a source that you've used (if it's online), as in

```
<blockquote cite="http://eserver.org/history/gettysburg-address.txt">Four
score and seven years ago, our forefathers brought forth on this continent
a new nation, conceived in liberty and dedicated to the proposition that
all men are created equal.</blockquote>
```

Although few popular browsers do much with the cite attribute, in the future it may become more common for browsers to provide a link or other behavior in response to this attribute.

The <address> Element

The <address> container element is used to create paragraph-like text that's specially formatted to stand out as information about the author of the page. In most browsers, the <address> element is displayed as an italicized paragraph. But, as with any logical style, browsers are free to display <address> text any way they want to.

An example of <address> might be

```
<address>Page created and maintained by Ed Smiley</address>
```

Traditionally, the `<address>` element is used toward the end of a Web page to give information like

■ When the page was last updated.

■ Who should be contacted concerning the page (usually the Webmaster's email address).

■ What the URL for this page is.

■ Phone numbers or physical addresses for the company or association.

Most of these elements aren't vital to your page's contents, but they're nice additions to consider. An example of a full address might be

```
<address>
This page last updated 6/12 at 9:08pm.<br />
Contact edsmiley@fakecorp.com with corrections or problems.<br />
FakeCorp<br/>
1732 93rd Street<br />
New York, NY 10025<br />
212-555-1200<br />
</address>
```

Notice the use of `<br />` to insert line breaks within an `<address>` element. This address is shown in Figure 5.8.

FIGURE 5.8

Generally, text within the `<address>` element is italicized.

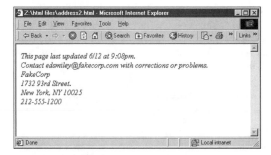

Marking Changes: `<ins>` and `<del>`

`<ins>` and `<del>` are elements that are particularly interesting in more formal business and academic settings. Ideally they're interim tags, to be used while you're working with an HTML document and before it's final.

You can use the `<del>` element to surround text that you feel should be deleted, and then use the `<ins>` element around text that should be inserted in its place. (They can also be used individually, if you're simply deleting or inserting text.) This is most useful when more than one person is working on the same HTML document and you want to see the changes. If you're familiar with the Track Changes feature in Microsoft Word, that's basically what you're doing with these elements.

Both elements can accept the `datetime`, `cite`, or `title` attributes, which you can use to better explain what you're doing. The `datetime` attribute is used to show the date and time of the insertion or deletion, using a somewhat clunky, but functional, approach:

```
2001-12-05T09:00:00-05:00
```

This stands for 9:00 a.m. EST on 12/5/2001. Note that the `-05:00` represents distance from mean (Zulu) time, so for PST, you'd use `-08:00` and so on. The `cite` attribute is used to reference an URL that includes an explanation of the insertion or deletion. The `title` attribute can be used to explain it within the tag. This is an example:

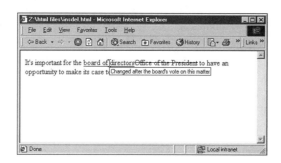

> **note**
>
> The `<ins>` and `<del>` elements can also be used around blocks of XHTML markup, like entire `<p>` container elements of text.

```
<p>It's important for the <ins
datetime="2001-12-05T09:00:00-05:00" title="Changed after the board's vote
on this matter">Board of Directors</ins><del>Office of the President</del>
to have an opportunity to make its case to the shareholders.</p>
```

This is shown in Figure 5.9.

FIGURE 5.9

The `<ins>` and `<del>` elements help you manage an ongoing discussion over text (or other elements) in a page.

```
Z:\html files\insdel.html - Microsoft Internet Explorer
File  Edit  View  Favorites  Tools  Help
Back  ·  →  ·  ⊗  ⤢  ⌂  | Search  Favorites  History  |  ⬜· ⬜  »  | Links »

It's important for the board of directors Office of the President to have an
opportunity to make its case t Changed after the board's vote on this matter

Done                                    Local intranet
```

Using Lists on Your Web Page

List elements, just as with paragraphs and preformatted text, are XHTML container elements that can accept other markup within their boundaries. XHTML lists require at least two elements, one that defines the type of list and one to contain each item within the list. Those contained items can be words, sentences, paragraphs, or other XHTML elements, such as images.

Most XHTML lists follow this format:

```
<list type>
<li>First item in list</li>
<li>Second item in list</li>
<li>Third item</li>
</list type>
```

Each of the `<li>` elements is an item, and each item begins on a new line. How that line begins depends on whether the list is ordered or unordered.

Ordered and Unordered Lists

It might be better to think of ordered and unordered lists as numbered and bulleted lists, respectively, especially when discussing their use in HTML documents. For numbered/ordered lists, the element is `<ol>`, and for bulleted/unordered lists, the element is `<ul>`.

For either of these lists, a list item is designated with the element `<li>`. In the case of ordered lists, the `<li>` tag inserts a number; for unordered lists, it inserts a bullet point.

This is an ordered list:

```
<ol>
<li>Item number one.</li>
<li>Item number two.</li>
<li>Item number three.</li>
</ol>
```

And this is an unordered list:

```
<ul>
<li>First item.</li>
<li>Second item.</li>
<li>Third item.</li>
</ul>
```

To see how these look in a browser, see Figure 5.10.

FIGURE 5.10

Ordered (numbered) and unordered (bulleted) lists.

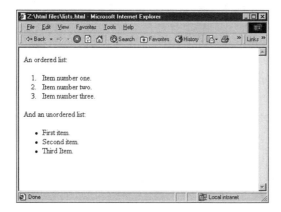

Aside from other XHTML markup, you can include other lists within lists, as long as they're carefully *nested* within one another. For example:

```
<ol>
<li>item 1</li>
<li>item 2</li>
<li><ul>
<li>item 3.1</li>
<li>item 3.2</li>
</ul></li>
<li>item 4</li>
</ol>
```

The rule is simple—you need to end the list that's nested within the original list before you can end the original list. In fact, you need to end the list item in which that nested list resides before you can move on.

Ordered List Attributes

You have the option of changing the way lists act and appear on the page. However, it's worth noting that these are transitional attributes, not compliant with the XHTML Strict DTD, so have the XHTML Transitional DTD specified if you're going to use them. The better approach is to use style sheets, as discussed in Chapter 10.

Most graphical browsers recognize some additional attributes for ordered list items, including start, value, and type. Likewise, unordered lists can accept the type attribute, which enables you to change the appearance of the bullet. Table 5.4 covers the attributes for ordered lists.

TABLE 5.4   Attributes for Ordered List Items

Tag	Display List Value As...
`<ol type="A">`	Uppercase letters
`<ol type="a">`	Lowercase letters
`<ol type="I">`	Uppercase Roman numerals
`<ol type="i">`	Lowercase Roman numerals
`<ol type="1">`	Numbers

In addition, the `start` attribute can be used to change the starting value for that list. For example, you could have a numbered list start at the value 10 by beginning it with this tag:

```
<ol start="10">
```

You can also use the `value` attribute to change the value of an individual list item. For example, this is how to change the numbering within the list:

```
<ol>
<li>Item #1</li>
<li>Item #2</li>
<li value="1">Item #1</li>
<LI>Item #2</li>
</ol>
```

Bullet List Attributes

This example is also transitional, so you should use a style sheet if you're trying to keep to the XHTML Strict DTD. If you're not, you can change the appearance of bullets in unordered lists with the `type` attribute. The bullet styles are as follows:

- *Solid circle*—`<ul type="disc">`
- *Solid square*—`<ul type="square">`
- *Open circle*—`<ul type="circle">`

Note that not all Web browsers can render these bullet styles, and not all do it correctly when they try. You might get squares for all these bullets, for example.

Definition Lists

The final list element is the definition list, which is designed to allow for two levels of list items: the defined term and its definition.

The elements for this list are the main list container element `<dl>` (definition list) and two list item container elements, `<dt>` (definition term) and `<dd>` (definition). The `<dt>` element is designed to fit on a single line of your Web page, although it wraps to the beginning of the next line if necessary. The `<dd>` element accepts a full paragraph of text. In most visual browsers, the definition text is continuously indenting beneath the `<dt>` term. For example:

```
<dl>
<dt><b>genus</b> <i>(n.)</i></dt>
<dd>A group or type marked by common
characteristics.</dd>
<dt><b>geocentric</b> <i>(adj.)</i></dt>
<dd>Of, related to or coming from the
center of the earth.</dd>
<dt><b>geography</b> <i>(n.)</i></dt>
<dd>The study of the earth, its topography
and its natural or manufactured
features.</dd>
</dl>
```

> **tip**
>
> Not all browsers display definition lists in the same way, so adding spaces to `<dt>` items to get them to line up with the `<dd>` text is often a waste of time.

Notice that standard XHTML markup is permissible within the boundaries of a definition list, and that using bold and italics for the defined terms adds a dictionary-like quality. This is shown in Figure 5.11.

FIGURE 5.11

A typical definition list.

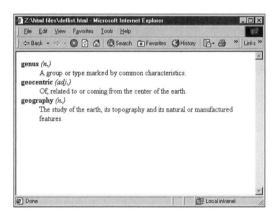

Just because definition lists allow for two different types of list items, you don't need to use both. Using just the `<dt>` element in your list, for example, results in a list not unlike an unordered list—except that nearly all browsers display it without bullets. For example:

```
<dl>
<dt>Uptown - above 60th Street
<dt>Midtown - 14th to 60th Street
<dt>Downtown - below 14th Street
</DL>
```

And, although the `<dd>` element isn't as useful, it could be used on its own to indent paragraphs repeatedly within the definition list structure.

Summary

In this chapter, you learned about quite of few of the basic HTML elements that are used to change the organization of text on your Web pages. The chapter began with a look at the heading elements, and then it explained the physical and logical elements that are used to emphasize and stylize text. You then saw the various elements used to alter the organization and appearance of paragraphs, followed by the elements used to create lists on the page.

In Chapter 6, you'll learn how to create images for your Web documents and add them using the `<img />` element and its attributes.

6

VISUAL STIMULUS—
ADDING GRAPHICS

The vast majority of Web pages you encounter have images that either enhance the appearance of the Web pages, add to their usability, or communicate information. Generally, these images are easy to create and easy to add to your Web document. All you need are the correct tools and the knowledge of a few additional XHTML elements. It's important to realize that your images are not visible to all of your Web users, however, so you'll want to compensate for non-graphical browsers. Fortunately, attributes that substitute text when images can't be displayed are built-in, as are other options for customizing the appearance of images on your pages.

Images on the Web

When you're talking about images on the Web (and in computing in general), what you're really talking about is a particular type of computer file. Such files can be any sort of visual element—a drawing, something placed on a digital scanner, a photo from a digital camera, even an image of text created in a graphics application—but that element is always in a particular file format.

This means that a text editor like Windows Notepad or Mac's SimpleText won't be able to read an image properly. Instead, you'd need to use an image-browsing application, an image-editing application, or a Web browser. Ultimately, it's the file format that differentiates the image document from a text document and, by extension, from an HTML document.

It's a simple matter to add images to your Web pages—all it takes is the `<img />` element. Realize, however, that you're not adding the images to your HTML document. You place a *pointer* in your HTML document, which tells a Web browser how to find and load the image from its location either on your Web server or on the Internet. The image file and HTML document need to exist separately (see Figure 6.1).

FIGURE 6.1

The image on this page is the result of an instruction in the HTML document to locate the image file and place it in the browser window.

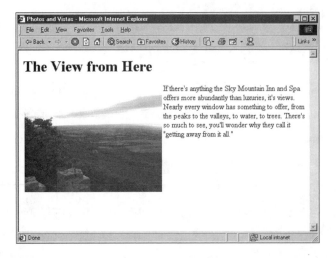

This issue of "where the image file is" can be a bit confusing, so let me clarify. Just as with any HTML document, an image file is referenced using a unique URL. This URL can point to an image file that's in the same folder or directory as the HTML document, one in a different directory on the same disk or Web server, or one that's somewhere else on the Internet. But the important issue is that you're using an URL. You'll see how exactly to do that later, in the section "The `<img />` Element." First, though, let's go through a quick primer on graphic file formats and how to create and/or translate images for the Web.

What Images Can You Use?

As mentioned, images are special files in particular formats that are recognized by Web browsers and other applications. On the Web, these file formats include JPEG, GIF, and PNG. But images can come in many other formats as well, such as PCX, TIFF, PICT, and so on.

For the sake of compatibility, however, only those first three formats are appropriate for use on your Web pages. If you have files in other formats, you'll want to translate them. Here's a look at the image formats that are Web-compatible:

- **JPEG (Joint Photographic Experts Group, pronounced "J-Peg")**—This format is generally used for photographs because it looks best at millions of colors. If you have an image that's been scanned using a scanner or taken with a digital still camera, it's possible that the image is already in JPEG format.

- **GIF (Graphics Interchange Format, pronounced "Jiff" or "Giff")**—This file type is best used for images that are computer-created—particularly text and mouse-drawn graphics that require fewer colors. GIF files are highly compressed, so they take less time to travel over the Internet—an important consideration. GIF also supports transparency within the image (so that images can appear to be sitting directly on the Web page's background) and animation.

You should avoid copying or translating images for your own use if you don't have the rights to do so. Web browsers and other applications will allow you to copy images from other Web sites, and you may have access to other images that you'd like to use on your Web pages. Many images, such as logos and photographs (among many others), are copyrighted and owned by individuals or corporations. Your best bet is to use only images that you create, not just translate or alter. Of course, I'm not an attorney, so consult one if you have a particular legal question.

- **PNG (Portable Network Graphics, pronounced "Ping")**—This format was actually created as a replacement for GIF, in part because GIF uses a patented compression scheme whereas PNG is free of patents. PNG also supports transparency and animation.

So, if you're creating an image in a drawing or photo-editing application, you'll likely choose PNG or GIF, particularly if it isn't a photographic-quality image. If the image is a photograph in another format, you'll likely use an image program to translate it into JPEG format, as discussed later in this chapter.

What Images *Should* You Use?

When you're choosing or creating the images for your Web page, you should focus on two basic issues. The images should be there for a good reason (not just to make the page look pretty) and should download quickly to the user's browser.

The photos, charts, and graphs that you use will likely improve both the appearance of your page and its ability to communicate with the reader. Text alone won't always hold a reader's attention, so images can be used to break up the text, summarize key points, or simply make the page more attractive.

Clear images communicate their function almost instantly. In fact, *icons*—which are simply small images similar to the folders and documents that appear in Microsoft Windows or the Macintosh OS—are often a clever way to get a point across graphically, while keeping your images small and to a minimum.

The images that communicate best may not even seem to be images at all—instead, they may be text. You'll find it's often convenient to create images that are largely text, if only to put more visually appealing text on your page. Figure 6.2, for instance, shows title text that looks a little more stylish than an HTML heading.

FIGURE 6.2

Images on a page can include stylized text.

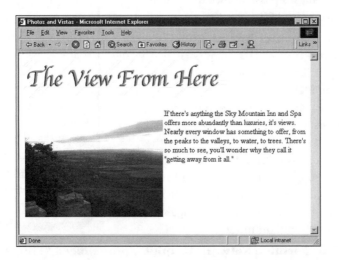

Although adding Web images to your pages is a fairly painless process, creating those images can be a bit tougher. The trick with Web images is to keep them interesting, entertaining, and useful, yet small and unobtrusive. It takes a bit of getting used to, but the best Web designers understand that having a balance is the most important element for successful images. Here are a few basic rules:

■ Images and drawn graphics should have a clear purpose on your page. Having images just for the sake of having pictures on the page should be kept to a minimum. Most Web surfers are looking for information or services, not cool images.

■ Image files should be small and load quickly. By the same token, your Web page should load quickly, too—which means it can't be overwhelmed with images.

■ Take advantage of technology to improve your images. Make sure you choose the correct image format for your graphic, and use your image-editing application to trim the image and make it as small as possible while still being useful. You should also consult Chapter 11, "Advanced Web Images and Imagemaps," to learn more about advanced issues that can make your images more highly compressed and efficient.

There are two measurements of image size on Web pages: the amount of the screen that an image takes up, and the storage space the image's file requires on the server computer. So, when we say you should have small images, it isn't only that the image shouldn't take up much space on the page. More importantly, it should be small in actual *file size*, which makes the image download to a user's Web browser more quickly.

How do you make files smaller? Some applications have special tools that help you shrink your images' file sizes. But mostly it's a question of choosing the correct image format (JPEG for photos, GIF or PNG for drawn or painted graphics and text), using the fewest number of colors possible, and cropping or trimming the images so that you only use as much space as necessary. For other hints and ideas, see Chapter 11.

Creating and Translating Web Images

Once you've considered the implications of using images on the Web, you can set yourself to the task of creating and/or translating images. You'll need a image-editing application (discussed in Chapter 3, "What You Need to Get Started"), and you'll need either some existing images or some ideas for creating new images. In this section, we'll discuss two different applications—Paint Shop Pro for Microsoft Windows and GraphicConverter for Macintosh.

Using Paint Shop Pro

Paint Shop Pro for Windows is the most popular shareware option for image editing, particularly among Web designers. And there's good reason—the basic tasks are simple.

If you already have an image you're working with, you should load that image into Paint Shop Pro by selecting **File**, **Open**. The image can be anything—a photograph, a drawing you've created in another application, or even an image that you've created in Paint Shop Pro. Once the image is loaded, you're ready to crop it and prepare it for the Web.

Cropping the Image

Cropping an image simply means selecting the portion of the original image that you'd like to use as the final image on your Web page. In many cases, it's a good idea to crop an image to the bare minimum you'd like to use. This is partly so that the image will fit well on your page, but also so that it's as small as possible while still communicating important information. With images that you create in other programs, you may also find it useful to crop each image so that less of its background will appear on the Web page.

In Paint Shop Pro, with the image loaded, select the Crop tool and drag an outline around the area that you'd like to keep. You do this by pointing at the top-left corner of the area, and then clicking and holding the mouse button while you drag to the bottom-right corner of the portion you'd like to keep. Release the mouse button and the area should be surrounded by a box (see Figure 6.3).

FIGURE 6.3

Selecting an area for cropping in Paint Shop Pro.

Crop tool

With the selection made, choose **Image**, **Crop** from the menu or double-click inside the box that you've drawn. The image is cropped to the portion inside the box. Choose **File**, **Save** to save the changes, or choose **File**, **Save As** to give the cropped image a new name, thus keeping the original image as well.

Resizing an Image

Often you'll find that even once you've cropped a high-resolution photo to the desired size, you've still got something that's a little too big to fit comfortably and effectively on your Web page. The solution is to resize the image, which is fairly simple to do in Paint Shop Pro.

With the image open in a document window, select **Image**, **Resize**. In the Pixel size section of the Resize dialog box, you can enter a new size, in pixels. Note that when you change the width, the height changes automatically. That's because the **Maintain Aspect Ratio** option is turned on at the bottom of the Resize dialog box. This ensures that a resized image won't be stretched or compressed in a way that makes it look distorted. (If you *want* distortion, turn this option off.)

If you'd prefer, you can click the radio button next to **Percentage of Original** and enter a new width or height. That way you can quickly change the size of the image without worrying about an exact size in pixels.

When you've made your changes, click **OK** and the image will change in size.

ALL ABOUT PIXELS

What's all this about pixels? Pixels are picture elements, which is a fancy way to say "dots." Images on your screen are composed of a certain number of dots. The more dots, the larger the image will appear.

Your computer display is set within your operating system, to display a fixed number of pixels—usually 1,024×768, or sometimes 800×600. (It may have a different setting, usually dependent on the size of the display.) Images from digital cameras can be "megapixel" images—1,024×768 at the lowest, with some of them pushing 2,048×1,536 or higher. Clearly, that's more pixels than you need for a Web image. The solution is to crop the images and/or resize them.

You may come across one other measurement, called pixels per inch (ppi). Different items have different pixel resolutions, which is why pixels can be so darned confusing. If you're asked by an application, images for a Web page generally don't need to be more than 72 ppi. As you'll see in Chapter 11, you can change the ppi of images to make them take up less storage space and travel over the Internet more quickly.

Adding Text

To add text to an image (or to create an image that's exclusively text), you simply click the **Text** button (it looks like a capital "A") and then click in the image window to begin adding text. When you click, the Text Entry dialog box will appear.

Enter the text you'd like to add to the image in the **Enter Text Here** entry box. Then use the commands elsewhere in the dialog box to fine-tune the appearance of the text, including font, size, style, alignment, and even kerning (space between characters) and leading (space between lines). When you're done, click **OK**.

After you click **OK**, your text becomes an object in the image, as shown in Figure 6.4. If you'd like to move the text, you can do that by pointing at the very middle of the text until you see the mouse pointer change into a four-way arrow. Now click and hold the mouse button, and then move the mouse around and you'll drag the text around on the image. When you get to its new home, release the mouse button.

> **note**
>
> One option enables you to *anti-alias* the text, which means to smooth the appearance of the text onscreen. This is a great idea for most Web images because the text looks more polished and professional.

FIGURE 6.4

Adding text in Paint Shop Pro.

Text tool

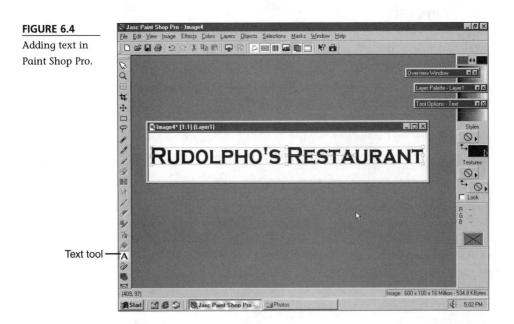

Saving or Translating the Image File

When you're ready to save an image for the Web, you'll want to select **File**, **Save As**, so that you can choose the appropriate image file format. In the Save As dialog box, enter a name for the image in the **File name** entry box. I recommend you avoid using spaces in the filename because they're a little tougher to deal with on the Web.

Now you'll see the **Save as Type** menu, which you can use to choose the file type. For photographic images, choose JPEG — JFIF (JFIF Compliant) as the type. For images you've created in Paint Shop Pro, choose either **CompuServe Graphics Interchange** or **Portable Network Graphics**. With that selection made, you can click **Save** to save your new image in its Web-compliant format.

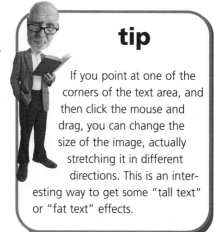

tip

If you point at one of the corners of the text area, and then click the mouse and drag, you can change the size of the image, actually stretching it in different directions. This is an interesting way to get some "tall text" or "fat text" effects.

Using GraphicConverter

GraphicConverter is the most popular shareware graphics solution for Macintosh, with both Mac OS 9 (and earlier) and Mac OS X versions available. To load your image into GraphicConverter, select **File**, **Open**. Once it's loaded, you'll be able to crop, resize, and save or translate it.

Cropping (Trimming) the Image

To crop an image in GraphicConverter, click the **Selection** tool in the toolbar (it looks like a dotted rectangle) and move the mouse pointer over to the image. Now draw a box around the portion of the image that you'd like to keep. You do this by pointing at the top-left corner of the area you'd like to keep, and then clicking and holding the mouse button while you drag to the bottom-right corner of the portion you'd like to keep. Release the mouse button and the area should be surrounded by a dotted line (see Figure 6.5).

note

You can do a lot more when saving images, including tricks to make them take up less space as files. See Chapter 11 for more details.

Selection tool

Selecting an area for cropping in Graphic-Converter.

To crop out the rest of the image and keep the outlined portion, choose **Edit**, **Trim Selection**. You'll see a new, smaller version of the image. Choose File, Save to immediately save the change. (If you'd like to give the cropped image a new name so that the original remains intact, choose **File**, **Save As**, as discussed later in the section "Saving or Translating the Image File.")

Resizing an Image

To resize an image in GraphicConverter, open the image in a document window and select **Picture**, **Size**, **Scale** from the menu. In the Scale dialog box, enter a new value in either the **Width** or **Height** entry box. The other value will change automatically as long as the **Keep Proportions** option is checked. Note that you can alter the units for the measurement you're changing by selecting **Pixel** or **Percent** from the pop-up menu that appears next to both the **Width** and **Height** entries.

When you're done making adjustments, click the OK button.

Adding Text

To add text to an image (or to create an image that's exclusively text), you simply click the **Text**

note

Typically, you won't want a photo to be more than a few hundred pixels wide by a few hundred pixels tall. In most cases, a 300×200 image will take up about 25% of the user's display. For more on pixels, see the "All About Pixels" sidebar earlier in this chapter.

button (it looks like a capital "A") and then click in the image window to create a text area. You can use the mouse to drag the sides of the text area to make it larger. Then, simply start typing the text you want to add to the image (see Figure 6.6).

Text tool

If you'd like to move the text area, place the mouse pointer over it until the pointer turns into a hand. Now click and hold the mouse button, and you'll see the hand turn into a fist. Move the mouse around to drag the text around on the image. When you get to its new home, release the mouse button.

If you'd like to change the style of the text, you can do so while the text area is still highlighted. (If it isn't, first click the **Selection** tool, and then click the text area again). Simply double-click the **Text** tool and a dialog box will appear in which you can change the font, size, alignment, and style of the text. When you're done, click the **OK** button.

note

Anti-alias means to smooth the appearance of text onscreen. This is a great idea for most Web images, as anti-aliasing text tends to make it look more polished and professional.

Saving or Translating the Image File

Once you have the image open and ready to save or translate, choose **File**, **Save As**. In the Save dialog box, enter a name for the image in the **Name** entry box. I recommend names without spaces because they're easier to add to your HTML documents. Next, select a format from the **Format** menu—JPEG/JFIF for photographic images, GIF or PNG for images you've created in GraphicConverter. (When you choose the format, a three-letter filename extension is appended automatically.) Click **Save**.

When you choose **JPEG/JFIF**, a dialog box appears. In that dialog box, you can choose the quality level of the image. The lower the quality, the smaller the file size of the image. You can also choose to use either QuickTime or JPEG 6.0 as the compression library—choose **JPEG 6.0**. Click **OK** to finish saving the image as a JPEG.

The `<img />` Element

When you want to insert a graphic file on a Web page, you actually do so with an URL. This URL is the specific location on the Internet where the graphic file is located. It can be on the same Web host computer that your HTML document is on, or it can be on a host somewhere else on the Internet.

The most basic `<img />` element can be used to create an *inline image*, which appears exactly where you place it relative to the text in the HTML document. The other kind of images, floating images, are discussed later in the section "Left- and Right-Aligning Images." The basic difference between the two types is that inline images aren't aligned against a margin—they're anchored in the text of the page. Floating images can be made to stick to the left or right margin.

To add an inline image to your page, you'll use the `<img />` element. This element acts as a placeholder in your text where the browser will put the graphic. The basic image element has the following syntax:

```
<img src="image_URL" />
```

The `src` attribute means *source* and refers to the location of the image (it's on some hard drive somewhere in the world). The actual URL for the image file replaces the words *image_URL*.

The *image_URL* can be a full URL with full machine name (such as `http://www.fakecorp.com/images/product1.jpg`). Alternatively, the URL can refer to the image file's *relative URL*. In this case, you refer to the file's location relative to the directory where the Web page is.

A relative URL is one that doesn't include an entire Internet address, such as `/images/product1.gif`. When you enter an URL in this way, the machine address portion of the URL (as in `www.fakecorp.com`) is assumed to be the same as that of the HTML document that includes the relative URL reference.

The following is sample HTML code for adding an inline graphic to the page (see Figure 6.7):

```
<p><img src="three.gif" />Rudolpho's offers excellent
vegetarian options, including a fabulous array of olive-based
appetizers, delectable breads and great house wines. The
mix-and-match pastas give you an array of choices for sauce
and pasta style and the atmosphere is the perfect blend of
sidewalk cafe and intimate conversation nooks. The only
downside -- weak service and a surprisingly woeful dessert tray.
Three stars.</p>
```

Notice that the `<img src />` element is using a relative URL. Actually, it could have just as easily been a complete URL like

```
<img src="http://www.fakecorp.com/three.gif" />
```

Both are similarly useful, but you only need to use a complete URL if the image you're loading resides elsewhere on the Internet. If it's in a subdirectory, something like this will work just fine:

```
<img src="/images/image1.gif" />
```

note

It's important to avoid linking to files using a direct file URL to your hard drive. (This will sometimes happen when you use less-sophisticated or older HTML editors.) Remember, your computer's hard drive isn't on the Internet—your Web server's hard drive is. So, if you create an image link like `<img src="file:///c|web_site/image.gif">`, your users will not be able to see the image once the page is uploaded to your Web server.

FIGURE 6.7

Notice that the image appears on the same line as the text. It's an inline image.

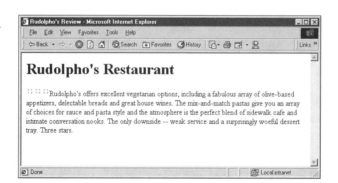

Alternative Text

Not everyone on the Internet has access to Internet Explorer, Netscape, or another graphical browser. In some cases you may be dealing with text-only Web browsers, such as those on cell phones, handheld computers, and "dumb" terminals at college campuses or libraries. In other cases, you may be dealing with sight-impaired users or others whose browsers offer assistive features.

So how can you accommodate these users, even when you use images in your Web pages? HTML provides a simple solution: the `alt` (alternative) attribute. This attribute defines a text string that replaces the image in browsers without graphics support. This text is often displayed in a box to separate it from the surrounding body text. Here's an example:

```
<img src="graph1.gif" alt="Chart shows sales up 25 percent in six months"
/>
```

You should consider `alt` a required attribute for well-formed XHTML code, and it offers the most benefit to the widest possible audience. In that spirit, it's also important not to place irrelevant text in the `alt` attribute (like "put text here" or "colorful bullet point"). Many assistive browsers will be forced to waste time by rendering that text in speech or in Braille, for instance. In other words, keep your `alt` text relevant and brief.

If you have a strong desire to explain an image in more detail, you can do so with another attribute: `longdesc`. This attribute enables you to specify an URL which can be linked to and explain the image in more detail, as in

```
<img src="graph1.gif" alt="Chart shows sales up 25 percent in six months"
longdesc="http://www.fakecorp.com/charts/chart1.html" />
```

Aligning Text and Images

On their own, Web browsers don't do much to help text and images share space on a Web page. Web browsers treat inline images like characters in the line of text. Often this doesn't look very good, particularly with photographs. Instead, you'd probably prefer an image to look more like an image on a magazine page, with the text wrapped around it.

Fortunately, you can do something about this. `<img />` comes with an attribute called `align`, which determines how text and images interact with one another on a Web page. Specifically, `align` controls how text that's placed on the same line as an image will line itself up along the vertical sides of the image.

The `align` attribute is written as

```
<img align="value" src="image_URL" />
```

The standard (inline) values for the align attribute are shown in Table 6.1.

TABLE 6.1   Standard Values for the `align` Attribute

Value	Effect on Text
`"top"`	Aligns the bottom of the text to top of the image
`"middle"`	Aligns the bottom of the text to the middle of the image
`"bottom"`	Aligns the bottom of the text to the bottom of the image

The `bottom` value is the default for `<img />`, so you don't need to specify it if that's what you want to use. When using any of the standard values, Web browsers leave white space around the text on the line, and the text wraps down to the next line beneath the bottom of the image. Figure 6.8 shows how a Web browser handles each of these attribute values.

FIGURE 6.8

The image is aligned to bot-tom, top, and middle, respec-tively.

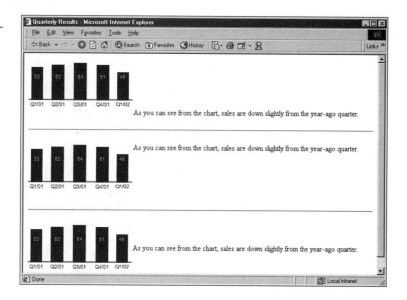

Right- and Left-Aligning Images

The `align` attribute can accept two other values, `left` and `right`, which change the image from an inline image to floating images. They won't appear exactly where you place the `<img />` element in the text, but rather on the selected margin near the text that surrounds the `<img />` element. In addition, the text will wrap around the image, somewhat like an image on a magazine page, as shown in Figure 6.9. Here's an example:

```
<p><img src="valley.jpg" align="left" />Views.
If there's
anything the Sky Mountain Inn and Spa offers
more abundantly
than luxuries, it's views. Nearly every
window has something
to offer, from the peaks to the valleys, to
water, to trees.
There's so much to see, you'll wonder why
they call it "getting
away from it all." </p>
```

Width and Height

Two other attributes for `<img />`, `width` and `height`, are worth mentioning. These two attributes are designed to make your Web page appear in the user's browser just a bit more quickly.

By telling the browser the size of the images (in pixels), the browser is able to mock up the layout and lay in the text before it finishes retrieving the images. This makes it appear that your page is loading more quickly in the browser window, and it allows the visitor to read text and click hyperlinks even as the page continues to download. Here's an example of the `width` and `height` attributes in action:

```
<p><img src="mountains.jpg" align="left" width="250" height="100" />
Views. If there's anything the Guest Cottage offers more abundantly
than luxuries, it's views. Nearly every
window has something to offer,
from the peaks to the valleys, to water, to
trees. There's so much to
see, you'll wonder why they call it
"getting away from it all."</p>
```

Note that the `width` and `height` attributes can actually be used to change the apparent size of an existing image and force it to conform to the pixel size that you specify. That means you could take an image that's 300 pixels wide and 150 pixels high and force it to appear 150 pixels wide and 75 pixels high simply by specifying those sizes:

```
<img src="bigimage.jpg" width="150" height="75" />
```

note

Older browsers will recognize two other attributes, `vspace` and `hspace`, which can be used to add space between a floating image and text. These commands are not well-formed code, however. In Chapter 10, "Get Splashy: Style Sheets, Fonts, and Special Characters," you'll see that style sheets can be used to create the same effect.

tip

Need to know the size of an image? In most cases, your image-editing application can help you. Just look for an Info command. In Paint Shop Pro, select **Image, Image Information**. In GraphicConverter, choose **Picture, Show Information**.

FIGURE 6.9

The top image is left-aligned; the bottom is right-aligned.

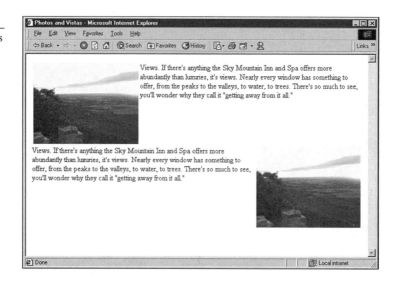

This is certainly possible, but it's not a great idea for one reason: file size. The file size of the image remains the same, regardless of the height and width specified. In the preceding example, you're forcing your visitors to download the full image and view it at half size. The better plan would be to crop or scale the image in an image-editing application, and then use that smaller image on your page.

Summary

In this chapter, you learned about the file formats that can be used on the Web, and how to modify and translate other images so that they can be saved in those formats. You also learned how to crop images and create images that include text. Then, you learned how to use the `<img />` element to add images to your Web documents, including many of the attributes associated with `<img />` that are used to align the image against text on the page, add alternative text, and specify the width and height of the image.

In Chapter 7, you'll learn how to add hyperlinks to your pages so that you can link to other Web pages, other Web sites, and even other Internet services.

7

BUILDING HYPERTEXT LINKS

Hypertext was the basic concept that propelled the idea of the Web forward, allowing information and ideas to be linked together in a way that hadn't happened before on the Internet. Combined with most Web browsers' graphical and multimedia capabilities, hypertext links (hyperlinks) make the Web an entirely new medium for communication and publishing.

How Hyperlinks Work

On the Web, hyperlinks are the basis of all movement and manipulation. Clicking a link on a Web page generally moves you to the related resource by loading that resource in your Web browser or in a helper application. Sometimes that's a new Web page; sometimes it's another Internet service, like an email message or an

FTP (file transfer protocol) server. Before the user can click a link, however, it has to be created by the Web author.

You use an XHTML element, the `<a>` anchor element, to create a hyperlink. The anchor requires the `href` attribute, which is used to tell the Web browser which new URL is being referenced by the hyperlink. So, to create a hyperlink, you'll first need to determine the URL for the target page or resource.

The Uniform Resource Locator

Every hyperlink contains a *Uniform Resource Locator*, or *URL*. The URL is the address of the Web page that appears in the Location or Address box near the top of your Web browser when you're surfing the Web. It's also the address that shows up, in many cases, at the bottom of your Web browser's window when you move the cursor over a hyperlink.

As mentioned in Chapter 1, "The Fundamentals of Web Publishing," the URL consists of two major items: the protocol and the destination (although they have all types of other names). The protocol tells you what kind of Internet resource you're dealing with. The most common protocol on the Web is http://, which retrieves HTML documents from the Web.

The destination can be a filename, a directory name, or a computer name. An URL such as `http://www.fakecorp.com/products/index.html` tells you exactly where the HTML document is located and what its filename is. If the URL is `ftp://ftp.netscape.com/`, the URL is telling the browser to access a computer named ftp.netscape.com using the File Transfer Protocol.

Relative Versus Absolute URLs

There's another distinction you can make when it comes to URLs for your hyperlinks. If a particular Web page's URL is basically the same as the current page—except, perhaps, for the filename—it's possible to use a *relative* URL to reference that page. Consider the following two pages:

`http://www.olelondonisp.net/drwatson/index.html`

`http://www.olelondonisp.net/drwatson/resume.html`

Both of these URLs are absolute URLs—they could both be used to reference their respective pages (index.html and resume.html) from anywhere on the Internet. But what if you're creating a hyperlink on the first page (index.html) that points to the second page (resume.html)? In that case, you could use a relative URL, because the rest of the information is the same.

It's a little like working with files in folders on your PC or Mac. If you save a file in a particular folder and then decide to open a new file, generally you don't have to go spelunking through your entire hard drive to find that folder again. Many applications will open right to the last-used folder.

A Web browser does the same thing. When it encounters an URL that's nothing more than a path or filename, such as resume.html, the browser will assume that the author meant "Use the current URL and directory, but open a new file." For instance, let's say the current page is stored in this directory:

`http://www.olelondonisp.net/drwatson/`

It's assumed that the relative link should simply be tacked onto that URL:

http://www.olelondonisp.net/drwatson/ + resume.html

This results in the following:

`http://www.olelondonisp.net/drwatson/resume.html`

So, you could use the following relative URL to refer to the second page from the first page:

`resume.html`

This is shown in Figure 7.1. If index.html and resume.html are in the same directory (and on the same Web server computer), everything will work fine.

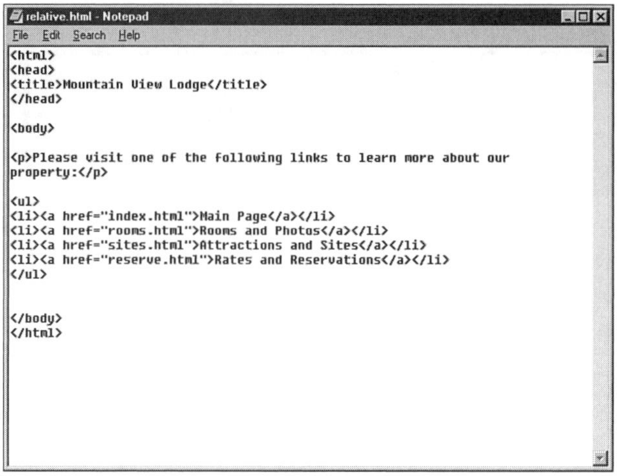

FIGURE 7.1

The links shown are relative links, which should work fine as long as those pages are in the same directory as the page being edited.

```
relative.html - Notepad
File   Edit   Search   Help
<html>
<head>
<title>Mountain View Lodge</title>
</head>

<body>

<p>Please visit one of the following links to learn more about our
property:</p>

<ul>
<li><a href="index.html">Main Page</a></li>
<li><a href="rooms.html">Rooms and Photos</a></li>
<li><a href="sites.html">Attractions and Sites</a></li>
<li><a href="reserve.html">Rates and Reservations</a></li>
</ul>


</body>
</html>
```

This relativity, if you will, means you can also reach other directories on the server using common notation. For instance, if you want to access an item that's in a subdirectory of the current directory, you could use an URL such as /pages/house.html or even `/assistants/roger/resume.html` to access those items. If those are valid subdirectories of the directory where the HTML document currently resides, those items will be accessed.

Similarly, you can use special notation to cause the URL to access a directory that's the parent of the current directory. For instance, suppose you're saving the current HTML document in the `products` directory, which is a subdirectory of the site's main (or root) directory. In that case, you could access the main index page using an URL like this:

`../index.html`

Likewise, you could access a subdirectory of the root directory using an URL like this:

`../service/contact.html`

The two periods at the beginning are standard notation that represents the *parent* of the current directory. They mean "go up one directory level." Figure 7.2 shows you where these files would be located to give you a sense of the hierarchy.

note

Using relative links can be a bit risky because they make it harder for you to move directories and subdirectories around on your site. If you reorganize your site at some point, your relative links may no longer work correctly.

FIGURE 7.2

If the current page is in the product's directory, its parent is the root directory of the Web site.

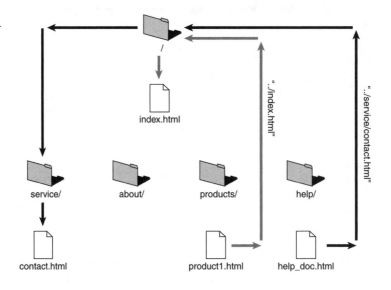

The <base> Element

You've already seen that relative URLs take some of the effort out of creating hyperlinks. But, as noted, relative URLs are always "relative" to the directory where the current HTML document is stored. But what if you'd like some other location to be the URL that gets added to your relative URL to make up the entire address? You can do that with the <base> element.

Take this example:

1. You've created a directory structure that begins at this URL:

   `http://www.fakecorp.com/`

2. Within that directory you've created some subdirectories, like images, about, and products.

3. You create a page called widget.html within a new_products subdirectory of the products directory. The URL to that file would be

   `http://www.fakecorp.com/products/new_products/widget.html`

4. Let's say you want to get to the contact.html page that's inside the about directory. One solution would be to use the two periods introduced earlier, which would result in a relative URL such as

   `../../about/contact.html`

5. Unfortunately, that's not much more fun than typing an absolute URL, such as http://www.fakecorp.com/about/contact.html. Plus, you're probably a bit more likely to commit a typo. But there is another option. You could use the <base> element to set the base URL to your site's root directory:

   ```
   <head>
   <base href="http://www.fakecorp.com/" />
   </head>
   ```

6. What this means is that all relative URLs will be relative to the base href URL instead of to the document's current location. So, to access that contact page, the URL would now be

   `about/contact.html`

Essentially, adding a <base> element means that the base URL is added together with any relative URLs to create a complete reference. In the example, the base URL http://www.fakecorp.com/ is added to the relative URL about/contact.html to create this absolute URL:

`http://www.fakecorp.com/about/contact.html`

Notice, though, that the `<base>` element will affect *every* relative URL on the page. You'll need to change any relative URLs that don't take the base URL into account. That said, the `<base>` element doesn't affect absolute URLs at all, so you don't need to worry about them.

Creating Links

Most hypertext links by themselves are added to HTML documents using the anchor element (`<a>`, `</a>`). This element surrounds the text that describes what the link points to. The URL itself must be in quotes, and it uses the `href` (hyperlink reference) attribute. A link in HTML takes the following format:

```
<a href="URL">put your link text here</a>
```

So, if you want to link the text "About our company" with the HTML document called `about.html` that resides in the root directory of the `www.fakecorp.com` machine, the HTML code would look like this:

```
<a href="http://www.fakecorp.com/about.html">About our company</a>
```

As mentioned earlier in this chapter, absolute URLs aren't the only ones you can use for hyperlinks. If, for instance, `team.html` is in the same directory and on the same machine as the page containing the following HTML code, the URL shown will work fine:

```
<a href="team.html">About our executive team</a>
```

Another interesting aspect of relative links is that they don't change just because you move the files. It's like furniture in your living room. If you moved from one address to another, chances are that the armchair and couch could still be found if you told a friend, "Look in the living room." If you used an absolute reference ("Go to 123 Main and look in the living room"), you'd have to change part of that reference when you moved to a new place.

tip

Try to make your link text descriptive. Links that say things such as "Click here" or "Follow this link" don't give the users enough information about what they are getting into.

note

Make sure you've enclosed *something* inside your anchor—whether it's text or an image element. If you don't put anything in there, you aren't giving your audience much of a target to click.

In the same way, you'd have to change an absolute URL, such as `http://www.oldfakecorp.com/about.html`, if you moved to a new server computer (such as `www.fakecorp.com`). If the URL were relative, however, it would still work fine in the new location.

One thing you *can't* do with a link is nest one link within another—you must close the first anchor element before starting another one. The following example is illegal:

```
Order <a href="product1.html">Product #1 or
<a href="product2.html">Product #2</a> from
our store.</a>
```

Instead, the link would need to be something more along these lines:

```
Order <a href="product1.html">Product #1</a>
or <a href="product2.html">Product #2</a> from
our store.
```

> **tip**
>
> You can also create links that point to any sort of file that a Web browser can display, such as a text file (.txt) or an image file (.jpg, .gif, .png). In fact, you can link to many types of multimedia files as well, and they'll be handed off to a helper application, if appropriate (see Chapter 13, "Adding Multimedia and Java Content").

Linking on the Same Page

Picture this—you've got a long Web page with different sections, and you want to include a link that takes the user to a different part of the page that is already being displayed. It's easy. You'll first name a portion of your page, and then you'll create an anchor that points to that named portion.

First things first. On some part of your page, you'll use the `<a>` element with the `name` attribute, as in

```
<a name="q1"><h2>Question 1</h2></a>

<p>What is the cause of the root of the problem?</p>
```

For the record, though, this actually isn't well-formed code for XHTML because XML doesn't really support the `name` attribute. Instead, you should use the `id` attribute, which is much more acceptable (as you'll see in later chapters). Furthermore, `id` (in this context) isn't implemented in many earlier Web browsers. So, for the foreseeable future, the solution is actually to include them both:

```
<a name="q1" id="q1"><h2>Question 1<h2></a>
```

And just to be perfectly clear, the name and ID specified can be anything alphanumeric that begins with a letter, and it can include dashes, underscores, periods, and colons. So "12" wouldn't be acceptable, while "question:one" or "myitem56" or "r134567" would all be acceptable.

Now, to reference that section with a link, you simply create an anchor tag that points to that name but includes the pound sign (#) as part of the URL:

```
<p>See <a href="#q1">Question 1</a> for more information.</p>
```

It may help to see all this in context. Figure 7.3 shows a sample HTML document that includes a number of named anchors on the same page.

FIGURE 7.3

Here's a page that includes multiple named anchors and links.

Named anchors can also be referenced when you're linking from other pages, even across the Internet. The named anchor simply becomes part of the URL that defines the page:

```
<p>For more, see <a
href="http://www.fakecorp.com/questions.html#q1">Question 1</a>
on the Questions page.</p>
```

In this example, the browser locates the page questions.html, locates the section of that page named "q1", and displays it in the browser window.

Building Links Using Images

If you'd like users to click an icon or a picture to move on to a new page or part of the current page, you can create a link that uses an image in the place of descriptive text. For instance, if you have an image named "icon.gif" you can use it as a link like so:

```
<a href="moutains.html"><img
src="mount1.jpg alt="Read about the
mountain range" /></a>
```

This places a highlighted border (most color browsers use blue by default) such as the one shown in Figure 7.4. This tells your user that the image can be followed by clicking it, just like any other hyperlink.

If you're working in transitional XHTML, you can add another attribute to your `<img>` element that can change the size of the border, in pixels, that appears around the image. The attribute, cleverly named `border`, accepts a number:

```
<a href="about.html"><img
src="button_about.gif" alt="About Us" border="0" /></a>
```

FIGURE 7.4

Images can be either large or small and still be clickable hyperlinks.

While the number can be any integer you desire, using 0 will keep the border from appearing at all on the page. In strict XHTML, this border issue should be handled with a style sheet, as discussed in Chapter 10, "Get Splashy: Style Sheets, Fonts, and Special Characters."

Using Special Links

URLs are so flexible that you can use them to create links to practically anything on the Net. You can create links to email, FTP, Gopher, Usenet newsgroups, and even Telnet sessions. This makes it possible for Web pages to put related information together on the same page. For instance, you could have a link to a Web page that describes a downloadable shareware program, a link to a Usenet newsgroup where that software is discussed, and a link to an FTP server where the program can be downloaded. In other words, your readers no longer have to fire up individual Internet programs to get to the information you want them to see.

This flexibility is part of what has made the Web browser the single most important Internet tool. From your browser, you can do just about everything else you can do on the Net, including accessing a variety of resources that technically aren't part of the World Wide Web. And when the browser doesn't support a service, generally it's launched in another application automatically, such as your email application or a multimedia viewer.

As a Web author, you can create links that lead your visitors to those resources. Regardless of the type of service accessed, each hyperlink uses the anchor element. From there, the only things that change are the protocols for the hyperlinks and the type of URL address used.

Creating a `mailto:` Link

Putting an email link in an HTML document is pretty easy. All you need is a valid email address, which is made up of four parts: the account or username, the @ symbol, the machine name, and the domain name.

Here's an example of an email address:

`questions@mac-upgrade.com`

The account name is questions and the domain name is `mac-upgrade.com`. In this example, there is no machine name. However, consider an email address like this:

`robert@mail.fakecorp.com`

In this case, `mail` is a machine name.

After you have a valid email address, you just use `mailto:` as the protocol for it in an anchor element. An example of an email link is as follows:

`<a href="mailto:questions@mac-upgrade.com">Send questions directly to me.</a>`

Figure 7.5 shows another example of a `mailto:` link. Many authors like to "sign" their home page by putting an email link at the bottom.

FIGURE 7.5

When users click an email link on your home page, a new message window will appear in their email applications.

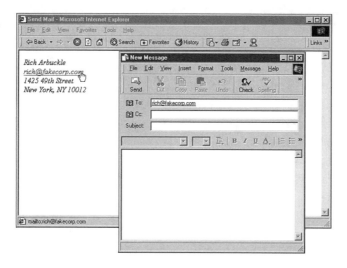

Want to specify the subject line? It won't work in all browsers, but the safest way to do this is to use the `title` attribute for the `<a>` anchor:

```
<a href="mailto:orders@fakecorp.com" title="I want the new book!">Order
the book</a>
```

Creating a Link to an FTP Site

FTP is mostly used to copy files between computers. Users of FTP have to log on to remote computers, often as guests, and get the files they want.

The only thing you need to put in a link to an FTP site is an Internet address to an FTP server computer. So, if a valid FTP site is `ftp.microsoft.com`, the link would look like the following:

```
<a href="ftp://ftp.microsoft.com/">Microsoft's FTP Site</a>
```

If you're inviting your Web visitors to download a particular file from your site, you should specify the file path for them. This keeps users from trying to find their way through unknown directories.

For example, let's say you have a compressed program (program.zip) in a directory called downloads (/downloads/) that you want people to access. A link to it might look something like the following:

```
<a href="ftp://ftp.fakecorp.com/downloads/program.zip">The program (PKZip
format)</a>
```

This tells the Web browser to connect with FTP, go directly to the correct directory, and immediately begin downloading the file.

ARE FTP SERVERS IMPORTANT?

If you're building a Web site for a company that has a lot of files to make available to customers or visitors, it's a good idea to put the files on an FTP server and then just include a link to that server on your Web page. This prevents your Web page from becoming cluttered with download links, and FTP servers are more efficient at sending files than HTTP (Web) servers are.

That said, smaller sites don't need to have FTP servers. The HTTP protocol is capable of transmitting binary files—particularly those that are in .exe form or have been compressed using PKZip (.zip) or StuffIt (.sit) compression engines. Then, a simple http:// link to the file will cause the receiving browser to download the file and save it to the user's hard disk. For example:

```
<a href="http://www.fakecorp.com/downloads/program.sit">Click to download</a>
```

This should work fine—the user will be prompted to select a place to store the file on his or her hard disk.

Gopher Servers

Before the Web came into existence, one of the most popular ways of storing and accessing information was through Gopher sites. Gopher is basically a collection of text-based menus that present information in a hierarchical format, as shown in Figure 7.6. As you might imagine, there aren't a ton of these sites left, thanks to the Web's popularity.

FIGURE 7.6

You can point your users directly to a Gopher server with a simple hyperlink.

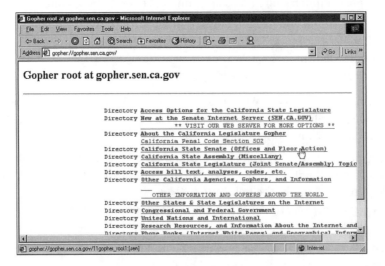

Gopher is very similar to the Web except that it doesn't have any built-in multimedia capabilities, such as graphics or sound. You can incorporate a link to a Gopher site on your Web page by adding an anchor around the computer's address and putting gopher:// in front of it. A Gopher link would look like the following:

```
<a href="gopher://marvel.loc.gov">The Library of Congress</a>
```

Link to Newsgroups

Usenet newsgroups are the discussion groups of the Internet. Although they're called "news," they're really centered around posting and replying to messages and having discussions. You may want to point people to a newsgroup because your home page relates specifically to what goes on in that group. Or, if you think that the users might have more questions than you can answer, you can include a link to a related newsgroup in hopes of decreasing the amount of email you receive.

Whatever the case, a link to a Usenet newsgroup is different from most other hypertext tags. To put in a link to a newsgroup, simply enter **news:** followed by the newsgroup name in the anchor. A typical newsgroup link would look like the following:

tip

While Usenet remains popular, many discussion groups have moved to the Web, where bulletin board software makes the discussions easier to follow and more graphical. See Chapter 17, "Forums, Chats, and Other Add-Ons," for a discussion of bulletin board options for Web sites.

```
<a href="news:alt.tv.startrek">Discuss Star Trek on Usenet</a>
```

In this case, the user's browser would do one of two things: Access its own news server (if one has been preconfigured) and attempt to locate the message group, or hand the command off to a helper application designed to access Usenet newsgroups.

If, for some reason, you were going to point the user to a particular news server computer instead of a particular newsgroup, you could do that using the double-slash version of the protocol:

```
<a href=news://news.fakecorp.com/>Visit our news server</a>
```

Links to Telnet Servers

A link to a Telnet server allows your user to log directly onto a computer that has a remote access server enabled. In most cases, this is a text-based remote access session, such as those between terminal computers and Unix or mainframe servers.

Indeed, no popular browsers support Telnet directly, so the user will likely need a Telnet helper application that will be launched when the link is clicked.

The syntax for a Telnet link is pretty straightforward: You just type **telnet://** followed by the remote computer's address as the URL. A typical Telnet link would look something like the following:

```
<a href="telnet://mac1.fakecorp.com/">Log into the corporate Telnet
server</A>
```

You can also create a link that automatically enters the logon name to use for guest accounts. All you have to do is specify the logon name they should use, followed by the @ sign before the machine name. So, if you want a person to access your computer with the logon name of guest, the HTML code would be

```
<a href="telnet://guest@mac1.fakecorp.com/">Log in anonymously.</a>
```

When the browser sees this, it notifies the user of the correct logon name.

Cool Tricks: Targets and Client-Pull

Before we finish this chapter, let's look at two unrelated but interesting things you can do with URLs and links. In one case, you'll augment the anchor element with another special attribute; in another, you'll use a completely different element to load a new Web page.

Open a New Window

We'll discuss targets for hyperlinks more in Chapter 12, "Creating Sites with HTML Frames," where you'll see how targets can be used to change pages in different frames within the Web browser. In this section, though, we're interested in one special case—opening a hyperlink in a new Web browser window.

To do this, you'll use the target attribute to the anchor element. The specific target in question is called "_blank", and it forces the linked page to appear in a new window. Here's an example:

```
<a href="http://www.w3.org/"
target="_blank">Click
```
```
here for more information on HTML and
XHTML.</a>
```

tip

You can specify the target attribute in the <base> element, too, if you'd like all hyperlinks on the page to open in new browser windows. For example, using `<base href="http://www.fakecorp.com/" target="_blank" />` in the <head> of your document would accomplish this.

Changing Pages Automatically

Using a process called *client-pull*, the `<meta>` element and its attributes enable you to load another HTML page automatically after a predetermined amount of time. You can also use these tags to reload, or *refresh*, the same HTML document over and over. It's called *client-pull* because the user's Web browser (often called the *client* in Internet-speak) is instructed to automatically load (or *pull*) a new page from the Web server without the user clicking anything or the Web server sending any special commands.

The client-pull concept is based on the `<meta>` element, introduced in Chapter 4, "Creating Your First Page," which is used in the head of your document. For client-pull, the `<meta>` element takes the attributes `http-equiv` and `content`. Client-pull follows this format:

```
<head>
<title>Title of Page</title>
<meta http-equiv="refresh" content="seconds; url="new URL" />
</head>
```

The `http-equiv` attribute always takes the value "refresh" in client-pull; it only loads a new document if the `content` attribute includes an URL. Otherwise, it refreshes (reloads) the current document.

The `content` attribute accepts a number for the amount of time (in seconds) you want the browser to wait before the next page is loaded (or the current page is refreshed). After that number, you type a colon and **url=** followed by a valid URL for the page that should be loaded automatically.

Here's an example that just refreshes the current page after waiting ten seconds:

```
<head>
<title>Page Title</title>
<meta http-equiv="refresh" content="10" />
</head>
```

In this next example, we'll use client-pull to load a new page after waiting 15 seconds:

```
<head>
<title>Page One</title>
<meta http-equiv="refresh" content="15;
url="http://www.fakecorp.com/index2.html" />
</head>
```

Summary

In this chapter, you learned how URLs are built and how they work together with the `<base>` and `<a>` anchor elements to make hyperlinks possible. You saw how to create hyperlinks that lead to outside Web sites, how to link to parts of a particular Web page, and how to use images as hyperlinks. Beyond that, you saw how to create hyperlinks to various types of Internet resources, as well as how to manage some automatic link-related tasks.

In the next chapter, you'll learn the basic XHTML table elements, which allow you to place data visually in rows and columns. You'll also see how to create the table and change its appearance using the `<table>` element and attributes.

8

TABLE BASICS

You've seen how lists and paragraph elements can be used to organize text logically on the page. The next level of complexity is the *table*, which can be used to divide a section of the Web page into different rows and columns. You can use the table elements to more precisely place rows and columns of data, text, links, and even images. In Chapter 9, "Advanced Table Elements and Table Design," you will see how you can use tables for something even grander—page layout.

Creating a Table

You use the table container element to hold together a group of other elements that define each individual row, and within each row, elements define each *cell*. Indeed, working with XHTML tables is very similar to working with a spreadsheet application. An XHTML table consists of rows and columns. Where a row and a column meet, you find a cell. Each individual cell is designed to be a container of data. XHTML table cells can contain nearly any text and XHTML elements, such as hyperlinks and images.

Tables take the following format:

```
<table>
<caption>Caption text for table</caption>
<tr><th>column head 1</th><th>column head
2</th><th>column head 3</th></tr>
<tr><td>cell1-1 data</td><td>cell1-2
data</td><td>cell1-3 data</td></tr>
<tr><td>cell2-1 data</td><td>cell2-2
data</td><td>cell2-3 data</td></tr>
...additional rows...
</table>
```

The main element is the `<table>` container. Using the optional `<caption>` element, you can add a line that explains the table or gives it a title. Within the `<table>` element, you add container elements for table rows, `<tr>`, and table data, `<td>`. Most tables also use the table heading element, `<th>`, which is useful for the title text for rows and columns.

Although these table elements have been around for many years now, there are some popular Web browsers that can have trouble with them—particularly, browsers in some mobile phones and Personal Digital Assistants (PDAs). If you'd like your pages to be visible to these users, you may opt for simpler layouts (using lists, for example). Or you can offer two pages, one that uses tables and one that uses the `<pre>` element.

The `<table>` Element

You begin any XHTML table with the `<table>` element, which is designed to contain all the elements necessary to create a table. Between the `<table>` and `</table>` tags, you use the `<tr>` table row container element to create each row. Then, each `<td>` container element defines a cell, in which you place that cell's data:

1. To begin a table, enter a set of `<table>`, `</table>` tags in your HTML document.

2. Between the table tags, add a set of `<tr>`, `</tr>` tags for each row you'd like in the table.

3. Now, in the first row definition, add a set of `<th>`, `</th>` table header tags for each column header (and, hence, each column) you'd like to define. Type the text for each column header inside each `<th>` element. (Remember, the `<th>` element is optional. In most graphical browsers, it simply makes the text boldface. Your first row can use the `<td>` element if desired.)

4. In all the remaining rows, add a set of `<td>`, `</td>` tags to define each individual cell. Between each set of `<td>` tags, enter the text and/or XHTML markup for that cell.

At this point, you need to be sure that your table has the same number of columns and/or column headings in each row. If your first row has three `<th>` elements, the second row needs to have three `<td>` elements, the third row needs three, and so forth. (You can skip cells, but we won't cover that until the section "Changing a Cell's Span" later in this chapter.) The table renders incorrectly if you don't define a consistent grid.

One example of a basic table using this format is the following:

```
<table border="1">
<caption>Regional Sales Teams</caption>
<tr><th>West</th><th>South</th><th>North
</th></tr>
<tr><td>Will H.</td><td>Sally
F.</td><td>Jude L.</td></tr>
<tr><td>Harvey D.</td><td>Paul
M.</td><td>Dale E.</td></tr>
<tr><td>Ryan C.</td><td>John
L.</td><td>Roger E.</td></tr>
</table>
```

So far, this isn't too tough. Once you're familiar with the concept, you can see how tables are similar to other containers, such as XHTML lists and paragraph elements. (In fact, as with list and paragraph elements, an XHTML table automatically begins and ends with space around it, separating it from other XHTML elements that come before or after it.) Figure 8.1 shows how this example might look in a browser.

Want a blank cell? You can create one using the *non-breaking space* entity code, ` `, within a cell definition. For example, `<td> </td>` should create a blank cell in most browsers.

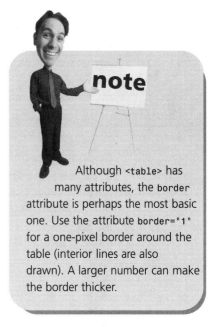

Although `<table>` has many attributes, the `border` attribute is perhaps the most basic one. Use the attribute `border="1"` for a one-pixel border around the table (interior lines are also drawn). A larger number can make the border thicker.

FIGURE 8.1

This basic
XHTML table is
a great way to
communicate
tabular data.

Captions and Summaries

The <caption> element is a container, inside which you type the name or a description for your table, along with any XHTML markup you'd like to use for that description. For example:

```
<caption><b>Consumer Retail Sales</b>, according to the <i>Wall Street
Journal</i></caption>
```

Just about any sort of markup tags are possible inside the <caption> element, although some—like list elements—wouldn't make much sense. You could use hyperlinks within the caption, however, which might be useful for referring the reader to another Web page for more information about the table, or to the source documents you use for data in the table.

If you use the <caption> element, it should come immediately after the opening <table> tag. Note that only one <caption> element is permitted per table.

By default, the caption text appears at the top of your table. If you'd like to force it to appear somewhere else (at the bottom of the table, for example), you can use the attribute align. Note that align isn't supported under the XHTML Strict DTD, but most browsers recognize it if you're using the XHTML Transitional DTD. The values for align include align="top" and align="bottom", which simply mean the caption appears at the top or bottom of the table. (In most browsers, the caption is automatically centered horizontally.) For example:

```
<caption align="bottom">Feed prices since spring, source: USA
Today</caption>
```

Each table you create can have a summary, which is a string of text that's used, in most cases, to help users of non-visual or assistive browsers (such as text-to-speech browsers) to recognize the purpose and structure of a table. The summary is added via an attribute to the <table> element, called summary. Place the summary text in quotes following the attribute. The following is an example:

```
<table summary="This table shows that sales in the Western region were 500
in spring and 600 in summer; sales in the Northern region were 300 in
spring and 400 in summer and sales in the Southern region were 200 in
spring and 650 in summer.">

<caption><b>Sales (in thousands) for Spring and Summer
Quarters</b></caption>

<tr><th>Quarter</th><th>West</th><th>North</th><th>South</th></tr>

<tr><th>Spring</th><td>500</td><td>300</td><td>200</td></tr>

<tr><th>Summer</th><td>600</td><td>400</td><td>650</td></tr>

</table>
```

Table Rows

The table row element can accept two attributes you may be interested in using, align and valign. These attributes are used to align the cells in that row horizontally and vertically, respectively. This is an example that uses align, shown in Figure 8.2:

```
<table border="1">

<tr align="center"><th>Year of Survery</th><th>Coffee
Preferred</th><th>Tea Preferred</th></tr>

<tr align="right"><th>1980</th><td>65%</td><td>35%</td></tr>

<tr align="right"><th>1990</th><td>60%</td><td>40%</td></tr>

<tr align="right"><th>2000</th><td>45%</td><td>55%</td></tr>

</table>
```

FIGURE 8.2

Cells are aligned to their right margins.

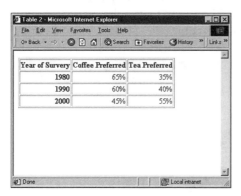

This align attribute can accept "center", "left", and "right" as values. valign can accept the values top, bottom, and center. You'll find this particularly useful when aligning images, as shown here:

```
<table border="1">

<tr valign="top">

<td><img src="image1.png"></td>
```

```
<td><img src="image2.png"></td>
<td><img src="image3.png"></td>
</tr>
</table>
```

Although the cells have to stretch to the height of the tallest image, all of the images in this example are aligned to the top of their respective cells to give the table a more uniform look. Figure 8.3 shows this top alignment, as well as the example with images aligned to `center`.

Table Cell Elements

You've already used the `<th>` and `<td>` elements to include headers and data in your tables. You may have noticed that, essentially, the only difference between the two is that `<th>` emphasizes the text (boldfaces it, in graphical browsers) and `<td>` does not.

> **tip**
>
> Like most XHTML elements, the spaces and returns you add in the middle of table row elements aren't rendered by the browser. So you can feel free to create spaces or returns between the various elements if it helps you when you're authoring the page. In particular, you may find it's helpful to place each cell on its own row as you get into more and more content and markup in each cell.

Technically, `<th>` is an element that the browser interprets as a header, so it displays text in a way that's distinct from the `<td>` element. In practice, this generally means it's boldface. In theory, however, it could mean the table is rendered very differently, particularly in non-graphical browsers, so you should only use the `<th>` container on cells that truly represent header data.

FIGURE 8.3

In the first table, cells are aligned to top. In the second, they're aligned to center.

Aside from accepting nearly any type of XHTML markup tags within them, both tags can accept two attributes that help you align data within the cell. These attributes are `align` and `valign`. For example:

```
<td align="center" valign="bottom">
```

`align` is used to align the data within the cell horizontally, accepting values of `left`, `right`, and `center`. Note that `align` in a `<td>` or `<th>` element is redundant if you've already used the `align` attribute with `<tr>`, unless you're specifically trying to override the row's alignment in a particular cell.

`valign` is used to align the data vertically within cells. Possible values are `top`, `bottom`, and `center`. Sometimes this doesn't actually look much different in a Web browser, especially if all your cells contain approximately the same amount of data. In the case of two cells that are different in the amount or size of the content enclosed, though, the `valign` attribute can make a significant difference in the appearance of the table. Figure 8.4 is an example of the `valign` attribute in action. Note the difference in the alignment of the second two images because the first image stretches the height of the overall row.

note

For best compatibility with assistive browsers, you should use `<th>` for the header data in your table whenever possible, if your columns and rows have headings. That helps assistive browsers organize and communicate the table data.

FIGURE 8.4

Cells vertically aligned to top, bottom, and center.

In addition to the alignment attributes, `<th>` supports another interesting attribute—the `scope` attribute. This allows you to specify the range of cells for which the `<th>` element is the header. It can accept the values `row` and `col` to specify that a particular `<th>` element is the header for its row, or its column, respectively. For example:

```
<tr><th scope="row">Processor</th><td>G9-1.6</td><td>G9-1.7</td></tr>
```

Changing a Cell's Span

Sometimes you need two or more cells with common borders (whether they're in the same row or the same column) to act as a single cell. You might fuse two cells together because they include the same information. Or, you might want to enter a single heading one time, and enable it to span over a number of columns.

Whatever the reason, attributes for the `<th>` and `<td>` elements enable you to force one cell to span more than one row or column. Those attributes are `colspan` and `rowspan`. The following is an example:

```
<table border="1">
<caption>PortaBook Specifications</caption>
<tr><th> </th><th>model 100</th><th>model 200</th></tr>
<tr><th>Processor</th><td>G9-1.6</td><td>G9-1.7</td></tr>
<tr><th>Hard disk</th><td>78GB</td><td>90GB</td></tr>
<tr><th>Video card</th><td colspan="2">Rageous 428p</td></tr>
<tr><th>AV Output</th><td rowspan="2">n/a<td>Yes</td></tr>
<tr><th>Docking port</th><td>Optional</td></tr>
</table>
```

Note that `colspan` is causing the entry `Rageous 428p` to span the second two columns of the fourth row—its function is fairly clear. The `rowspan` attribute can be a little more obscure—it's spanning the second column of the sixth and *seventh* rows. That means, in the second row, the entry `Optional` actually appears in the third column, even though it seems that only two cells are defined in that row. Remembering not to put a cell there (or realizing your mistake if you get an odd-looking table) goes along with the territory when you decide to use `rowspan`.

Viewed in a browser, the table looks like the one in Figure 8.5.

FIGURE 8.5

The colspan and rowspan attributes can force a cell to take up two or more columns or rows.

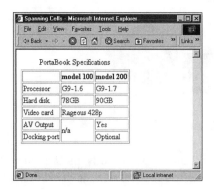

Cell and Row Colors

As you're working with your tables, you may want to change the background color of some of your rows or even of individual cells. Each of the elements is able to accept a bgcolor attribute that can be used for this. The bgcolor attribute is not compatible with the XHTML Strict DTD, however, so you only want to use it with the XHTML Transitional DTD.

The bgcolor attribute accepts a color name as its value and works with the <table>, <tr>, and <td> elements, as shown in this example:

```
<table>
<tr><th>Region</th><th>June</th><th>July
</th><th>August</th></tr>
<tr
bgcolor="yellow"><th>North</th><td>600,000
</td><td>400,000</td><td>800,000</td></tr>
<tr><th>South</th><td>300,000</td><td>
200,000</td><td>400,000</td></tr>
<tr
bgcolor="yellow"><th>East</th><td>230,000
</td><td>490,000</td><td>980,000</td></tr>
<tr><th>West</th><td>320,000</td><td>120,000
</td><td>490,000</td></tr>
</table>
```

> **tip**
>
> Aside from color names, the bgcolor attribute also accepts three two-digit hex numbers that represent the RGB (red, green, and blue) values for a particular color. For example, bgcolor="#FFFFFF" creates a white background. (For more on this, see Chapter 10, "Get Splashy: Style Sheets, Fonts, and Special Characters.")

As you can see in Figure 8.6, one reason to change the background color of your tables it to shade alternating rows of data. As accountants and engineers have known for years, it's easier to communicate information in tables when alternating colors make the individual rows of data stand out.

FIGURE 8.6

Using background colors, you can make a table a bit easier on the eyes.

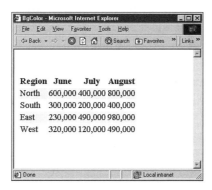

Additional Table Attributes

Now that you have created a basic table, you can move on to a more advanced understanding of the `<table>` element itself and its optional attributes. You've already seen some of them, including `align` and `border`, but a few others are worth examining:

- ▦ `width`—Sets the relative width of your table as part of the browser window (or an absolute width), usually in pixels. The values can be either percentages, as in `width="50%"`, or an integer representing pixels.

- ▦ `border`—Defines the width of the border surrounding the table. The value is a number (integer) in pixels.

- ▦ `align`—Not strict XHTML, but it can be handy if you're using the XHTML Transitional DTD. `align` can be used much as it's used for the `<img>` element, enabling you to create a "floating" table that enables text to wrap around it.

- ▦ `cellspacing`—Tells the browser how much space to include between the walls of the table and between individual cells. The value is a number (an integer) in pixels.

- ▦ `cellpadding`—Tells the browser how much space to use between data elements and the walls of the cell. The value is a number in pixels.

- ▦ `rules` and `frames`—Used to determine which lines are drawn between cells (rules) and around the table (frames). This one is exclusive to visual browsers, but it's allowed under the XHTML Strict DTD.

Let's take a look at each attribute briefly.

The `width` Attribute

By default, a table in XHTML takes up only as much space as needed to display the data in the cells of its longest row. Only when the table has filled the width of the browser window does it begin to wrap the data in its cells to a second line. Expanding the size of the browser window (if the user still has room on his display) rearranges the text in those cells accordingly.

With the `width` attribute, you can take a little bit more control over how the table looks. The value that `width` accepts is either an integer representing the number of pixels wide that the table should be, or the percentage of the page that the table should take up. In this second case, the table is still free to grow or shrink when the user changes the size of her Web browser window, but within certain constraints.

For example, a table that takes up 75% of the browser window could be created with the following table definition, which is shown in Figure 8.7:

```
<table width="75%">
<tr><th>Region</td><th>June</th><th>July
</th><th>August</th>
<tr bgcolor="yellow"><td>North</td><td>
600,000</td><td>400,000</td><td>800,000
</td>
<tr><td>South</td><td>300,000</td><td>
200,000</td><td>400,000</td>
<tr
bgcolor="yellow"><td>East</td><td>230,000
</td><td>490,000</td><td>980,000</td>
<tr><td>West</td><td>320,000</td><td>120,000
</td><td>490,000</td>
</table>
```

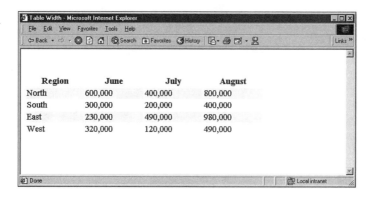

> **tip**
>
> With absolute values for `width`, you can also include a suffix that defines the units used, as in `px` for pixels or `in` for inches (for example, `width="3.5in"`). Absolute values for table widths are not recommended, because tables should react to user input (like a user changing his browser window size). That said, it's a fairly common practice to use absolute values, particularly when designing entire pages using tables (as discussed in Chapter 9).

Note that the `width` attribute forces the table to that width, even if the data doesn't need that much room. For example, a table with a `width="100%"` attribute takes up the entire width of the browser window, regardless of the amount of data in the cells.

FIGURE 8.7
Using the `width` attribute, you can force tables to different sizes.

Region	June	July	August
North	600,000	400,000	800,000
South	300,000	200,000	400,000
East	230,000	490,000	980,000
West	320,000	120,000	490,000

The `border` and `align` Attributes

By default, most browsers render a table without lines defining its perimeter and cells. Using the `border` attribute, you can change this so that a table has lines that separate cells from one other. You can also specify the width of the line that surrounds the table on the outside, in pixels. For example:

```
<table border="8">
```

The align attribute can be used with the `<table>` element to either center the table on the page or cause the table to become a floating object, with text wrapping around it on the left or right. Although this can be handy for page presentation and layout, it's not compatible with the XHTML Strict DTD and you should only use it if you're working under the XHTML Transitional DTD.

The following is an example of both attributes, the result of which is shown in Figure 8.8:

```
<table border="8" align="center" width="50%">
<caption>Candy Sales Per Student Per Type</caption>

<tr>
<th>Type</th><th>Melissa</th><th>Brian</th><th>Roger</th>
</tr>

<tr>
<th>Chocolate Bars</th><td>50</td><td>25</td><td>50</td>
</tr>

<tr>
<th>Fruit Chews</th><td>50</td><td>45</td><td>30</td>
</tr>

<tr>
<th>Lollipops</th><td>15</td><td>25</td><td>40</td>
</tr>

</table>
```

FIGURE 8.8

A table with a thick border, centered on the page.

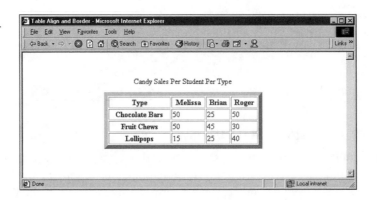

The `cellpadding` and `cellspacing` Attributes

Although the `border` attribute is used to set the pixel width of the lines that enclose cells in your table, the `cellpadding` and `cellspacing` attributes give you fine control over the amount of space used in other parts of the table. The `cellspacing` attribute specifies how much space is between cells, in pixels. As shown in Figure 8.9, including the `cellspacing` attribute also increases the size of the interior border walls, even if the actual `border` attribute is set to a low number. For example:

```
<table border="1" cellspacing="10">
```

However, `cellspacing` is equally effective when you aren't using a border on your table at all:

```
<table cellspacing="10">
```

The `cellpadding` attribute is used to specify the amount of space that should be displayed between a cell's wall and the contents of that cell. (Again, this measurement is in pixels.) The default setting for `cellpadding` (that is, if you don't include the attribute at all) is 1. You can set `cellpadding="0"`, but that causes the items in each cell to bump up against the border. The following example is the second table shown in Figure 8.9:

```
<table border="1" cellpadding="10">
```

FIGURE 8.9

Two tables: `cellspacing` with a border and `cellpadding` with a border.

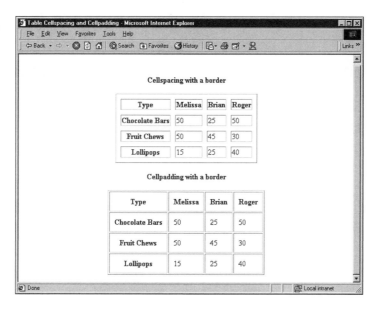

Summary

This chapter taught you the basics of creating an HTML table, from entering the `<table>` element to adding the row (`<tr>`), heading (`<th>`), and data cell (`<td>`) elements. You also learned some of the attributes for cells and rows, including alignment, background colors, and attributes that enable you to span more than one row or more than one column with a single cell. Then, you saw some of the more involved attributes for a `<table>` element, including those that alter the spacing of cells and the borders between them. This has all been primer for Chapter 9, where you'll learn some advanced uses for tables, including formatting entire pages using table elements.

IN THIS CHAPTER

- The basics of designing a Web page with a table
- Creating page sections, setting table widths and heights, and border appearance
- Examples of using table design for different types of pages

9

ADVANCED TABLE ELEMENTS AND TABLE DESIGN

In Chapter 8, "Table Basics," you learned the basics of table design and saw how to create tables that communicate information in rows and columns. Obviously, that's a primary use of the HTML table elements. In this chapter, you'll be introduced to one of the other common uses of table tags—formatting entire pages. Using the table tags gives you some interesting options for controlling the appearance of your Web page, including the placement of paragraphs, interface controls (such as hyperlinks for different pages in your Web site), and even images. You'll look at many of those possibilities in this chapter.

Table Design Theory

Since the HTML tables standard appeared on the scene, the sophistication and professionalism of Web pages have improved dramatically. With the control over cells that the standard offers, it's easier to put pictures, text, lists, and links wherever you want them on the page. In this way, you can create an *all-page table*, or a table that is used to control the design of the entire Web page.

You do this by aligning cells, creating spanning cells (or fusing cells together), and adding the appropriate cell padding and spacing, as you saw in Chapter 8. You can add some other tricks as well, including nested tables, which enable you to place one table inside another.

At its most basic, though, using tables for layout simply gives you rows and columns with which to work. As with a page in a newsletter, newspaper, or magazine, you can visually divide your Web page to make it easier to read or to guide the eye to different elements, such as the hyperlinks used to change pages. For example, take this page on a fictional realtor's Web site that's designed to display the particulars of a home that's for sale:

```
<table border="1" cellpadding="5">

<!-- Top control area -->
<tr>
<td colspan="2" align="center">
<a href="index.html">Home Page</a> |
<a href="homes.html">Home for Sale</a> |
<a href="info.html">Homebuyer Information</a> |
<a href="rates.html">Mortgage/Rates Info</a> |
<a href="contact.html">Contact Me</a>

</tr>



<!-- Main body of page -->
<tr>
<td rowspan="2" valign="top">
<h1>Farmhouse Living</h1>
<p>This 3/2 traditional has a full basement (modern
touches like Italian lighting and Berber carpet) for
a media room, home office or an unemployment den for
that English-major college grad of yours. Screened porch
```

```
in back overlooks a nice badminton/croquet lawn
complete
with a walking garden on the side and a dog
run in the trees.
325 Main Street. $129,000.</p></td>
<td>
<img src="house2.jpg" width=250
alt="Exterior of House" />
</td>
</tr>

<tr>
<td>
<img src="fall1.jpg" width="250" alt="Side
Garden" />
</td>
</tr>
</table>
```

As you create more and more complicated page tables, you'll find it's helpful to use the comment element liberally throughout, if only to remind you what a particular row or cell is meant to do.

Figure 9.1 shows this example as displayed in a browser window.

FIGURE 9.1

Here's a page that uses a simple table to separate elements.

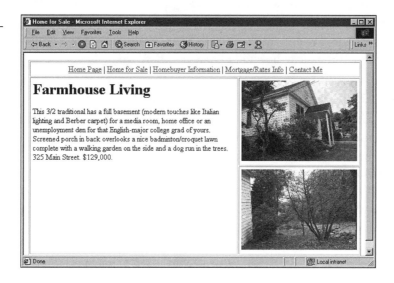

Here's a quick walkthrough of what's being done to create this table:

1. It begins with a standard `<table>` opening tag, which includes a border definition and a setting for cell padding.

2. Next, the first row is defined, followed by a single data cell that spans two columns. Within that data cell is the markup, text, and anchors that define the top-of-the-page links used to move between the pages on this Web site.

3. That cell and row are closed, and then the next row is defined. Note that this row will have two different `<td>` elements, meaning it will have two columns. (That's why the previous row's data cell spanned two columns.)

4. In the first cell, text is entered. If more than one paragraph is required, standard `<p>` containers can be used.

5. In the second cell, `<img />` elements will cause images to appear on that side of the table. (Note that the width of the images will dictate the width of this column—and, hence, the width of the other column—as mentioned in Chapter 8.)

6. Finally, the second row is closed and the table is closed.

This page is really a simple layout, but tables allow you to add the navigation toolbar at the top, which is separated out into its own table row. Next, in the second row, the table is divided into two columns, separating the description from the images that appear along the side. (The only other way to do this would be to use floating images [those using an `align="right"` or `align="left"` attribute], which wouldn't align themselves as neatly.)

It's a clean, inviting interface that's easy to work with. But let's back up a little bit and look at exactly how to put together these types of pages.

Using Images in Tables

Using an HTML table to display images really offers some advantages. It's nice to have such exacting control over the placement of the images. Plus, tables make it easier to align text and images so the user knows how they're related to one another.

For example, another page that our fictional real estate agent might want to post on the Web is a listing of all available homes. Using a table, the home images and descriptions are simple to align:

```
<table border=1 cellspacing=2 cellpadding=2 width="100%">
<tr><td colspan="2"><h1>Current Home Sale Listings</h1></td></tr>
<tr>
<td>
<p>This 3/2 traditional has a full basement (modern
touches like Italian lighting and Berber carpet) for
a media room, home office or an unemployment den for
```

```
that English-major college grad of yours. Screened
porch in back overlooks a nice badminton/croquet lawn
complete with a walking garden on the side and a dog
run in the trees. 325 Main Street. $129,000.</p>
</td>
<td>
<img src="325main.png" alt="Front of 325 Main Street" />
</td>
</tr>
<tr>
<td>
<p>You don't see garden estates at these prices anymore.
Brick fenced entry (with a fancy remote control) opens to
a winding drive up the front lawn to this colonial in the
best Jeffersonian tradition. Inside, you'll find formal
living and dining, a basement game room (perfect for
media or art projects) and a downstairs master suite with
whirlpool tub. This one even has extras like a butler's pantry
(for storing all those family-sized cans of ravioli-os) and a
second, back staircase for creeping quietly down in the middle
of the night to get one more small sliver of homemade pie. And,
best yet, a babbling brook right there on the property.
19 E. Gables Road. $279,000. </p>
</td>
<td>
<img src="brook.png" alt="Babbling brook" /><br />
</td>
</tr>
</table>
```

Figure 9.2 shows this one in action. Note how the table tags make it easy to align images with text.

Nesting Tables

Here's another bit of theory to ingest before we move on—I've mentioned that a table cell can accept all sorts of data. As it happens, this includes a second table. When you place one table inside another, you're said to be *nesting* the tables. It can get a little confusing in your raw HTML code, but you'll find that nesting tables is an invaluable solution to a number of layout problems.

FIGURE 9.2

Tables can help you align images and text in creative ways.

For starters, you'll recall from Chapter 8 that a table can have a width. Let's say you want a particular *cell* to have a fixed (or specific) width. You want to create two cells—one that's about 25% of the page and one that's about 75%. The 25% side will be used as a sidebar of sorts, perhaps for navigation. The 75% side will be used for the text you're interested in putting on the page. Figure 9.3 shows a table that fits this description.

One way to do this is to use the width attribute for the <td>, as in <td width="75%">. Sure, that seems easy, but unfortunately, it's not strict XHTML. If you're using the transitional DTD, you could use the width attribute.

The other solution is to use a nested table. Because the <table> element can legally accept a width attribute (in XHTML), you can put a table in one of the cells and thereby define its width. The code in Listing 9.1 matches up with Figure 9.3.

note

If you add cell padding or cell spacing to your original table, note that those pixels will affect the overall width of the column that includes your nested table. For instance, with 3 pixels of cell padding, a column with a 150-pixel nested table will actually be 156 pixels wide. In other words, to be exact, you may need to do a little math or go without cell padding or cell spacing.

FIGURE 9.3

Here's a table where the width of the cells has been specified.

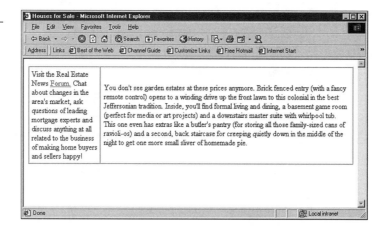

LISTING 9.1   Nesting a Table Within a Table

```
<table width="100%" cellpadding="0"cellspacing="0">
<tr>

<td>
   <table width="150" cellpadding="3">
   <tr>
   <td>markup for left side</td>
   </tr>
   </table>
</td>

<td>
   <table cellpadding="5">
   <tr>
   <td>markup for right side</td>
   </tr>
   </table>
</td>

</tr>
</table>
```

In this case, the nested tables are used simply to create single cells over which you have some formatting control. By setting the left-side table to 150 pixels, you're able to fix its width. The rest of the overall page table will still resize to the browser window, but this left-side table is fixed.

Okay, so you've seen a basic nested table. But what about a table that has even more functionality—for instance, one that's used for formatting *inside* the cell? In place of the left-side table in Listing 9.1, consider what the page might look like with the following table in its place:

```
<table width="150" cellpadding="2"
border="1">
<tr bgcolor="yellow"><td>Home
Listings</td></tr>
<tr><td>
129k, 3/2, Sumner<br />
139k, 4/2, Ridgewood<br />
142k, 4/2, Highland<br />
159k, 4/2/2, Haven<br />
179k, 5/2.5, Haven<br />
229k, 5/3/2, Laurel<br />
</td></tr>
<tr bgcolor="yellow"><td>Call for more: 645.3567</td></tr>
</table>
```

> **tip**
>
> As shown in the example, you can use white space in your HTML document, both hard returns and spaces, to help you remember which rows and columns are related to which tables. It's important to keep track, because forgetting a </td>, </tr>, or </table> tag will likely cause your page to fail in the Web browser (or at least look very odd).

Figure 9.4 shows this table in action. (Note that I've made each of the listings a hyperlink for Figure 9.4, although I left the anchor elements out of this listing for clarity.) This little nested table replaces the left side with something more interesting: an interface control.

While you're nesting tables, don't forget the possibilities presented by *floating* tables, which are aligned to the right or left using the align attribute with the <table> element. Floating tables are great for adding tabular information in a way that's a bit more visually pleasing. Text wraps around the table, while other markup can be used to call attention to the table's contents. For instance, using the code in Listing 9.1, slip a floating table into the right-side nested table, as shown in Listing 9.2.

FIGURE 9.4

Here a complete table is nested on the left side.

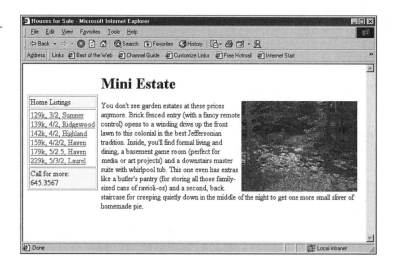

LISTING 9.2   Add a Floating Table to the Mix

```
<table width="100%" cellpadding="0"cellspacing="0">
<tr>

<td>
   <table width="150" cellpadding="3">
   <tr>
   <td>markup for left side</td>
   </tr>
   </table>
</td>

<td>
   <table cellpadding="5">
   <tr>
   <td>
       <!-- Here's the floating table -->
       <table align="right" cellpadding="5" width="200" border="1">
          <tr bgcolor="yellow"><td>19 E. Gable Road</td></tr>
     <tr><td><b>Price:</b> $279,000</td></tr>
     <tr><td><b>Appraisal:</b> $309,000</td></tr>
     <tr><td>Owner is moving to Florida and interested in a
quick sale. Call 645.3567 and ask for Andy</td></tr>
```

LISTING 9.2   (continued)

```
</table>

<h1>Your Own Mini-Estate</h1>

<p>You don't see garden estates at these prices anymore.
Brick fenced entry (with a fancy remote control) opens to a
winding drive up the front lawn to this colonial in the best
Jeffersonian tradition. Inside, you'll find formal living and
dining, a basement game room (perfect for media or art
projects) and a downstairs master suite with whirlpool tub.
This one even has extras like a butler's pantry (for storing
all those family-sized cans of ravioli-os) and a second, back
staircase for creeping quietly down in the middle of the night
to get one more small sliver of homemade pie.</p>

      </td>
      </tr>
      </table>
   </td>
   </tr>
   </table>
```

Remember that it's the `align="right"` attribute to the table that makes it a floating table. The result of all this nesting is shown in Figure 9.5.

FIGURE 9.5

You can nest a floating table (on the right) for an interesting effect.

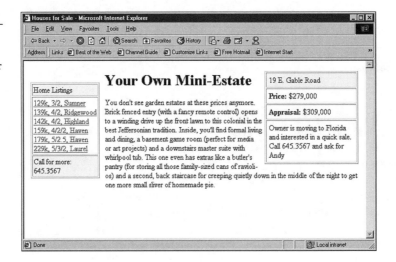

Grouping Columns and Rows

So far, most of the markup you've seen is actually the basic table elements used for larger chunks of text and images—that's most of what table-based layout is about. There are a few more elements to discuss, however, and you'll find that they're important as your tables grow in complexity. These new elements will enable you to group your rows, defining different portions of the table (and hence the page). Other elements enable you to better group and define your columns, as you'll see in this section.

Table Row Groupings

Table row groupings are reasonably straightforward. They're designed to help you group your rows into different sections of the table, just as you group different elements into a head and body in an HTML document. In this case, the elements are `<thead>`, `<tfoot>>`, and `<tbody>>`. The idea behind these elements is to enable a Web browser or other application to consider the header and footer to be separate from the body, so that, for instance, the body of the table can scroll while the header and footer stay in place. Likewise, a browser can decide that the header and footer information on each page of a multi-page table will appear when printed, just like the header and footer of a typical word processing document.

Each of these elements is a container, and each one is designed specifically to hold certain types of table rows and data. Note also that you still need to use the `<tr>` container element for each row, and that each of these row grouping elements should have at least one row contained within it. Also, if you plan to include a table header and a table footer, there's one oddity—the footer needs to be typed in first, before the body, so that the browser knows it's there. Here's an example:

```
<table border="1">
<thead>
<tr>
<th colspan="2">Customer</th><th rowspan="3">Sales Month:</th>
</tr>
<tr>
<th>September</th><th>October</th><th>November</th>
</thead>
<tfoot>
<tr>
<td colspan="4">Source: New York Gazette-Tribune</td>
</tr>
</tfoot>
```

```
<tbody>
<tr>
<td>NonCo, Inc.</td><td>450,000</td><td>350,000</td><td>50,000</td>
</tr>
<tr>
<td>RichCo, LLC</td><td>345,000</td><td>230,000</td><td>12,400</td>
</tr>
<tr>
<td>FakeCorp, Ltd.</td><td>120,000</td><td>543,000</td><td>10,000</td>
</tr>
...additional rows...
</tbody>
</table>
```

This is a fairly simple example, and one you might not encounter too often. After all, the vast majority of HTML documents you create probably won't be designed to show page after page of scrolling tables of numbers. That's pretty dull for a Web page.

Instead, one place you'll likely want to consider using these row grouping tags is when you're building a full page using table elements, and you'd like a non-scrolling header and footer. (Remember, of course, that the browser isn't required to render them as non-scrolling.) Defining your document in this way—with a banner image in the header, for instance, and navigation links in the footer—gives you some extra flexibility without affecting older browsers that don't recognize the row groupings. Here's one way such a table could be created:

```
<table cellpadding="5">
<thead>
<tr><td colspan="5"><img src="top_banner.png" alt="Flatland Real
Estate"/></td></tr>
</thead>

<tfoot>
<tr>
<td><a href="about.html">About</a></td>
<td><a href="listings.html">Land and Homes</a></td>
<td><a href="buyer.html">Buyer's Broker Services</a></td>
<td><a href="seller.html">Sell Your Home</a></td>
<td><a href="mortgage.html">Mortgage Info</a></td>
</tr>
</tfoot>
```

```
<tbody>
<tr>
<td colspan="5">
<img src="fall1.jpg" width="250" alt="Side Garden" align="right" />
<h1>Farmhouse Living</h1>
<p>This 3/2 traditional has a full basement (modern touches
like Italian lighting and Berber carpet) for a media room,
home office or an unemployment den for that English-major
college grad of yours. Screened porch in back overlooks a
nice badminton/croquet lawn complete with a walking garden
on the side and a dog run in the trees. 325 Main Street.
$129,000.</p></td>
</tr>
</tbody>
</table>
```

In many browsers, the header and footer will appear in their proper places independent of the body of the table, as shown in Figure 9.6.

FIGURE 9.6
Using row groupings can augment the look and organization of your all-page table.

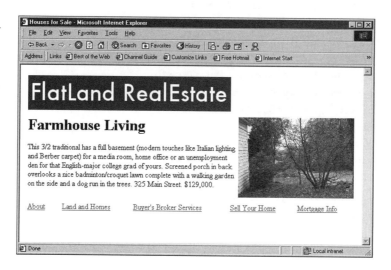

Column Groupings

You'll find that column groupings are a touch more complex, if only because they offer a few more options and reasons for being. You may have noticed already that columns seem to be afterthoughts with the XHTML spec, because most of what gets defined are rows and data cells. You can group columns, however, and you can select individual columns (or groups of columns) for certain types of markup, as you'll see.

In this section we're dealing with two different elements, the <colgroup> and <col> elements. The <colgroup> element is used to create groups of columns, to which you can then assign other attributes. (Or, future browsers may recognize groups of columns for some reason, although none of them really do that now.) The <col> container can be used on individual columns to assign properties without putting them in a particular group.

With <colgroup>, you'll use the span attribute to assign the number of columns in a particular group. For example, take a table that has five columns in it. Here's an example of <colgroup> being used to break it into two different groups (see Figure 9.7):

```
<table border="1" cellpadding="5">
<colgroup span="3" align="center"> </colgroup>
<colgroup span="2" align="right" width="100"> </colgroup>
<tr><th>Quantity</th><th>Prod ID</th><th>Description</th>
<th>Unit Price</th><th>Sub-Total</th></tr>
<tr><td>12</td><td>0876547</td><td>#4 wing nuts</td>
<td>$1.00</td><td>$12.00</td></tr>
<tr><td>10</td><td>0876501</td><td>#4 wood screws </td>
<td>$1.50</td><td>$15.00</td></tr>
<tr><td>20</td><td>0887965</td><td>ProBuild Hammer</td>
<td>$9.50</td><td>$190.00</td></tr>
<tr><td>5</td><td>0927125</td><td>Caulking gun</td>
<td>$4.00</td><td>$20.00</td></tr>
<tr><td>10</td><td>1034526</td><td>3-Pk Masking Tape</td>
<td>$2.00</td><td>$20.00</td></tr>
</table>
```

FIGURE 9.7

Using <col-group> to define and align groups of columns.

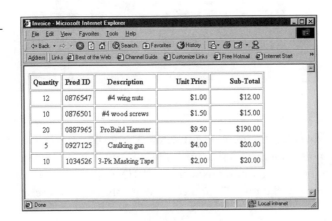

Note that `<colgroup>` can accept an `align` attribute and/or a `valign` attribute, which is applied to each of the columns specified in the span of the element. All the groups are defined first, before the first row definition. (They're defined before the applicable `<thead>` or `<tbody>` elements as well.) The `<colgroup>` element can also include a `width` attribute, which defines a default width for each of the columns in that group. For instance, `<colgroup span="4" width="10">` would set each of those columns to a default width of 10 pixels.

The other element, `<col>`, is used inside a `<colgroup>` element when you'd like to define the characteristics of columns individually *within* their group. In other words, if you have a column that needs a different setting from the one that's specified in the `<colgroup>` element, you can use `<col>`. Here's an example, using the data that was used for Figure 9.7:

> **note**
>
> The `<colgroup>` element can accept a special width value, written as `width="0*"` (as can the `<col>` element, discussed next). That tells the browser to determine the default width based on the least amount of space required by the lengthiest entry in that column. If the longest entry requires 50 pixels, for instance, that's what the width of the column will be.

```
<table border="1" cellpadding="5">
<colgroup span="3" align="center">
<col width="50" />
<col span="2" width="100" />
</colgroup>
<colgroup span="2" width="150">
<col align="center" />
<col align="right" />
</colgroup>
<tr><th>Quantity</th><th>Prod ID</th><th>Description</th>
<th>Unit Price</th><th>Sub-Total</th></tr>
<tr><td>12</td><td>0876547</td><td>#4 wing nuts</td>
<td>$1.00</td><td>$12.00</td></tr>
<tr><td>10</td><td>0876501</td><td>#4 wood screws</td>
<td>$1.50</td><td>$15.00</td></tr>
<tr><td>20</td><td>0887965</td><td>ProBuild Hammer</td>
<td>$9.50</td><td>$190.00</td></tr>
<tr><td>5</td><td>0927125</td><td>Caulking gun</td>
<td>$4.00</td><td>$20.00</td></tr>
<tr><td>10</td><td>1034526</td><td>3-Pk Masking Tape</td>
```

```
<td>$2.00</td><td>$20.00</td></tr>
</table>
```

In this example, we still have two column groups. However, some of the columns are getting a bit more individual attention. In the first group, the first column is getting a different width from the second two columns; in the second group, the two columns have the same width, but different alignment properties. The `<col>` element can handle the same attributes as `<colgroup>`, including span. The only major difference is that `<col>` doesn't define a new group—it only sets attributes for columns. Refer to Figure 9.8 to see how these changes affect the table.

FIGURE 9.8

Using `<col>` to set attributes within the column groups. Note the column width and alignment differences when compared to Figure 9.7.

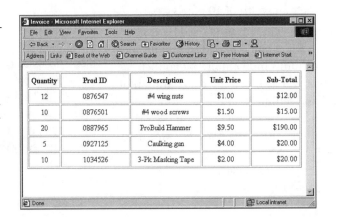

So far, most of what we've seen of `<colgroup>` and `<col>` has affected a basic data-focused table, but these elements can be just as effective with an all-page table that's used for page layout. You've got some interesting options for managing entire columns of markup with a few easy elements. Here's an earlier example updated to manage the columns:

```
<table border="1" cellspacing="2"
cellpadding="2" width="100%">
<colgroup>
<col width="500">
<col align="center">
</colgroup>
<tr><td colspan="2"><h1>Current Home Sale
Listings</h1></td></tr>
<tr>
```

tip

As you'll see in Chapter 10, "Get Splashy: Style Sheets, Fonts, and Special Characters," `<col>` isn't completely dissimilar from other elements that are used for style and attribute markup, such as `<span>` and `<div>`. In fact, you'll likely find yourself using `<col>` with style sheet markup.

```
<td>
<h1>Farmhouse Living</h1>
<p>This 3/2 traditional has a full basement (modern
touches like Italian lighting and Berber carpet) for
a media room, home office or an unemployment den for
that English-major college grad of yours. Screened porch
in back overlooks a nice badminton/croquet lawn complete
with a walking garden on the side and a dog run in the
trees.</p>
<td>
<img src="325main.png" alt="Front of 325 Main Street" /><br />
<b>325 Main Street. $129,000</b>
</td>
</td>
</tr>
<tr>
<td>
<h1>Mini Estate</h1>
<p>You don't see garden estates at these prices anymore.
Brick fenced entry (with a fancy remote control) opens to
a winding drive up the front lawn to this colonial in the
best Jeffersonian tradition. Inside, you'll find formal
living and dining, a basement game room (perfect for media
or art projects) and a downstairs master suite with whirlpool
tub (see photo). This one even has extras like a butler's pantry
(for storing all those family-sized cans of ravioli-os) and a
second, back staircase for creeping quietly down in the middle
of the night to get one more small sliver of homemade pie.</p>
</td>
<td>
<img src="brook.png" alt="Babbling brook " /><br />
<b>19 E. Gables Road. $279,000.</b>
</td>
</tr>
</table>
```

Figure 9.9 shows how this looks in a browser.

FIGURE 9.9
Here's an example of `<col-group>` and `<col>` for a table that's focused more on page layout than tabular data.

Frames and Rules

One last set of attributes can be used both for advanced tabular data and page layout tables. These attributes are `frame` and `rules`. The `frame` attribute is used to determine which lines around the *outside* of a table are rendered when the `border` attribute is used. The `rules` attribute is used to determine which lines are drawn *inside* a table, between cells, when `border` is used.

An example might be

```
<table border="1" frame="hsides" rules="rows">
...table markup...
</table>
```

The result is a table that has only an outline of the table and its columns, as shown in Figure 9.10. (Compare it to Figure 9.9, which shows the full set of border lines.)

Each attribute offers a number of options. The `frame` attribute, which deals with the four outer sides of the table, is set to show them all by default when the `border` attribute is used. Other values for `frame` are

- `void`—No sides of the table are rendered
- `above`—The top of the table is drawn
- `below`—The bottom is drawn
- `hsides`—The left and right sides are drawn

- ▓ `vsides`—The top and bottom are drawn
- ▓ `lhs` or `rhs`—Left or right side only, respectively

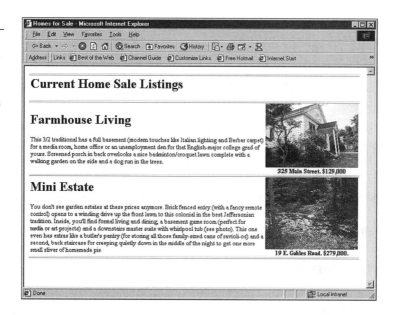

You can also use the values `box` or `border` to draw all four sides. (This might be necessary in some scripting, for instance, although in regular markup you'd simply omit the `frame` attribute.)

For the lines inside your table, you can vary the value you assign to `rules`. Those potential values include

- ▓ `none`—No lines drawn inside the table
- ▓ `groups`—Lines will only appear between row groups—those defined by `<thead>`, `<tfoot>`, and `<tbody>`—and column groups defined by `<colgroup>` containers
- ▓ `rows`—Lines only appear between rows
- ▓ `cols`—Lines only appear between columns
- ▓ `all`—Lines appear on all sides of every cell, as in the default value

note

It's worth noting that the `frame` attribute for the `<table>` element has nothing to do with the HTML Frames elements discussed in Chapter 12, "Creating Sites with HTML Frames." In this case, the `frame` attribute is meant to suggest the outline of cells and rows in an HTML table.

Although these attributes are part of the strict XHTML specification, be aware that you can also accomplish some of these visual changes with style sheets, as discussed in Chapter 10. That probably would be preferable if you're working with late-model visual Web browsers. (Non-visual and older Web browsers will ignore all these attributes anyway.)

Table Design Examples

Now that you've learned a good bit of the theory behind table design and the bulk of the elements and attributes you can use for a table, let's turn our attention to some slightly more complex examples. You'll find that HTML table elements are useful for a wide variety of page design approaches. Almost anytime you want some control over the placement of paragraphs, images, and other rows or columns of data, a table is the right choice. Let's look at two examples—one that focuses on dividing the page into rows, and one that focuses on creating and managing columns.

A Row-Centric Table

This fairly clean-looking page example is designed for that fictional real estate agent. In this case, you'll notice that the page is rather *row-centric*. By that I mean that most of what you're seeing are a bunch of rows, each one with really only a single column of data. When you need multiple columns, you simply nest another table with as many columns as desired. This is one way to design reasonably simple-looking pages that still use tables for fine control over the layout. (And you can usually keep the rows and columns straight in your head when you think this way.)

Note also that this page sets a border of 0 for the main table, so as to offer white space around most of the elements. As part of the example, the row grouping elements are used, so that a browser that wanted to could render the header (image and links) and footer (contact address information) separately, non-scrolling or on each page of a printout. See Listing 9.3 for the entire document (in strict XHTML), including the declarations that are required for such documents (and were introduced back in Chapter 4, "Creating Your First Page").

LISTING 9.3   A Row-Centric All-Page Table Design

```
<?xml version="1.0" encoding="iso-8859-1"?>
<!DOCTYPE HTML PUBLIC "-//W3C//DTD HTML 4.01//EN"
   "http://www.w3.org/TR/html4/strict.dtd">
```

LISTING 9.3 (continued)

```
<html xmlns="http://www.w3.org/1999/xhtml">
<head>
  <title>Inside the House</title>
</head>
<body bgcolor="#ffffff">

<!-- Start the whole-page table -->
<table border="0" width="100%" cellpadding="10">

<thead>
<!-- Top banner image -->
<tr>
<td align="center"><img src="images/heading.jpg" /></td>
</tr>

<!-- Control center row -- >
<tr>
<td align="center">
<a href="index.html">Main Page</a> |
<a href="house.html"> The House </a> |
<ahref="area.html">Moving to the Area</a> |
<a href="terms.html">Terms of Sale</a> |
<a href="map.html">Directions</a>
</td>
</tr>
</thead>

<tbody>

<!-- Thumbnail images in a nested table -->
<tr>
<td align="center">
<table width="450" border="1" cellspacing="2" cellpadding="5">
  <tr>
    <td width="33%"><img src="images/master.jpg" /></td>
    <td width="33%"><img src="images/kids_bedroom.jpg"  /></td>
    <td width="34%"><img src="images/living_room.jpg" /></td>
  </tr>
```

LISTING 9.3   (continued)

```
<tr>
   <td width="33%" valign="top">Master Bedroom includes
luxury bath with whirlpool tub</td>
   <td width="33%" valign="top">Second Bedroom features
good light and cool breezes</td>
   <td width="34%" valign="top">Rustic living area includes
stone fireplace with gas logs</td>
</tr>
</table>

</td>
</tr>

<!-- Main body text and floating table-->

<tr>
<td>
 <h1>Your Own Mini-Estate</h1>

   <table align="right" cellpadding="5" width="200" border="1">
         <tr bgcolor="yellow"><td>19 E. Gable Road</td></tr>
    <tr><td><b>Price:</b> $279,000</td></tr>
    <tr><td><b>Appraisal</b> $309,000</td></tr>
    <tr><td>Owner is moving to Florida and interested
in a quick sale. Call 555.1023 and ask for Rich</td></tr>
    </table>

   <p>You don't see garden estates at these prices anymore.
Brick fenced entry (with a fancy remote control) opens to a
winding drive up the front lawn to this colonial in the best
Jeffersonian tradition. Inside, you'll find formal living and
dining, a basement game room (perfect for media
or art projects) and a downstairs master suite with whirlpool tub.
This one even has extras like a butler's pantry (for storing all
those family-sized cans of ravioli-os) and a second, back staircase
for creeping quietly down in the middle of the night to get one
more small sliver of homemade pie.</p>
```

LISTING 9.3   (continued)

```
</td>
</tr>
</tbody>

<!--Last row, info line -->
<tr>
<td align="center">
<address>For more information or for an appointment,
call 945.555.1023 or send e-mail to
<a href="mailto:rich@fakeestate.com">Rich Salesguy</a>
with the subject line "Mini Estate." Thanks!</address>
</td>
</tr>

</body>
</html>
```

The result is shown in Figure 9.11.

FIGURE 9.11

Here's the page as shown in Listing 9.3. Note the nested tables.

Focusing on Columns

Being row-centric is great for basic tables, but it falls down a little when you decide you'd like to organize your page into multiple columns. A columnar approach is popular for sites that would like to look a lot like a newsletter, or otherwise organize a lot of information in as little space as possible. That's partly why this design approach is popular with portal sites, such as Excite (http://www.excite.com/) and Yahoo! (http://www.yahoo.com), and with news sites such as the New York Times site (http://www.nytimes.com/).

If you'd like to try this design, you'll find it's certainly possible. For the most part, you'll simply have very large data cells, with <td> container tags many, many lines apart. It can be a little tough to see this when you look at the raw HTML code, because columns that appear side-by-side in a Web browser must be defined one after the other in your HTML document.

But it won't be that tough, particularly if you use HTML comments liberally to remind you where you are in your all-page table. See Listing 9.4 for a sample of a column-focused page. Figure 9.12 shows what the results look like in a Web browser.

In my experience, browsers can be a little independent-minded when it comes to the align attribute. You may find that your columns look a little different in different browsers. It's also important to know that <colgroup> and <col> are relatively recent additions. The solution, in some cases, is to use <td width="xx"> on cells within your table. Because a column must be as wide as its widest cell, generally you can get away with specifying the width of just your top data cells in each column. I've used that technique in this listing instead of relying on <colgroup> and <col>.

LISTING 9.4   Here's a Page Specifically Divided into Columns

```
<?xml version="1.0" encoding="iso-8859-1"?>
<!DOCTYPE HTML PUBLIC "-//W3C//DTD HTML 4.01//EN"
   "http://www.w3.org/TR/html4/strict.dtd">

<html xmlns="http://www.w3.org/1999/xhtml">
<head>
<title>Real Estate News!</title>
</head>
```

LISTING 9.4 (continued)

```
<!-- Begin Page Table -->

<table width=100% border="0" cellpadding="5" cellspacing="0" bgcolor="#eeeeee">

<!-- Begin top rows -->
<thead>
<tr>
<td align="center" colspan="3">Updated: 10/14/02 2:15 PM EDT</td>
</tr>

<tr>
<td align="center" colspan="3"><img src="title.png" alt="Real Estate News" /></td>
</tr>

<tr>
<td align="center" bgcolor="#eeeeee" colspan="3">
<a href="http://www.fakeestate.com/">Home</a> |
<a href="reports/mortgage.html">Mortgage Report</a> |
<a href="column/index.html">Nancy's View</a> |
<a href="recent.html">Archives</a> |
<a href="http://www.fakeestate.com/cgi-bin/forums">Forums</a>
</td>
</tr>

<tr>
<td colspan="3"> </td>
</tr>
</thead>
<!-- End top rows -->




<!-- Begin main row -->
<tbody>
<tr>

<!-- Begin left-side column -->
```

LISTING 9.4   (continued)

```
<td valign="top" bgcolor="#eeeeee" width="150">

<b>Just posted, new message areas!</b><br />
<p> Visit the Real Estate News
<a href="http://www.fakeestate.com/cgi-bin/forum">Forum.</a>
Chat about changes in the area's market, ask questions of
leading mortgage experts and discuss anything at all related
to the business of making home buyers and sellers happy!</p>

<b>Cool Links</b><br />
<p>Check out these other interesting sites for news and views about real estate:</p>

<p>
<a target="_blank" href="http://www.realworldestate.com/">World of RE</a>
</p>

<p>
<a target="_blank" href="http://www.mortgage-planet.com">Mortgage Planet</a>
</p>

<p>
<a target="_blank" href="http://www.realfakedeal.com">Real Deal RE</a>
</p>

<p>
<a target="_blank" href="http://www.fixituppers.com">FixItUppers.com</a>
</p>

</td>

<!-- End left-side column -->


<!-- Begin middle column -->

<td valign="top" bgcolor="#ffffff">
```

LISTING 9.4 (continued)

```
<h1>Closing Costs Head Down</h1>

<p>Thanks to local competition and a soft national economic outlook,
many banks are lowering or rebating key closing costs to move more
traffic to their banks and encourage new and existing home purchases.
In some cases, the advantages are available for individuals interested
in refinancing their homes.</p>

<p><a href="news/10.14.closing.html">Read more...</a></p>


<h1>Insurance Investigation Begins</h1>

<p>The State Attorney General is looking into the practices of two
regional title insurance companies that may have overcharged customers
in the past five years. Spokespeople for both companies say they're
working with the state government to uncover the errors.</p>

<p><a href="http://www.stategov.gov/page/news.html">Visit the state site...</a></p>


<h1>Nancy: Doing the Books</h1>

<p> In this week's column, Nancy takes a look at some of the personal
accounting options you have for tax time and personal budget management.
The end goal? Putting together the perfect portfolio for increasing the
amount a bank is willing to lend you.</p>

<p><a href="columns/10.14.nancy.html">Read Nancy's column...</a>


<!-- End middle column -->

</td>
```

LISTING 9.4 (continued)

```
<!-- Begin right-side column -->

<td width="150" valign="top" bgcolor="#eeeeee">

<img src="images/feature.jpg" width="100" alt="featured home" />

<p><b>Featured Property</b></br>
This week's featured listing is a 4/2/2 with a finished, walk-out basement,
13 acres and it's own swimming hole fed by the Rogers River. If you've ever
wondered what those relaxation books mean by "walking meditation" wait until
you take a stroll on your own riverfront property.</p>

<p><a href="features/10.14.property.html">[4/2/2 Riverfront]</a></p>

<!-- End right side column -->

</tbody>
</td>
</tr>
</table>


</body>
</html>
```

FIGURE 9.12

Here's the page as shown in Listing 9.4, with its column-focused newsletter look.

Summary

In this chapter, you learned some of the advanced techniques for using table elements to organize and lay out an entire page. You began with some theory—a look at the techniques involved in adding images to tables, using nested tables and grouping the columns and rows within your table so that they can be labeled and altered. Then, you saw how those techniques can all come together in some example table-based layouts, including one that focused on formatting rows and one that focused on creating columns on the page.

In the next chapter you'll be introduced to style sheets, the modern approach to changing the look and feel of your pages.

IN THIS CHAPTER

- The basics of creating style sheets (including the theory behind them)

- The building blocks of style sheets (including `<style>`, `<span>`, and `<div>`), as well as a discussion of linking versus embedding style sheets

- Creating new classes and adding inline style attributes to other HTML elements

- The various properties and styles you can render using style sheets

- Adding special characters and symbols to your document's text

10

GET SPLASHY: STYLE SHEETS, FONTS, AND SPECIAL CHARACTERS

HTML, in its most ideal form, is application-neutral. Pages created in HTML (and even more so in XHTML) should render as completely and informatively on a cell phone's display or a palm-held computer as they do in a full-fledged graphical browser application on a Windows or Macintosh computer. As mentioned in previous chapters, this is done by separating the styling of a page from the content and organization of that page. This chapter discusses that styling, and also touches on the less ideal ways that you can style your page—the transitional options.

Style Sheets in Theory

Early versions of HTML didn't have much control over the look-and-feel of the page. In the early 1990s, most Web pages were fairly basic-looking. You had a text font (generally Times or similar), a monospaced font (usually one with a typewriter look to it), and many of the basic HTML elements you've seen in this book, such as headings, lists, images, and hyperlinks. Heck, it even took a while before HTML tables appeared in the specification.

As the Web became more popular as a commercial medium, the graphics designers started to get their hands in Web design, and the Web browser companies—particularly Netscape and Microsoft— began to oblige them with proprietary elements that did more to change the look of a page. These elements included `<center>`, `<font>`, and the once-popular and always-maligned `<blink>` element.

Although some of these elements were included in HTML specifications (notably HTML 3.2), they were frowned upon by the HTML gurus, in part because they encouraged graphic-focused coding. For instance, the following markup became a popular approach to creating headings that cut the `<h1>` elements out of the mix:

```
<font face="Arial, Helvetica"
size="+2">Welcome to the Site</font><br />
```

Because of this, browsers that don't recognize the `<font>` element (again, a handheld computer comes to mind) not only ignore the `<font>` element, but also they don't communicate the fact that the enclosed text is supposed to be a header. If `<h1>` is used, both the graphical and *non-graphical* browsers can figure out a way to tell the user, "Hey, this is a header."

note

What do I mean by non-graphical browsers? They're browsers that don't display different fonts or font sizes, and in many cases can't support images. This might include Web browsers built into handheld computers (such as Palm or PocketPC devices). Non-graphical browsers can also include assistive browsers that are speech-enabled or communicate in Braille. These browsers can't recognize elements such as `<font>`, but they may have a way to communicate the difference between `<h1>` and `<h2>` elements.

What Are Style Sheets?

Although the `<font>` element and its ilk were (and are) immensely popular for visual browsers, these style-only elements would be ignored by non-graphical browsers, at best, or would be a problem, at worst. So, some solution needed to be reached. That solution is *style sheets*, which enable the Web developer to use the strict XHTML elements, such as `<h1>`, while also being able to style that element, such as

```
<h1 style="font-family: Arial, Helvetica">Welcome to the Site</h1>
```

Everyone is happy—users with graphical browsers see pretty fonts, and users with non-graphical browsers still have an `<h1>` element that enables them to recognize this line as a heading and format it appropriately, even if they're forced to ignore the style attribute.

That's the theory behind the style sheet—you separate the look-and-feel of the page from the organization and content of the page. It's a strong enough theory, in fact, that it's required for strict XHTML—you can only use those older formatting tags if you specify a transitional DTD.

Why Use Style Sheets?

Style sheets are helpful in a few other ways. They can actually be separated from the HTML document entirely. As you'll see in this chapter, the `style` attribute isn't the only way to assign styles. You can set up an entire Web site to know that a `<p>` container (or nearly any other element) should be in a certain font, color, size, or some other visual, aural, or tactile property. So, style sheets can make it easier to set a particular series of style guidelines for your Web site and force all your pages to adhere to it.

Separating style tags from organizational tags maintains another goal of HTML and XHTML—making the code human-readable. Consider the following line:

```
<p><font face="Arial, Helvetica, San Serif" size="+2" color="green">Thanks
for visiting. Please sign the guest book below and let me know if there's
anything else you'd like to see on the site.</font></p>
```

This isn't impossible to read and decipher, but it's even easier to read if you specify in the style sheet definitions that the `<p>` element has a certain font face, size, and color, using a definition at the top of the page like this:

```
<style>
p { font-family: Arial, Helvetica, San Serif; font-size: 16pt; color:
green }
</style>
```

Now, for the body of the document, you'll only need to enter this:

```
<p>Thanks for visiting. Please sign the guest book below and let me know
if there's anything else you'd like to see on the site.</p>
```

And, if that happens to be the style you want for your entire page, or your entire Web site, suddenly all <p> elements can be defined with those characteristics. Even if that *isn't* the style you want for every single one of your paragraphs, you can still define a style ahead of time and then assign it to a particular element or selection with a minimum of hassle. In other words, style sheets are definitely a timesaver, and they're great for giving your pages a uniform look.

Finally, style sheets are useful in a grander, industry-wide sense because they stop the browser companies from coming up with as many proprietary (and often incompatible) elements. In the mid-1990s, creating proprietary elements became something of a horserace, with Netscape and Internet Explorer diverging on the different ways that you aligned and styled text and other items. With the style sheet approach, there's a set standard for everything and, perhaps surprisingly, there are only a few actual XHTML elements to learn in order to implement style sheets.

Understanding CSS and XHTML

As with XHTML and HTML, the style sheet language we'll be dealing with has a set specification—*CCS2*, or *Cascading Style Sheets 2*. This standard is what's used most often in Web publishing, and it's the standard that most modern visual Web browsers recognize. (Some browsers support only CCS1, but not too much has changed in CCS2, so most of that markup will be recognized.)

The CSS approach is fairly straightforward. You'll find that the specification offers a number of properties, each of which can accept a range of values. Those properties are used as part of the style attribute for a given XHMTL element; that element is then styled by the browser, if possible. Here are a few examples:

```
<h1 style="font-family: Arial, Helvetica, Sans Serif">Your Restaurant
Reviews</h1>
<p style="font-size: 12pt">Welcome to the section of the site where you
review the restaurants.
If you disagree with something we've said, have a different take on a dish
or if you'd like to
let everyone know about a find you've made, do it here!</p>
```

Using style sheets isn't required in XHTML documents—you can simply go without this level of formatting. And if you do decide to format, technically you don't have to use CSS. You could use a different style sheet specification, if you declare it in your Web browser's <head> section. That said, most Web browsers are designed to recognize CSS, not other style sheet specifications, so CSS is the best bet.

CSS has been supported in Web browsers since around the 4.0 level of Netscape and Microsoft's applications. At this point, you can be assured that the basic formatting of your page, using style sheets, is recognized by upwards of 90% of the graphical Web browsers out there. In other words, you can leave the `<blink>` and `<font>` elements behind for good!

If you're concerned about CCS2 versus CCS1, don't be. Very little has changed between the two specifications. CSS2 really just builds on the CSS1 specification, particularly in more complex operations—style elements for tables, for non-visual presentation (audio and Braille, for instance), and for some advanced topics such as CSS-based positioning and internationalization. The non-visual CSS properties are in Chapter 14, "Site-Wide Styles: Design, Accessibility, and Internationalization." CSS positioning is discussed in the online chapter, "Adding Dynamic HTML Elements." (See the Introduction to this book for details on how to download additional chapters online.)

What Style Sheets Replace

Before we dig deeper into style sheets, let's back up and cover some of the older elements and attributes that have remained among the favorite methods for styling a Web page. Many pages (including some of mine!) continue to use the `<font>` element, along with some attributes that are officially discouraged as of XHTML 1.0 (and, in some cases, the HTML 4.0.1 standard that preceded it).

The `<font>` element can accept a number of different attributes, including `face`, `size`, and `color`. The `<font>` element is a container that is placed around the text that it is to affect, as in

```
<font face="Arial, Helvetica" size="+2">Welcome to My Site</font>
```

For the `face` attribute, you can include a list of font family names. If the first name isn't installed on the user's system, the second name listed will be used, if possible. You can also use the names "Sans Serif" and "Serif" to use the default fonts of those types assigned in the browser. For size, you can specify a size from 1 to 7, or you can tell `font` to render the text in a size that is a certain number larger or smaller than the current size. (For instance, if the `<font>` element appeared within an `<h1>` element, the attribute `size="-2"` would make the font of that `<h1>` element two "sizes" smaller.) The `color` attribute can accept color names (red, green, blue, aqua, yellow...) or hexadecimal values (discussed in the "Understanding Color Values" section later in this chapter).

The `<center>` container element is one popular way to center nearly any markup that appears between the tags—images, text, hyperlinks, and even multimedia objects. `<center>` is easily replaced with the `<div>` element (discussed in the next section), so it shouldn't be missed.

A few other attributes in the past have included the `<blink>` container (causes text to blink on and off), the `<s>` and `<strike>` containers (make text appear as strikethrough text), and the `<u>` container (underlines text) .

As has been noted in previous sections, many of the elements we've learned about thus far have been able to accept an `align` attribute in previous HTML specifications. That isn't allowed in strict XHTML, but it's easy enough to fix with style sheets. Likewise, many elements (including the `<body>` element, `<p>` element, and others) that have accepted a `bgcolor` attribute (background color) in the past now rely on style sheets for that option.

Creating Style Sheets

Now that you've seen some of the theory of style sheets, let's move on to the elements and attributes that actually enable you to put style sheets to use. That includes a quick discussion of the different methods you can use to implement styles:

- **The style attribute**—Using the style attribute for various XHTML elements, you can add style to an individual element or container.

- **Defining element styles**—Using special style definitions, you can define elements—such as `<p>`, `<blockquote>`, `<h3>`, and so on—so that they have a particular styling on the entire page, or even throughout your Web site. If you'd like every paragraph to use a particular font, for instance, you can create a style sheet definition that does that.

- **Defining element classes**—Finally, you can create new *classes* that are styled, and elements can be assigned particular classes. If you create a particular class of `<p>` element that is red text, for instance, you can then use that class definition when you're creating a red paragraph on your page. Other paragraphs (or other elements) can be styled differently, if desired.

So, you have all these options. Beyond that, you can also decide how you're going to make those style sheet definitions available. You have two basic choices. First, you can *embed* the style information in each individual Web page. You'll do that either by adding style information in the `<head>` of the document, or by adding style information to any of the individual elements in your page using the `style` attribute.

Second, you can *link* to a style sheet, which enables you to create a central style sheet document and use it for multiple pages. We'll cover all of those eventualities in the upcoming sections.

The `style` Attribute

Let's begin with the most basic way that you can embed styles in your Web document—using the `style` attribute. The `style` attribute is a simple way to tell almost any XHTML element, "Hey, I'd like to apply a style sheet style to you." Most XHTML elements can accept a `style` attribute, which can then be used to style that element. For instance, you've seen `<p>` and `<h1>` elements accept the `style` attribute earlier in this chapter. But other elements can accept the `style` attribute as well. The following would suppress the underlining of the hyperlink:

```
<a href="index.html" style="text-decoration": none">Click to visit the
online store</a>
```

Or the following would change the background color of the selected table cells:

```
<tr><td style="background: yellow">100</td><td>200</td><td
style="background: yellow">300</td></tr>
```

To add more than one element at a time, simply separate the properties and their values using a semicolon:

```
<p style="align: left; font-style: italic; font-weight: bold; background:
yellow">
Here's some bold, italic text on a yellow background.</p>
```

You'll find that the `style` attribute is a simple way to quickly add a few different style properties within your page. However, it doesn't substitute for creating an overall style definition using the `<style>` element, as discussed next.

The `<style>` Element

The `style` attribute is useful for the occasional property change, but when you're really serious, it's time to think about using the `<style>` element. This element, which is placed in the `<head>` of your document, is where you can embed style definitions that can be used throughout the page. The basic format is this:

```
<head><style type="text/css">
p { font-style: small-caps }
</style>
<style type="text/css">
Element {property: setting}
</style>
</head>
```

It's fairly straightforward. For example, if you'd like to set every paragraph on the page so that its text is in small caps, you'd create the following `<style>` element in the head of the document:

```
<style type="text/css">
p { font-style: small-caps }
</style>
```

The typed element (such as the "p" in the preceding example) is called the *selector* in CSS-speak, and anything between the brackets is called the *definition*. The overall entry is a *rule*.

Selectors should be familiar to you—they're the letters that make up XHTML elements, such as p, h1, and ul, which you've seen in earlier chapters. When you create a rule, you're assigning a particular style definition to an element of your choosing, as in

```
ul { list-style: disc }
```

The <style> element can have more than one rule. Each rule technically ends with a closing bracket, so you could place more than one rule on a single line. But, it's best to format each definition on its own line, as in

```
<style type="text/css">
p { font-style: small-caps }
h1 { color: blue }
ul { list-style: disc }
</style>
```

Also, a particular definition can have more than one property within it. Properties are separated by semicolons, but you might consider placing each property on a separate line to make it more readable:

```
<style type="text/css">
p { font-style: small-caps;
    background: yellow;
    padding-left: 12px
    }
</style>
```

Again, all that spacing isn't required, but you can see that it helps make the rule clearer.

It's worth noting that you can assign the same definition to a number of elements at the same time simply by adding more selectors, separated by commas. For instance:

```
<style type="text/css">
p, h1, h2, h3, blockquote, ul, ol  { font-family: Arial, Helvetica }
</style>
```

This approach enables you to quickly set the font or a similar attribute for a group of elements at once, making them all more uniform on the page.

Finally, part of the point of calling the standard Cascading Style Sheets is to suggest that there's a certain amount of *cascading* (or, more technically, *inheritance*) going on. For instance, if a particular font style is assigned to a <table> element, elements within that table—row and cell definitions—are also assumed to have those characteristics.

The same is true, for instance, for the <body> element, which can be used to set some overall defaults for your page, such as font properties, background colors (or images), and so forth. Once these properties are set, all other elements within the <body> element will inherit these properties unless they're specifically overridden with either a definition of their own or the style attribute. For example, the following style definition would cause the main body font to be a sans-serif font (Arial, Helvetica), but would override that for unordered lists (ul), using Times or Times New Roman instead:

```
<style>
body { font-family: Arial, Helvetica; font-size: 12pt }
ul { font-family: Times New Roman, Times}
</style>
```

Creating Special Classes

Beyond simply redefining the properties of existing XHTML elements, you can go further with style sheets by creating new *classes*. In essence, these classes enable you to assign to a particular style a particular element sometimes, while leaving the original element's definition alone. For instance, consider this code snippet:

```
<head>
<style>
h1.red { color: red }
</style>
</head>
<body>
<h1>This Heading is the Default Color</h1>
<h1 class="red">This Heading is Red</h1>
</body>
```

Using the h1.red selector instead of just h1 means you're not assigning a style that will appear every time you use <h1>. Instead, it will only appear when you use the class attribute to specify that style rule. You can use this approach in many different ways, not the least of which is to define more than one class for the same element:

```
<style>
p.body { font-family: Times New Roman, Times; font-size: 14pt }
p.footnote { font-family: Arial, Helvetica; font-size: 10pt }
</style>
```

In this case, all you have to do is change the `class` attribute's value for a particular `<p>` element and that element's content will change appearance.

You can also create a class that isn't tied to a particular element, which enables you to add that class to any element in the body of the page that you'd like to style. For example:

```
<style>
.small { font-family: Arial, Helvetica; font-size: 10pt }
</style>
```

This rule could be used to change the formatting of pretty much any container that handles text, such as `<ul class="small">` to `<blockquote class="small">` and so on.

Using the `<span>` Element

When you're working with style sheets, you'll find that a new element, `<span>`, can come in handy. In essence, `<span>` is used to apply style sheet formatting to whatever markup you'd like to use it for. Anything from a single letter to entire paragraphs can be contained by the `<span>` element, which can then be used to apply a certain style or style class to the selection.

You've got four ways to define and use `<span>`. The first method is to simply use it with the `style` attribute for a quick styling fix, as in

```
<span style="font-style: small-caps">
```

This text is in small caps.

```
</span>
```

Just as you can define the style for almost any other element, you can define the style for span, as in

```
<style>
span { font-family: Arial, Helvetica; font-
size: 12pt }
</style>
```

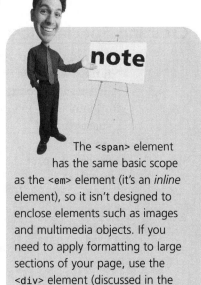

The `<span>` element has the same basic scope as the `<em>` element (it's an *inline* element), so it isn't designed to enclose elements such as images and multimedia objects. If you need to apply formatting to large sections of your page, use the `<div>` element (discussed in the next section).

You can then use <span> on its own as a simple way to apply some different formatting to a selection, such as

```
<p><span>Coming soon: More interesting content!</span></p>
```

So, that's one way to use <span>, but it's probably not the most interesting way because it limits you to a single style definition. The second way to define <span> is to create classes of the <span> element, the same way you might create a class for a <p> or <ul> element:

```
<head>
<title>Drop and Small Caps</title>
<style>
span.dropcap { font-family: Times New Roman, Times; font-size: 28pt;
float: left}
span.smallcaps {font: Arial, Helvetica; font-variant: small-caps }
</style>
</head>
```

With those rules in place, you could use the <span> element with a class attribute to change the appearance of the enclosed markup, as in

```
<p><span class="dropcap">I</span><span class="smallcaps">t was a dark and
stormy night.</span>
The clouds rolled in - thundered in - and the bleak black was only
occasionally interrupted
by bright flashes of fear.</p>
```

Putting these rules together with such markup, you'd end up with a page that looks similar to Figure 10.1.

FIGURE 10.1

Here you can see the <span> element at work, changing the markup using universal style classes you've created.

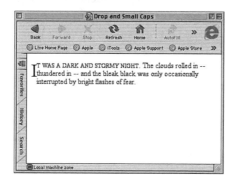

The third thing you can do with <span> is use it with a defined standalone class, such as

```
<style>
.dropcap { font-family: Times New Roman, Times; font-size: 24pt; text-
align: top }
</style>
```

Using `<span class="dropcap">`, you can apply this styling to a section of text, just as you could use the `class` attribute with another text container tag to apply the drop-cap style.

Using the `<div>` Element

Another style-related element is `<div>`, which is short for "division," and can be used to create sections within your entire Web document. The `<div>` element can be used to apply almost any formatting to nearly any elements that it contains, including tables, images, and multimedia objects. You could think of `<div>` as sort of a user-defined element that's one rung below the `<body>` and `<head>` elements in significance. (In specifications-ese, it's called a *block-level* element, which means it automatically has white space around it, like a `<p>` or `<blockquote>` element.)

The `<div>` element can be used in a way that's similar to `<span>`. Style sheet rules can be defined for it, and then the `class` attribute can be used to apply those styles to the enclosed markup. For instance:

```
<h1>Dining Out</h1>
<div style="background-color: yellow">
<p>Some tips for a better business dining experience:</p>
<ul>
<li>Call ahead and check to see if the restaurant takes reservations.</li>
<li>For six or more people, request special accommodations, such as
seating in a quiet area, banquet room or near a window with a view.</li>
<li>If you call early enough (before dinner) you can also ask for a quick
rundown of their house and recommended wine selections. Then, look them up
and have an idea if they're good recommendations.</li>
<li>Know whether the restaurant offers vegetarian, kosher, diabetic or
other dietary considerations, particularly if you aren't familiar with all
of your diners.</li>
<li>Consider any other special needs in your party (wheelchair access,
special seating) and request or discuss those items ahead of time.</li>
<li>Discreetly hand your credit card to the head waiter when you're first
```

```
seated, or otherwise let him or her know that you'll be taking the check.
This can avoid tussles at the end of the meal.</li>
<li>Tip well, including bartenders and bar wait staff if you wait for your
table in the bar or lounge area.</li>
</ul>
</div>
```

As you can see from this listing and from Figure 10.2, the `<div>` element can be used around multiple types of container elements, such as `<p>` and `<ul>` containers. The `<div>` element is designed to do just this—to create artificial divisions for styling and alignment purposes.

As with other elements, including `<span>`, the `<div>` element can be defined with a style rule, it can be assigned classes directly, or it can work with independent class rules.

tip

`<div>` can accept an `align` attribute that is recognized in many browsers, even those that predate style sheet support. Use `<div align="center">`, `</div>` to center all markup—paragraphs, tables, images—contained in the `<div>` element. (This is preferable to the `<center>` element, which is not a recommended part of the HTML or XHTML specification.)

FIGURE 10.2

Using the `<div>` tag enables you to span multiple elements with a style definition.

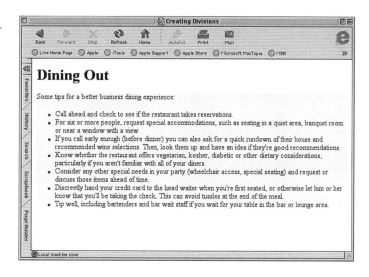

Dining Out

Some tips for a better business dining experience:

- Call ahead and check to see if the restaurant takes reservations.
- For six or more people, request special accommodations, such as seating in a quiet area, banquet room or near a window with a view.
- If you call early enough (before dinner) you can also ask for a quick rundown of their house and recommended wine selections. Then, look them up and have an idea if they're good recommendations.
- Know whether the restaurant offers vegetarian, kosher, diabetic or other dietary considerations, particularly if you aren't familiar with all of your diners.
- Consider any other special needs in your party (wheelchair access, special seating) and request or discuss those items ahead of time.
- Discreetly hand your credit card to the head waiter when you're first seated, or otherwise let him or her know that you'll be taking the check. This can avoid tussles at the end of the meal.
- Tip well, including bartenders and bar wait staff if you wait for your table in the bar or lounge area.

Linking Versus Embedding

There's one other issue before we move on to the various styles that are available for use—and it's a fairly important issue. It turns out that you have two different methods for style sheet definitions available to you. So far, you've seen many examples of the first option—embedded style sheet definitions, using the `<style>` container within the head of the document. This is particularly useful if your style sheet only applies to the page in which it's embedded.

Of course, many of us don't design Web sites that way. Our Web sites will often have common elements and styles on many, most, or all the pages. In that case, you may find it more convenient to create a more universal style sheet, and then link to it from within each document.

This linking approach offers two advantages. First, the obvious advantage is that you don't have to add the `<style>` container to the top of each page that you create. Second, using a single document for your style sheet definitions means you can quickly and easily alter the look-and-feel of your entire Web site with a simple change to the style sheet document. Plus, it's easier to manage a large Web site, even one developed by different Web authors and designers, if they are all expected to link to a predetermined style sheet.

Of course, even with linked style sheets, you can override a given style with a `<span>` or `<div>` element or by using the `style` attribute within an element. Likewise, you can still use the `<style>` element on individual pages to add to the style sheet document or to override portions of the linked style sheet document.

So, how do you link? First, you need to create the style sheet document. It should be plain ASCII text, just like an HTML document. Save the file with a `.css` extension, such as `styles.css`. The file can include rules that define element styles and rules that define classes. Within the style sheet, you can also use a special comment tag if you choose—text between `/*` and `*/` is ignored, as in

```
/* Begin rules for headings */
h1 {
 font-family: Arial, Helvetica;
 font-size: 24pt;
 font-weight: bold;
 word-spacing: 2pt;
 }
```

Once the file is created and saved, you can link to that file using the `<link />` element, which is placed in the head of your document:

```
<head>
<title>Main Page</title>
<link rel="stylesheet" href="http://www.fakecorp.com/styles.css">
</head>
```

Note that the URL to which you link can be a relative URL, but it would vary depending on where in your site's hierarchy you've saved the style sheet file. If you use the `<base>` element on your pages, you can use a relative URL that builds on the `<base>` element, as discussed in Chapter 7, "Building Hypertext Links."

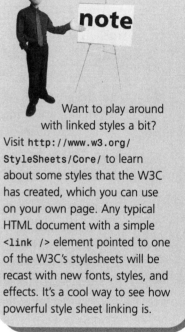

Properties and Styles

Now that you've seen the different ways to add styles to your pages, let's take a look at the variety of styles that you can add using CSS1 and CSS2. This section doesn't cover them all; only the most popular. However, you can visit `http://www.zvon.org/xxl/css1Reference/Output/index.html` for an excellent reference to the CSS1 specification. (It also has links to a CSS2 reference.) The official CSS2 specification is at `http://www.w3.org/TR/CSS2/`.

In the following sections, I'll touch on some of the styles for text, fonts, backgrounds, and links, and for working with borders, margins, and padding.

Want to play around with linked styles a bit? Visit `http://www.w3.org/StyleSheets/Core/` to learn about some styles that the W3C has created, which you can use on your own page. Any typical HTML document with a simple `<link />` element pointed to one of the W3C's stylesheets will be recast with new fonts, styles, and effects. It's a cool way to see how powerful style sheet linking is.

Text Styles

The text styles in the CSS definition are those that enable you to determine how text will be rendered, positioned, and aligned on the page. These styles can be used with nearly any XHTML element, giving you control over how text and inline images appear in your document. Table 10.1 shows many of these text styles.

TABLE 10.1   CCS Text-Style Properties

Property	Value	Example(s)
word-spacing	Number and units	1pt, 4em, 1in
letter-spacing	Number and units	3pt, 0.1em, +1
line-height	Number and units	
text-decoration	Value	underline, line-through, box, blink
text-transform	Value	capitalize, lowercase, uppercase, none
text-indent	Number and units or percentage	1in, 5%, 3em
vertical-align	Value or percentage	baseline, sup, sub, top, middle, 50%
text-align	Value	left, right, center, justify

The properties word-spacing, letter-spacing, line-height, and text-indent accept length values, which include a number and the units of length. An example of this would be extra point-size spacing:

```
p.wide { letter-spacing: 2pt }
```

When creating CSS-compliant rules, length (among many other values) includes both a number and the measurement unit. The number can be either positive or negative; there should be no space between the number and the unit. Unit measurements you can use include px (pixels), in (inches), mm (millimeters), cm (centimeters), pt (points), em (the height of the current font), and ex (the height of the current font's letter "x").

text-decoration is used to change the appearance of text in your document, and it includes the values listed in Table 10.1. The value normal is also possible.

The vertical-align and text-align properties give Web designers much-desired control over centering and justifying text in a document. Vertical alignment is best used with elements that appear inside another element. For instance, this style definition creates a class of the <em> element that can be used as a superscript:

```
em.super { vertical-align: super }
```

So, adding this class within another paragraph creates text that is superscript compared to the surrounding text:

```
<p>The only thing we have to fear is fear itself. <em class="super">F.D.R,
public speech, 1933</em>.</p>
```

Font Properties

While the <font> element is frowned upon, that doesn't mean there isn't an entire Web out there with defined fonts and snazzy-looking paragraphs! One way to get in on the action is to define fonts—including font family, size, weight, color, and more—using style sheet properties to create rules. With fonts in particular, remember inheritance. You can specify font properties for the `<body>`, for instance, and then override that specification for elements or classes that need to be different from the main body. Table 10.2 offers some of the font-related CSS styles and shows how they can be used.

TABLE 10.2   CCS-Defined Style Properties

Property	Value	Example(s)
`font-family`	Name of font	`Helvetica, Serif, Symbol`
`font-size`	Number/percentage	`12pt, +1, 120%`
`font-weight`	Number/strength	`normal, bold, bolder, 100, 900`
`font-style`	Name of style	`italic, oblique, normal`
`font-variant`	Name of style	`normal, small caps`
`font`	Combination	`12pt Serif`
`color`	Word/hex number	`red, green, blue, #FF00FF`

Here's a quick rundown of all these style sheet properties:

The `font-family` property allows you to choose the name of the font that you'd like text to appear in. With any `font` property, you want to be as general with font family names (such as Helvetica or Courier) as possible because the user's browser will have to decide what that font name's closest counterpart is on the user's system. So, avoid names like "Helvetica Oblique" or "Courier Heavy 12."

In fact, `font-family` allows you to specify alternative font names for different computer systems, like this:

```
<style type="text/css">
  p.standard { font-family: Helvetica,
Arial, sans-serif }
</style>
```

The `font-family` property can also accept one of five generic font names: `serif`, `sans-serif`, `cursive`,

note

Font family names with spaces should be put in quotes, like `"Century Schoolbook"`, when found in a style definition rule. When they're used with the `style` attribute, you can use single quotes, as in `style="font-family: 'Century Schoolbook', serif"` because the `style` attribute itself requires double quotes.

fantasy, and mono-space. If you stick with these generic names (or at least include them in your list of values), you'll always have at least some measure of predictability in your visual browser.

font-size can be a percentage, point size, or word size, such as larger or smaller. font-weight refers to the boldness of the font, with possible values like bolder, lighter, or numerical values from 100–900. (Normal is 400.) font-style values determine the italic nature of the font. Possible values are italic, oblique, and normal.

The font-variant property is simply used to set the font to either normal or small caps.

The font property is basically a shorthand reference for the four that appear preceding it in the table. You can simply use any of the related values for the catch-all font property, effectively describing its entire appearance in one definition. The font property's implementation can be problematic in different browsers, so it's recommended that you define font properties separately (particularly font-family and font-size) for cross-platform compatibility.

Background and Color Properties

Style sheets can be used to give unprecedented control over what appears in the background of your Web page. Not only can you specify a color or an image for the background, but you can also decide how the image will be repeated, whether it acts like a "watermark," and other characteristics.

Although background properties are popularly applied to the <body> tag (so that they affect the entire document), background properties can actually be assigned to nearly any XHTML element, from inline elements (<em> or <span>) to block elements such as <p> or <h1>. This makes it possible to set highlighting colors around individual words or background colors for blocks of text in paragraphs, lists, and elsewhere. Table 10.3 discusses the background properties.

TABLE 10.3   CCS Background Properties

Property	Value	Example(s)
background-color	Color name of RGB value	white, #0000FF
background-image	url( )	url(image.gif), url(http://www.fakcorp.net/bgnd.jpg)
background-repeat	Word value	repeat, repeat-x, repeat-y, no-repeat
background-attachment	word value	scroll, fixed
background-position	Direction or percentage	top, left center, 20%, 65%
background	Combination	white url(image.gif) repeat-x fixed

The possible values for color include `black`, `red`, `maroon`, `white`, `green`, `olive`, `lime`, `aqua`, `teal`, `blue`, `navy`, `yellow`, `brown`, `gray`, `silver`, `orange`, `purple`, and `fuchsia`. If you opt to use a `red-green-blue` (RGB) value for your colors, you can do that in one of two ways. You can either use a three-digit hexadecimal number in the form `#0F0F0F`, or you can specify a 256-color value for each of red, green, blue, as in `"color: rgb(255,255,0)"`.

As for the background colors, you may find them interesting but largely unnecessary. That's because you can use the `background` property as a shorthand reference to all (or any) of the other properties:

```
<style type="text/css">
  body.back_image { background:
url(http://www.fakecorp.com/images/back.gif)
white repeat-x fixed }
</style>
```

If you need or want to use the precise `background` property, here are some quick explanations of the less obvious ones:

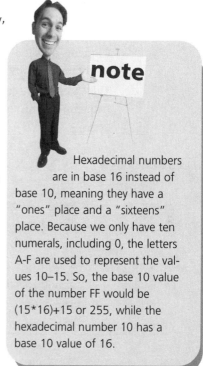

note

Hexadecimal numbers are in base 16 instead of base 10, meaning they have a "ones" place and a "sixteens" place. Because we only have ten numerals, including 0, the letters A-F are used to represent the values 10–15. So, the base 10 value of the number FF would be (15*16)+15 or 255, while the hexadecimal number 10 has a base 10 value of 16.

- `background-repeat`—This property uses one of four codes (shown in Table 10.3) to determine how a background image will be repeated to *tile* itself over the entire browser window area. `repeat-x` sets it to repeat horizontally; `repeat-y` sets it to repeat only vertically.

- `background-attachment`—Determines whether or not the background image will scroll along with the rest of the Web document (scroll), or if the page scrolls over the background as it stays in place (fixed).

- `background-position`—Accepts direction names or percentages to determine the position of the top-left corner of the background image.

Alignment and Block Appearance Properties

XHTML elements that include white space around them tend to be called *block* elements because in effect, they create a box of text (and other markup) that can then be considered an object on the page. (Just to confuse matters, the CSS specification refers to blocks as *boxes*, so this section really talks about *box* properties.) And because the box is an object, there are certain ways you can alter its alignment and appearance, including setting margins, padding the box, adding a border, and so on. While you saw some of these properties for tables in Chapter 9, "Advanced Table Elements and Table Design," it's interesting to note that with style sheets, you can apply them to any block-level element.

The CSS style sheet definition creates a number of properties specifically designed to help you control the appearance of these boxes. Table 10.4 shows you the box properties.

TABLE 10.4 CCS Box Appearance Properties

Property	Value	Example(s)
margin	Length or percentage	1in, 5% 10%, 12pt 10pt 12pt 10pt
padding	Length or percentage	1in, 5% 10%, 12pt 10pt 12pt 10pt
border	Width/style/color	medium dashed red, 2in grooved, blue
width	Length/percentage	.5in, 10%
height	Length/percentage	10em, 12pt
float	Direction	left, right, none
clear	Direction	none, left, right, both

The margin and padding properties work in very similar ways, with the number of values included in the definition determining which sides of the page are being affected:

- A single value, such as {margin: 5pt}, means that margin is applied to the top, right, bottom, and left sides of the page.

- Two values, such as {padding: .5in .4in}, means the initial value is applied to the top and bottom, while the second value applies to the right and left.

- Three values, such as {padding: .5in .4in .3in}, means the first number applies to the top, the second to the right and left, and the third to the bottom.

- Four values, such as {margin: 5em 4em 6em 9em}, means the numbers apply to the top, right, bottom, and left, respectively.

The difference between the two properties is that margin applies extra space outside the borders of the current element, while padding applies spaces between the edges of the element's box and the text it encloses.

Note that both of these properties can also be broken out into directional versions, such as `"margin-left: 12px"` or `"padding-bottom: 1in"`, which is useful when you need to specify only one side for margin or padding.

The `border` property is a shortcut property, like `background`. In `border`'s case, it can accept values for the width, style, and color of the border of a particular element. The width can be `thin`, `medium`, `thick`, or a length; the color can be any color name or set of hexadecimal pairs; and the style values include `none`, `dotted`, `dashed`, `solid`, `double`, `groove`, `ridge`, `inset`, `outset`. For example:

```
p.redborder {border: red dashed 20px}
```

The `border` property is a shortcut for many different properties, including a series of `border-size` properties (`border-left-size`, `border-right-size`, and so on) and `border-width` properties (`border-bottom-width`, `border-left-width`, and so on). Even as a shortcut property, you can include directions, such as `"border-left: 12px blue dotted"` and so on.

The `width` and `height` properties can be used to specify the width or height of any block element, using either a length or percentage. (The value `"auto"` can also be used in individual cases to override a setting and change the width and height to normal.)

The `float` property can be used to allow text to flow around an element. This works the same way that `align="left"` and `align="right"` do for the `<img />` element, except that the `float` property works for any element:

```
h2.wrap { float: left }
```

And finally, the `clear` property can be used to determine whether or not an element will allow other elements to float to one side of it (that is, whether or not the element will wrap around other elements). If `clear` has a value of `left`, the element is moved below any floating element to its left; if the value is `right`, the element is moved below any images floating to the right. For instance, with the style rules:

```
<style type="text/css">
  img.right { float: right }
  h2.no_wrap { clear: right }
</style>
```

Adding this markup would create a page that looks like Figure 10.3:

```
<h2>3 Bedroom Traditional</h2>
<img class="right" src="house1.jpg">
<p>This 3/2 traditional has a full basement (modern touches like Italian
lighting and Berber carpet) for a media room, home office or an
unemployment den for that
```

English-major college grad of yours. 325 Main Street. $129,000.</p>
<h2 class="no_wrap">Mini Mansion</h2>
<p> This one even has extras like a butler's pantry and a second, back staircase for creeping quietly down in the middle of the night to get one more small sliver of homemade pie. And, best yet, a babbling brook right there on the property. 19 E. Gables Road. $279,000.</p>

FIGURE 10.3

With clear, the second <h2> heading refuses to wrap next to the floating image, beginning below the image instead. (Note the extra white space above the "Mini Mansion" heading.)

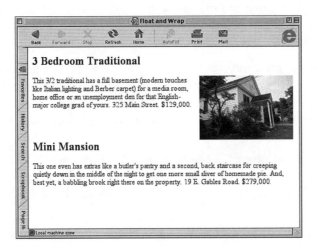

Styles for Links and Objects

Changing the style of your hyperlinks may be some of the easiest fun you can have with style sheet properties. Not only can you choose the colors that your links appear in, but you can use style sheets to change the appearance of a link when someone points the mouse at it—a popular way to make pages appear a bit more active. This is done using something called *pseudo classes*—specifically, those designed for links and similar objects.

The pseudo classes are shown in Table 10.5.

TABLE 10.5   Pseudo Classes

Property	Explanation
:link	Properties of the hyperlink before it's clicked
:visited	Properties of the hyperlink after it's clicked
:hover	Properties of the link or object while the mouse pointer is over it

Property	Explanation
`:focus`	Properties of the link or object while text is being entered or it's selected by the keyboard
`:active`	Properties of the link or object while it's being selected (that is, while the mouse button is down or the Enter key is pressed)

These classes can be defined in style sheet rules with `color`, `font`, and `background` properties, as in

```
<style type="text/css">
a:link { color: red; background: white }
a:visited { color: pink; background: white }
a:hover { color: blue; background: yellow }
a:active { color: orange; background: yellow }
</style>
```

When defined in this way, the styles are automatically assigned to `<a>` elements used throughout the page.

First Letter and First Line

Two other pseudo classes might grab your attention. The `:first-letter` and `:first-line` classes can be used to create drop caps, small-cap introductions, or similar effects. For instance:

```
<style type="text/css">
p.drop:first-letter {
    font-family: Times, "Times New Roman";
    font-size: 450%;
    float: left;
    margin-right: 5px;
    }
</style>
```

This would create a drop-cap at the beginning of each paragraph, with the attribute `class="drop"` as part of the `<p>` element. The same sort of thing would work for `first-line`.

Special Table Styles

Many of the text and box styles discussed so far can be used on markup that appears inside tables. But what about using styles with the table elements themselves, particularly `<table>`, `<td>`, and `<tr>`? All of these elements can be used with the background, color, and box style properties discussed earlier in this chapter.

With table rows especially, you may find it useful to define style rules that can be used for background colors, alignment, and more. For example:

```
<style>
tr.yellow { background-color: yellow }
</style>
```

This definition creates a class of `<tr>` that can be used to create rows that have a yellow background. Other background and box properties could also be used with the `<tr>` element or with individual `<td>` elements.

While it's clear that the `<tr>` element can accept many style properties to style each row, what about defining styles for columns? If you use the `<colgroup>` or `<col />` elements discussed in Chapter 9, you can assign style properties to them. For instance, you could give a particular column a background color. First, define the style:

```
<style>
col.yellow { background-color: yellow }
</style>
```

Then, using the `<col />` element, you can assign a particular column the style class that you've created:

```
<table>
<colgroup>
<col />
<col class="yellow" align="right" />
</colgroup>
<tr><td>January</td><td>$100.50</td></tr>
<tr><td>February</td><td>$50.95</td></tr>
<tr><td>March</td><td>$1000.55</td></tr>
</table>
```

Because the second `<col />` element is the one that has been assigned a style class, the second column will appear with a background color.

You may want to change the border and margin characteristics of your table, which you can do with the `border` and `margin` properties discussed earlier in the section "Alignment and Block Appearance Properties." You'll find that you can alter both the `<table>` and individual `<tr>` elements with those styles, as well as the `<col />` element. For instance:

```
<table style="border: solid red">
```

This opening tag begins a table with a solid red border around it. Whether or not the table has interior lines would rely on the `border` property with individual `<col />` and `<tr>` elements. (Note also that the current versions of most Web browsers differ in their implementation of table borders. You might want to stick with the table `border`, `frame`, and `rules` attributes discussed in Chapter 9 for a while longer.)

In my experience, Listing 10.1 generates a red border around all cells in Internet Explorer 5 (and higher), but only a red border around the entire table in Netscape 6. Ideally, it would create a border around all cells.

LISTING 10.1   Using Border Properties with HTML Table Elements

```
<!DOCTYPE html PUBLIC "-//W3C//DTD XHTML 1.0 Strict//EN"
    "http://www.w3.org/TR/xhtml1/DTD/xhtml1-strict.dtd">

<html xmlns="http://www.w3.org/1999/xhtml">

<head>
<style>
.redborder { border: solid red }
</style>

</head>

<body>

<table class="redborder">
<colgroup>
<col  class="redborder"/>
<col class="redborder" />
</colgroup>
<tr class="redborder"><td>January</td><td>$100.50</td></tr>
<tr class="redborder"><td>February</td><td>$50.95</td></tr>
<tr class="redborder"><td>March</td><td>$1000.55</td></tr>
</table>

</body>
</html>
```

Special Characters

In previous chapters, you've seen ways to add special quotation marks (using the `<q>` element), and I touched briefly on the use of the non-breaking space (` `). There are many other special characters you can add to your HTML document, although how to add them may not be readily apparent.

What do you do if you need to render a character that can't be typed into a plain-text document? Or what about special characters, such as < and >, that XHTML uses as part of its own syntax? You add them using special *entities* that look much like the non-breaking space already discussed. This can be used to solve one thorny problem—how to actually display XHTML elements in an HTML document. For example, consider these two lines:

```
Students should remember to use the <b> and
</b> elements.

Students should remember to use the
&lt;b&gt; and &lt;/b&gt; elements.
```

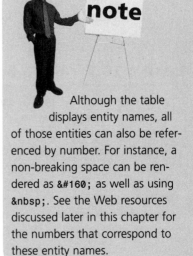

note

Although the table displays entity names, all of those entities can also be referenced by number. For instance, a non-breaking space can be rendered as ` ` as well as using ` `. See the Web resources discussed later in this chapter for the numbers that correspond to these entity names.

In the first line, the word and is in boldface. In the second line, the entities `&lt;` and `&gt;` are used to represent the less-than and greater-than signs, respectively, so that they aren't interpreted as XHTML by the browser. Instead, when the browser displays the second line, it will look like the first line does on this page.

All entities begin with an ampersand and end with a semicolon. Some use letters between those two symbols, while others use numbers. Table 10.5 shows some of the other named entities you can use in your pages.

TABLE 10.6   Named ISO Entities for HTML Documents

Entity Name	What It Represents
` `	Non-breaking space
`&lt;`	Less-than sign (<)
`&gt;`	Greater than sign (>)
`&frasl;`	Forward slash (/)
`&amp;`	Ampersand (&)

Entity Name	What It Represents
&copy;	Copyright symbol
&trade;	Trademark symbol
&reg;	Registered trademark symbol
&para;	Paragraph symbol
&lsquo;	Left single quotation mark
&rsquo;	Right single quotation mark
&ldquo;	Left double quotation mark
&rdquo;	Right double quotation mark
&yen;	Yen currency symbol
&euro;	Euro currency symbol
&pound;	English Pound currency symbol
&cent;	Cent currency symbol
&ndash;	En dash ( )
&mdash;	Em dash ( )
&iexl;	Inverted exclamation point
&iquest;	Inverted question mark

Aside from these entities, there are many others, including special language characters. For instance, to represent n~, which is the letter n and a tilde, you can use ñ in your document. For an uppercase N~, you would use Ñ in your text. Entities work similarly for other language characters, such as ö for ö (an o with an *umlaut*) or é for é (an e with an *acute* accent).

Other types of diacritical marks are supported, along with codes for Greek letters, mathematical characters, and many other special marks and symbols. For easy-to-follow references, see http://www.w3schools.com/html/html_entitiesref.asp or http://hotwired.lycos.com/webmonkey/reference/special_characters/. For a comprehensive look at the definitions of these entities, see http://www.w3.org/TR/REC-html40/sgml/entities.html.

Summary

In this chapter you learned the theory behind style sheets, why they're recommended, and how they can be implemented on your pages. You learned what the Cascading Style Sheets specification is, as well as some of the XHTML elements, such as <span> and <div>, that work hand-in-hand with style sheet concepts. The second portion of this chapter was devoted to the myriad styles that can be used to dress up your pages, including text, font, background, and block properties. You learned some of the special pseudo classes, which can be used for special effects in style sheet-enhanced pages. And you learned some special ways that style sheet properties can be applied to HTML tables. Finally, you were introduced to the entity codes you can use in HTML documents to represent special characters.

In Chapter 11, "Advanced Web Images and Imagemaps," you'll learn a little more about Web images, including how to optimize them for quick downloading and how to turn them into clickable imagemaps.

IN THIS CHAPTER

- Making your images better, smaller, and faster
- Creating and using animated image sequences
- Creating clickable imagemaps for Web site navigation

11

ADVANCED WEB IMAGES AND IMAGEMAPS

Chapter 6, "Visual Stimulus—Adding Graphics," discussed the basics of creating Web images and putting them on the page, but there's a lot more to cover. Creating and translating images that work well on the Web is an art and a science. You want images that look good, but you want the image files to be small so that they transfer very quickly over the Internet. You can do much more with images than simply create them and post them on the Web. You can animate them, in certain cases, and you can use certain HTML elements to turn images into clickable *imagemaps*, in which different parts of the image can be used as hyperlinks to different URLs.

Making Your Images Better

In Chapter 6, you learned the basics of choosing your image format, saving images, and translating them. You also saw how to crop and resize images; two steps that can help reduce their file size. In this section, let's dig in and a take a look at some of the more advanced options you find in our two graphics editors of choice: Paint Shop Pro for Windows and GraphicConverter from Macintosh. (Getting these applications is also discussed in Chapter 6.)

The issues covered include optimizing your images by tweaking settings in the graphics application. You then see the myriad of options that you're likely to encounter when saving or translating images, and how those options can affect the final images you decide to put on the page.

Optimizing Web Images

Aside from cropping and resizing your images, probably the most important considerations are to use as few colors as possible (in most cases) and to lower the resolution of the images to the appropriate dots per inch (dpi) for onscreen display.

Color Depth

Using fewer colors is generally appropriate for GIF and PNG format images. JPEG images, if they're photographic, almost always require millions of colors. (You can translate JPEG to 256 colors, but photos look pretty bad at that setting.) *Colors* means the palette of colors available to the image. If you use fewer colors in the palette, it's likely that the image is smaller in file size because very similar colors are made the same. The size of the palette is called the *color depth*.

In Paint Shop Pro, you can change the color depth of an image by opening the image and choosing **Colors**, **Decrease Color Depth** from the menu. You're then presented with some choices in the Decrease Color Depth dialog box, shown in Figure 11.1.

In this dialog box, you likely want to choose the **Standard/Web-safe palette** in the first column of options, because the Web is the destination for this image. The Web-safe palette is recognized by Web browsers as the most accurate across different platforms.

tip

After a color change has been put into place, you can choose Edit, Undo Decrease Colors to undo that change, so you can return the image to its original palette and experiment with other changes.

FIGURE 11.1

The Decrease
Color Depth dia-
log box.

Next, you choose a reduction method, which you can experiment with if desired.
The Nearest Color method is the most self-explanatory—when it's tossing out a particular color that's not supported by the smaller palette, it chooses the color that's
closest. The other two are different approaches that diffuse colors and *dither*, or vary
a pattern of dots, to get slightly different resulting colors.

In GraphicConverter, choose **Picture**, **Colors**. In the menu that appears, choose the
Change to... option that you'd like to try—that selection is the number of colors
used in the image. Note that you can also use the **Picture**, **Colors**, **Minimize
Color Table** option to use the smallest palette of colors possible.

Remember, if you're dealing with color photographs, lowering the color palette often
doesn't work, partly because JPG works only with millions of colors or 256 colors,
and partly because photos just look bad when you take out color information. If
you're creating images from scratch in GIF or PNG, however, lowering the color
palette should be helpful. In fact, generally you can start with a lower color palette
(say, 256 colors or the Web-safe 216-color palette) when you first create a new image
document. In both Paint Shop Pro and GraphicConverter, you can choose a color
depth in the New dialog box.

Resolution

Although you don't often change the color depth of scanned or digital camera
images, you may often want to change their resolution. Many images that are captured via scanner or camera use more resolution information than is necessary for
them to be displayed onscreen. In general, images for the Web only need to be 72
dots per inch (dpi, sometimes also pixels per inch, or ppi), instead of the 200 dpi or
higher that is often used for scanned images destined for a printer.

To change the resolution in Paint Shop Pro, select **Image**, **Resize**. Turn on the
Actual/Print Size radio button, and then change **Resolution** to 72 ppi. Click **OK**.
Now you likely need to resize the image, because changing the resolution in Paint
Shop Pro makes it larger. Choose **Image**, **Resize** again, and then turn on the **Pixel
Size** radio button. Enter the pixel size you want for either the width or the height. If
the **Maintain Aspect Ratio** option is checked (as it should be), the other measure-
ment changes automatically. Click **OK**, and your image is now the correct size and
the correct resolution for the screen.

In GraphicConverter, select **Picture**, **Resolution**. In the Resolution dialog box, enter 72 in each of the fields, leave the **Convert picture** option checked, and then click **OK**. The image is converted to the new resolution.

Image Compression and Progressive Encoding

When you save your Web images, you still aren't finished making decisions, particularly if you're dealing with JPEG images and (to a lesser extent) PNG format documents. That's because you've got some additional choices to make in the Save dialog box of your image-editing application.

Compression

When saving JPEG images, usually you can choose a quality setting. The lower the quality, the more *compressed* the image file is, and the smaller its file is. It's a direct trade-off, but one you might consider if you find that, even after cropping, sizing, and changing the resolution of an image, you're still stuck with an image file that's too big.

In Paint Shop Pro, you can change the compression setting when saving a JPEG image. First, choose **File**, **Save As**. If the image isn't already in JPEG format, choose **JPEG-JFIF Compliant** from the **Save As Type** menu. Now click the Options button. In the Options dialog box, note the Compression Factor slider. The more you drag that slider to the right, the higher the compression and the lower the quality. Make your selection, click **OK**, and then save the file.

> **tip**
>
> Paint Shop Pro has a neat feature, the Optimizer, which can help you make JPEGs that are small in file size but still good-looking. Click Run Optimizer in the Options dialog box and the Optimizer appears. (Note that it also has a wizard option, which can walk you through the optimization process.)

In GraphicConverter, you also set compression options when saving. Choose **File**, Save As, and make sure **JPEG/JFIF** is selected in the **Format** menu. Now click the **Options** button. In the JPEG/JFIF dialog box, use the Quality slider to choose the balance point between compression and quality. Note that with the **Calculate File Size** option turned on, you can see the approximate size of the file that you are saving (see Figure 11.2).

FIGURE 11.2
The JPEG/JFIF
dialog box
shows you both
file size and a
preview image.

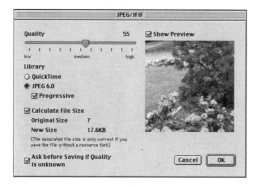

Saving Progressive Images

In the options for saving JPEG, GIF, or PNG images in an image editing program, generally you'll find a setting that enables you to make the image *progressive*, or *interlaced*. What this means is simple—the image can appear in a browser window as it downloads, instead of appearing only after the entire image has been received by the client computer. This makes your Web page appear in the browser a bit more quickly, while giving the user a sense of what the image will look like before it has completely appeared.

Both Paint Shop Pro and GraphicConverter make a progressive option available in the same option dialog box you access to set compression for a JPEG image. (GraphicConverter's is shown in Figure 11.2.) PNG and GIF images can also be progressive (with GIFs, the option is generally called interlaced), so look in the Options dialog box when saving them.

Image Transparency

Although image transparency doesn't really make an image download any faster or appear any more quickly in a Web browser window, it's still an interesting effect to play with. Transparency is supported in the GIF and PNG formats, enabling you to select *one* color within the image and make it transparent so that any background images or colors show through it.

This is most useful for creating images that appear to "float" on the page. Or, with the right shading and photographic qualities, a portion of the image might actually appear to be sitting on the Web browser's background, as shown in Figure 11.3.

FIGURE 11.3

The image's background is transparent, so the rest of the image appears to be sitting on the page.

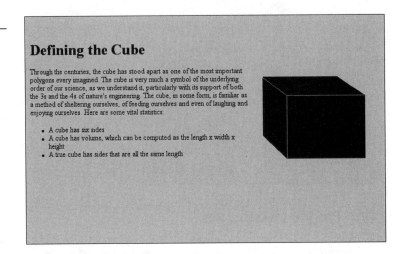

Defining the Cube

Through the centuries, the cube has stood apart as one of the most important polygons every imagined. The cube is very much a symbol of the underlying order of our science, as we understand it, particularly with its support of both the 3s and the 4s of nature's engineering. The cube, in some form, is familiar as a method of sheltering ourselves, of feeding ourselves and even of laughing and enjoying ourselves. Here are some vital statistics:

- A cube has six sides
- A cube has volume, which can be computed as the length x width x height
- A true cube has sides that are all the same length

The transparent color you choose needn't be the background color—you can make other parts of the image transparent, if you have a reason to. Only one color can be transparent, however, so you might need to plan ahead when creating the image. If your background is two-tone, you need to change that before you can make the whole thing transparent.

In Paint Shop Pro, you can make a color transparent by selecting **Colors**, **Set Palette Transparency**. You might then be told that the image needs to be converted before transparency can be added. This is particularly true if the image started as a high-color photograph. (See the "Color Depth" section earlier in this chapter for details.)

After you have the image in the correct format, you see the Set Palette Transparency dialog box (see Figure 11.4). You can choose no transparency, set it to the current background color (which you often do), or set it to a particular color. If you'd like to choose a particular color, you don't have to enter its number by hand (unless you happen to know the number). Instead, you can simply move the mouse pointer to the image and click the color you want to turn transparent—its number appears in the dialog box. When that's done, click the **OK** button.

In Paint Shop Pro itself, the portion that is now transparent turns a pinkish color. That color will be transparent after the image is saved as a GIF or PNG and displayed in a Web browser.

In GraphicConverter, transparency is even a bit easier. With the image on the screen, simply click the transparency tool in the toolbar—it looks like a magic wand with the letter "T" as part of the icon. Now drag the pointer to the color in the image that you want to turn transparent and click the mouse button. Immediately, that color turns gray, indicating that it's transparent. You can click another color to change the selection, or you can save the image as a PNG or GIF and it's ready to be displayed.

FIGURE 11.4

In Paint Shop Pro, you can click the image to select the transparent color.

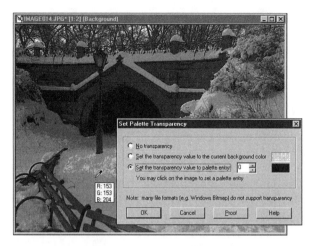

Creating Animated Images

The GIF format (specifically, GIF89a) supports a certain level of animation, akin to a flipbook animation you might have sketched into the corner of your grade school textbooks. By creating a series of images that are quickly displayed one after another on the screen, you can use these image formats to create the appearance of animation. If you've spent some time browsing the Web, no doubt you've seen this animation, generally in the form of Web advertisements.

Creating your own animations requires nothing more than some dedication and an animation application. Although many animation applications are pricey options from big-name graphics companies such as Macromedia and Adobe, others are available as shareware. In fact, most distributions of Paint Shop Pro include Animation Shop, which is a good option for Microsoft Windows users. For Macintosh, you might consider GifBuilder (`http://homepage.mac.com/piguet/gif.html`), which is freeware, or VSE Animation Maker (`http://www.vse-online.com/`), which is shareware.

note

Animation can be time-consuming because you need to create a series of GIF images or frames, usually by painting them. You'll find that the more sophisticated applications enable you to set the duration or frames, and to automatically add transitions and effects that make fewer painted frames appear more "animated" and interesting. But such animation applications tend to be pricey.

To create an animated GIF, generally you need to begin by either creating a series of GIF images (in Paint Shop Pro or GraphicConverter, for example) or creating image frames within the animation tool. Then those frames are put together in sequence and saved as an animated GIF. You can then add the GIF to your pages with a standard `<img />` element. The following is a quick look at the process in different applications.

Jasc Animation Shop

Animation Shop makes GIF animation fairly easy to accomplish. You begin by creating a new project (File, New), and then either drawing frames on the screen or importing them using the **Animation**, **Insert Frames**, **From File** option. Animation Shop can also be used (via the **File**, **Open** command) to open and work with animations in the popular FLI and FLC animation formats.

tip

If you're creating a banner advertisement, try the Banner Wizard (**File**, **Banner Wizard**). It walks you through the process of creating a fairly simple banner advertisement, complete with transitions.

After you've created the project, you see each frame in the window. (You need to scroll to see more than the first few frames.) Using the tools in the toolbar, you can add text, draw, paint, and otherwise make changes to each frame. To add more frames, choose **Animation**, **Insert Frames**, **Empty**, and then use the dialog box to specify the number of frames that you'd like. Remember, each frame represents another progressive change in the animation, so you may need to create a few frames if your animation is complicated.

After you've created your frames, you can select a frame and then select **Effects**, **Insert Image Transition** to add a transition effect. Or choose **Effect**, **Insert Image Effect** if you'd simply like to add a special effect to that frame. You've got a few different effects to choose from.

To test your handiwork, choose **View**, **Animation**. Now you see the VCR-like controls spring to life, enabling you to play your animation to test it. If it's moving too quickly, you may need to change the duration of some or all the frames. You can do that by selecting **Animation**,

note

Looping means the animation will play again once it's completed. In some cases, you can choose to have an animation loop one time, a fixed number of times, or continuously.

Frame Properties and changing the settings in the dialog box. To determine whether or not the animation will *loop* and to choose a transparency color (if desired), choose **Animation**, **Animation Properties**.

To save your animation, choose **File**, Save. With CompuServe Graphics Interchange selected in the **Save As Type** menu, you can name the image and click **Save** to save it as a GIF. Then you simply add it to your page as you would any GIF image.

VSE Animation Maker

Animation Maker isn't as full-featured as Animation Shop, but it's relatively inexpensive. With Animation Maker, you can create individual frames using paint and text tools, or you can import a series of images (PICT images are supported) using the **Frame**, **Open PICT** and **Insert** command.

Animation Maker doesn't have built-in transitions, but you can double-click a frame in the Frames window to change the percentage of time it spends on the screen, give it a name, and see its size. To control the overall speed of your animation, you choose **Set**, **Speed**, and then select how many frames per second (or seconds per frame) you want the animation to be. To test the animation, click the **Play** arrow in the main window or select **Set**, **Play Animation**.

When you're done creating the animation, choose **File**, **Save As**, **GIF**. In the Save GIF file dialog box, you can turn checkboxes on and off to make selections about the comments and delay times. Then you can select a transparent color, if desired, and finally click **Save** to view a Save As dialog box so that you can name the file. When saved, you can add the GIF to your Web page using a standard `<img />` element.

> **tip**
>
> If you'd like to create an animation that loops continuously, choose **Set**, **Settings**, and then, in the Loop section, decide if the animation should loop infinitely or just a set number of times. You can also specify a comment in this dialog box.

Using Imagemaps

One other use for images on Web pages that hasn't been touched on yet is the *imagemap*. Put simply, an imagemap enables you to define different portions of an image as hyperlinks that point to different URLs. The sections of such an image are often called *hot zones*, and they're defined using the imagemap specifications.

You have two different imagemap approaches to consider: client-side and server-side. *Server-side* imagemaps are the older type. In essence, they rely on the server computer (specifically, a *map server*) to recognize and deal with the clicks that a user makes. Most graphical Web browsers now support the client-side approach, which simply means that the browser itself can recognize where the user clicks and launches the specified URL. This section focuses on client-side maps because they are the dominant type. Server-side maps are discussed briefly at the end of this chapter.

Creating a Client-Side Imagemap

To begin creating a client-side map you need an appropriate graphic. You can create one in an image-editing application, or you can use an existing photo or image and overlay it with hot zones.

These hot zones are defined by x,y coordinates, where 0,0 is the top-left corner of the image. Using these coordinates and telling the browser what shape the hotzone should be makes it fairly simple to create a clickable image. The only real catch is figuring out what the various coordinates should be. One way to do this is to use your image-editing application. You can find the x, y coordinates in both Paint Shop Pro (in the bottom-left corner of the image window) and GraphicConverter (in the top-right corner of the image window, using the **Picture**, **Show Position** command). You can point to various parts of your image to learn the coordinates, and then jot them down for use in the imagemap.

You can also work with a map-editing program, such as MapEdit (`http://www.boutell.com/mapedit/`), which is available for both Windows and Macintosh. Using MapEdit, you can create hot zones (the clickable shapes that work as hyperlinks) that you'd like to use for your map. In fact, MapEdit actually saves the client-side imagemap information to your HTML document, enabling you to skip some of the steps in the rest of this chapter. (You probably want to read them anyway, just to see what's going on.)

You may find that other map-editing applications create a *map definition file*. This is the file that's generally used for a server-side imagemap, but it contains the coordinate information that you can use for a client-side map.

Then, to add the client-side map to your page, you use a new attribute to the `<img />` element, called usemap, along with an entirely new element, the `<map>` container element. Inside the `<map>` element, you use `<area />` elements to specify the coordinates and URLs for each of the hot zones.

Adding usemap to `<img>`

To create a client-side imagemap, you need to add the new attribute usemap, as follows:

```
<img src="map_image.gif" usemap="#map_name" />
```

Notice that the point of usemap is to specify a named link for the map definition information that you'd like to use. Elsewhere in the document, you enter the map definition itself in a `<map name="`*`map_name`*`">` element that has the same name specified in the usemap attribute. An example of the `<img />` element might be

```
<img src="main_banner.gif" usemap="#banner_map" alt="Top banner for
navigation" />
```

This element goes in the HTML document at the point where the image for the imagemap will appear. This `<img />` element displays the image and tells the browser that this is a client-side imagemap. Before you have a complete imagemap, however, you need to create the definition that the browser uses for that map.

The `<map>` and `<area>` Elements

The `<map>` container is used to create each of the hot zones that are used as hyperlinks in your imagemap. Each zone is created using an `<area />` element, which defines the shape, coordinates, and URL associated with that hotzone:

```
<map name="map_name">
<area shape="shape_type" coords="coordinates" href="URL" alt="text" />
<area shape="shape_type" coords="coordinates" href="URL" alt="text" />
...
</map>
```

If your map-editing application created a map definition file, you'll find that most of the information required for your `<map>` definition is in that file. If not, the coordinates you approximated in your graphics editing application should suffice. Based on those numbers, you can come up with `<area>` elements that define each of the hot zones in your imagemap.

First, though, you need to know something about the shapes that are supported. The shapes for client-side hot zones differ a bit from those for server-side maps, which is important to know if you're using an imagemap editor to determine coordinates. Only three basic shapes are accepted by the shape attribute, and then the numbers are given to the coords attribute. The three basic shapes are as follows:

> **tip**
>
> The `<map>` element can be anywhere in the document. Often, it's easiest to put it at the top of the body section, so you can get to it quickly. It doesn't display anything in the browser window, so its placement won't affect other elements.

- `rect`—The rectangle requires the coordinates for the top-left corner and the bottom-right corner. For example, 0,0, 10,10 places the left and top lines of the rectangle at 0,0 and the right and bottom lines at 10,10.

- `circle`—A circular hot zone requires three different coordinates: center-x, center-y, and a radius. An example might be 100,100,20, which would represent a circle with a center at 100,100 on the page, and a radius of 20 pixels.

- `polygon`—The third shape, a polygon, enables you to specify a shape with any number of sides. Each vertex requires a pair of points as its definition. The coordinates 100,100,200,200,0,200 would create a three-sided polygon (a triangle) with its top at 100,100, its bottom right at 200,200, and its bottom left at 200,0.

> **tip**
>
> The simpler your imagemap is, the better. For the most part, today's imagemaps use rectangular hot zones because rectangles are easy to define, they're button-like, and there isn't much novelty left in the idea of complicated clickable images. You may find a good reason to use the other shapes, particularly when you're creating clickable photos or educational sites. For basic navigation, though, rectangles are easy.

The `href` attribute is used to assign an URL to each hot zone. If no URL is desired, the attribute `nohref="nohref"` can be used to define a particular hot zone that doesn't reference a URL.

For example, consider a bar that you might put at the top of your site as a graphical navigation option:

```
<body>
<img src="banner.gif" usemap="#banner_map" alt="navigation banner"
border="0" />


<h1>The Movie Site</h1>


<p>Welcome to the Movie Site, the number one place on the Internet for
information about movies, stars, directors and more.</p>


<map name="banner_map">
<area shape="rect" coords="45,45,115,70" href="films.html" alt="Film
Details" />
<area shape="rect" coords="150,45,220,60" href="actors.html" alt="Actor
Bios" />
```

```
<area shape="rect" coords="260, 45, 330, 70" href="directors.html"
alt="Director Filmographies" />
<area shape="rect" coords="370, 45, 440, 70" href="producers.html"
alt="Producer Info" />
<area shape="rect" coords="480, 45, 550, 70" href="reviews.html" alt="User
Reviews" />
<area shape="rect" coords="0, 0, 585, 75" href="help.html" alt="To Help"
/>
</map>
</body>
```

Figure 11.5 shows this image.

FIGURE 11.5

An imagemap that might be used for navigation.

Notice in the previous example that the last area element has coordinates that cover the entire image. According to the client-side specification, the area that's defined *first* takes precedence when two areas overlap. So, if someone clicks in one of the first four hot zones, they'll be taken to the appropriate URL. If they miss a hot zone, though, they'll be taken to a document called help.html, where you can tell them how to use the map correctly.

tip

If you elect not to create your own default hot zone, client-side maps automatically ignore clicks that fall outside your other hot zones.

Working with Server-Side Maps

Most likely, you don't need to work with server-side imagemaps. For years now, the HMTL standard and Web browsers have supported client-side maps, which are more efficient and effective. At this point, they're really only useful when very old Web browsers are used to access the map.

If you do need to work with a server-side map, it certainly isn't difficult. All you have to do is add the `ismap="ismap"` attribute to your `<img />` element, and then wrap the `<img />` element in an anchor element that points to an imagemap definition file that's stored on the server. When the server detects that an imagemap definition file is being requested, it automatically launches the imagemap server, which then handles all the hot zone requests. For example:

```
<a href="/maps/topbanner.map">
<img src="topbanner.gif" ismap="ismap" alt="Banner image" />
</a>
```

You need to ask your ISP or administrator how and where to store imagemap definition files, as it can vary somewhat depending on the Web server application and platform. You need to create the map definition file by using a map editor application such as MapEdit, mentioned earlier. That map definition file is the one that you store on the server and access via the anchor element.

Summary

This chapter began by discussing some of the advanced techniques you can use to make the image files on your Web pages smaller, faster, and more efficient. You also saw how to create transparent colors within images, and how to animate GIF format images. Then you saw how to create imagemaps, which enable you to create clickable hot zones on your images, hyperlinking to different URLs.

In Chapter 12, "Creating Sites with HTML Frames," you'll see how to create a Web interface using the `<frameset>` element, which divides a single browser window so that multiple HTML documents can be displayed at once.

PART III

BUILDING YOUR SITE

12

CREATING SITES WITH HTML FRAMES

For a long time, Web authors were plagued with a particular problem—they wanted to display many similar documents via their Web sites, offering common controls (in the form of hyperlinks or imagemaps) that quickly allowed the viewer to move through the pages. For instance, imagine you're designing a site that displays a number of very similar documents, such as articles, and you'd like the visitor to have a standard set of hyperlinks that can be used to view the next document, the previous document, or a particular article.

Using the standard approach of individual Web pages, you would be forced to replicate these links or controls on every page, or use some other sneaky approach (such as a server-side include, discussed in Chapter 17, "Forums, Chats, and Other Add-Ons"). With the advent of the HTML Frames specification, however, it was possible to split the browser window to allow more than one Web page to appear at a time. One frame could include navigation links, while another could display each article.

Suddenly, with the ability to split the window into frames, Web authors had a whole different option for designing their sites. This continues into the XHTML standard. That doesn't mean frames are always recommended, however, as you'll see in this chapter.

The Great Frames Debate

For a while, the problem with HTML frames was that many browsers couldn't view them. The frames specification was added after HTML 3.2 standard, which was created around 1997. (At that time, frames were already popular, but only with Netscape users.) Frames have been formalized in the HTML 4.0 standard, and most browsers have handled frames well. Interestingly, frames still remain just a bit controversial. Before we get to that, though, let's understand what frames are.

What Frames Are

The HTML frames specification enables you to display two or more pages in the same Web browser window at the same time. Those pages have separate URLs, separate scroll bars (if necessary), and otherwise act pretty much independently. Figure 12.1 shows a site that's using a frames interface.

FIGURE 12.1

A Web page that's using frames to make multiple documents easily accessible.

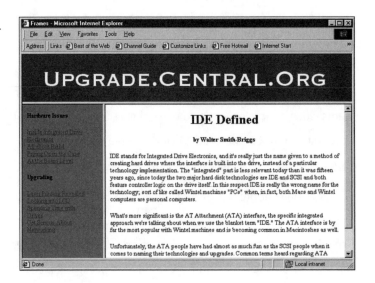

Splitting the page into frames is done by replacing the <body> element in your Web page with an element called <frameset>. The <frameset> container is designed to hold individual <frame /> elements, which then define the frames on the page and determine which URLs are loaded in the frames as default pages.

Once you've created those frames, the individual pages within the frames can include hyperlinks that specify which frame another URL should be loaded into. For instance, you could have a frame that you've determined is the "main viewer" frame where your documents will appear. (In Figure 12.1, this is the frame where the IDE Defined article appears.)

On the document used as an index, you can include hyperlinks that load different pages in that main viewer window, giving you an effect that's a little like a remote control changing channels on a television screen. In Figure 12.1, the document that contains the links All About RAM and Prying Open the Case is such an index. It's not the same HTML document as the article that appears in the main viewer. What's more, each of the hyperlinks in that index document uses a target attribute to specify that its URL will be loaded in the main viewer frame. So, clicking a link on the left side changes the article that appears on the right side.

Note also that the frames often have their own scroll bars and, in many cases, moveable dividers. While viewing a page that uses frames, you can often click and drag on the divider to change the size of the frame.

What's Wrong with Frames?

So far, frames sound cool, don't they? It seems odd that they'd be controversial, but there are some reasons why they are. First, using frames will sometimes make it more difficult for the viewer to discover the full URL to a particular page, because a frameset can be used to view many different pages at once. When you load a new document in one frame on the page (for instance, in that "main viewer" frame), the user may have trouble accessing that frame's page again directly via URL. (It's usually possible, but not as easy as using a bookmark or favorite.) Instead of showing that page's URL in its address bar, many Web browsers will display the URL to the frameset document itself. (In some browsers, this problem can extend to printing the individual frames.)

tip

When you're Web surfing, you can usually get around this issue by right-clicking the frame in Windows, or Ctrl-clicking it in the MacOs. You'll probably see an option such as **Open Frame in New Window**, which enables you to view the page, view its URL, and create a bookmark of that document.

The other issue is more basic—some people just don't like visiting sites that use frames. They'd prefer not to be forced to scroll around on different parts of their Web browser page, or be overwhelmed with different frames that act independently. Because framesets access a number of different URLs at once, they can be slower than typical Web pages. Your users with slow connections might find them annoying for that reason.

The solution, generally, is to use HTML frames only when you have a good reason, and not just because the technology is there. You can also take pains not to load another Web site's page into your frameset, which really tends to irritate people. You'll see how to avoid that in this chapter. Finally, when you do use frames, they should be as simple and cleanly designed as possible.

When Should You Use Frames?

So, you've seen the "don'ts"—what are the "dos"? While you're never *required* to use HTML frames, it's not a bad idea under a few particular circumstances:

- **Making documents available by index**—One common use for frames is to make many similar documents available using a convenient interface (as shown in Figure 12.1). Using frames in this way enables you to keep the index or table of contents readily available to the viewer, while the main frame is updated with different content.

- **Discussions or annotations**—Another reason to use frames is that it enables you to load two different pages at once on the same page. For instance, you could add annotations or explanations in one frame while the other frame holds a historical text or document that's being studied.

- **Fixed elements**—Let's say you'd like to place a banner image at the top of your Web page and have the content of the page (or the content of multiple pages) scroll beneath the banner image, instead of having the banner image move offscreen when you scroll the page. If you have two frames, one of them can hold that banner image (or anything else, such as hyperlinks or contact information) while the other frame holds a document that can scroll independently of that image. Figure 12.2 shows an example.

With HTML frames, you should always offer options to your visitors. In effect, you can do a few simple things that enable your visitors to "opt out" of the frames interface, if desired. You have a few different ways of doing this, which we'll explore later in this chapter.

FIGURE 12.2

With the banner image fixed at the top of the page, it's possible to scroll another document beneath it.

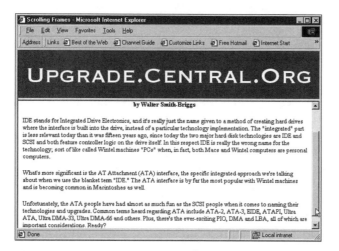

Adding Frames to Your Site

As you've already seen, creating HTML frames means adding some elements to your repertoire, including the <frameset> and <frames /> elements. Before you do that, however, you'll need to specify a new DTD and set up your Web document accordingly.

To work with framesets and be XHTML-compliant, you'll need to use the XHTML Frameset DTD, which enables you to create frames while using the transitional set of elements and attributes. The frameset DTD is added in the same way that the strict or transitional DTDs are added to your page, using a short entry at the top prior to the <html> open tag:

```
<!DOCTYPE html PUBLIC "-//W3C//DTD XHTML 1.0 Frameset/EN"
 "http://www.w3.org/TR/xhtml1/DTD/frameset.dtd">

<html xmlns="http://www.w3.org/1999/xhtml">
```

Creating the Frameset

Now you've defined this HTML document as a frameset document. The next step is to actually add the frameset by simply replacing the <body> element with the <frameset> element:

```
<!DOCTYPE html PUBLIC "-//W3C//DTD XHTML 1.0 Frameset/EN"
 "http://www.w3.org/TR/xhtml1/DTD/frameset.dtd">
<html xmlns="http://www.w3.org/1999/xhtml">
<head>
<title>Review.Central.Org</title>
```

```
</head>
<frameset>
</frameset>
</html>
```

The `<frameset>` element can accept two attributes: `cols` and `rows`. With an individual `<frameset>`, you can only define it as being broken into columns or rows. If you need both, you'll use multiple `<frameset>` elements, as you'll see in a moment. For now, though, notice what happens if you include a frameset definition that looks like this:

```
<frameset cols="25%, 75%">
</frameset>
```

The result is shown in Figure 12.3. (Note that if you try this example in a browser, it won't work until you've added some `<frame />` elements inside the `<frameset>` container. This is the basic structure, though.)

FIGURE 12.3

Here's an example of using a `<frameset>` element to create columns.

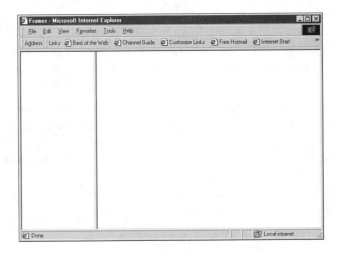

The `<frameset>` element will accept as many rows or columns as you want to create, and they don't need to be percentages, either. You can use specific pixels, such as `rows="10,200,30,300"`. This would create four rows. The top row will be 10 pixels high, beneath that will be a row that's 200 pixels high, and so on. Also, you can use an asterisk ("*") as a placeholder, which tells the `<frameset>` element to create a row or column that fills the rest of the space. For example, `cols="200, 400, *"` would create a third column that takes up any space that's left after the first 600 pixels. It works just as well with percentages, as in `rows="25%, 35%, *"`, with the added advantage of not forcing you to perform actual arithmetic.

`<frame>` and `<noframes>`

The `<frameset>` container doesn't do much for you on its own—you need to add additional elements before anything appears on the page. The `<frameset>` element supports two major elements: `<frame />` and `<noframes>`. The `<frame />` element is used to define frames within the document, while the `<noframes>` element is used to offer text and markup that can be seen by browsers that don't support frames. The first you might consider adding is the `<noframes>` element, such as

```
<frameset>
<noframes>
<p>This site requires HTML frames support. If your
browser doesn't support frames, you can access the
<a href="/articles/index.html">article index</a>
directly.</p>
</noframes>
</frameset>
```

Technically, the `<noframes>` container element could hold an entire page's worth of markup, if you thought that would be appropriate. In practice, however, you'll probably find it useful to create a special page that supports visitors who can't view frames. For instance, you could create an index that's loaded in the left column of your frameset, but that could also be used, in a browser window all by itself, as an index for accessing other pages. We'll discuss this idea more in the section "Offering Options to Users."

Meanwhile, the next step within that frameset container is to add `<frame />` elements that define the rows or columns that you'd like to add to your page. For instance, if you've defined the frameset as having two columns, you'll add two `<frame />` elements, one for each column's definition:

```
<frameset cols="25%, 75%">
<frame src="index.html" />
<frame src="viewer.html" />
<noframes>
<p>This site requires HTML frames support. If your
browser doesn't support frames, you can access the
<a href="/articles/index.html">article index</a>
directly.</p>
</noframes>
</frameset>
```

Generally speaking, the `<frame />` element is used to define the original source HTML document that is to be displayed in that frame of the frameset via the `src` attribute. The `src` URL can be either a relative URL, as shown in the example, or an absolute URL, such as `http://www.fakecorp.com/index.html`.

Those source files should be full-fledged HTML or XHTML documents, complete with a DTD, `<html>` container, `<head>` and `<body>` containers, and so on, just like all the XHTML-compliant documents you've created thus far. For example, the page `index.html` might look like this:

```
<!DOCTYPE html PUBLIC "\//W3C//DTD XHTML 1.0 Strict//EN"
"DTD/xhtml1-strict.dtd">
<html xmlns="http://www.w3.org/1999/xhtml">
<head>
<title>Index Frame</title>
</head>
<body>
<h1>index.html</h1>
</body>
</html>
```

Granted, this is not a terribly useful index page, but it shows you how the frameset works, as shown in Figure 12.4.

FIGURE 12.4

Now all the columns have URLs associated with them, and those URLs' documents are displayed by default.

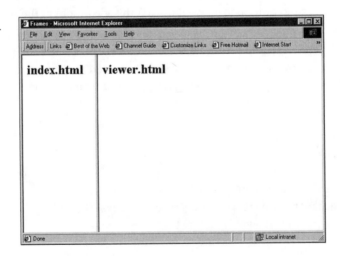

Naming and Targeting Frames

So far this frames thing is interesting, but you might have noticed one problem—the frame definitions are static. In other words, how do you go about actively loading a new page in a particular frame? It's a two-step process. First you name the frames, and then you target those frames with your URL.

By using the name attribute, you assign the frame a name in a way that's similar to naming a section of a page for an internal link. (If you're working under the XHTML frameset DTD, you should also include the id attribute with an identical value as the name attribute for future compatibility. The name attribute was officially replaced by id, but most browsers still recognize name and will for a long time.)

Here's our example as it's progressing:

```
<frameset cols="25%, 75%">
<frame src="index.html" />
<frame src="viewer.html" name="doc_viewer" id="doc_viewer" />
<noframes>
<p>This site requires HTML frames support. If your
browser doesn't support frames, you can access the
<a href="/articles/index.html">article index</a>
directly.</p>
</noframes>
</frameset>
```

Note that I've named the second frame "doc_viewer" while leaving the first frame unnamed. In this scenario, that first frame doesn't need a name because it will always be the index page that's assigned by default. However, I'll be creating links on that index page that will target the "doc_viewer" frame.

Targeting is done with the target attribute to the <a> anchor element. On the index page (in this example), I create a hyperlink that looks something like this:

```
<a href="story1.html"
target="doc_viewer">Read Story #1</a>
```

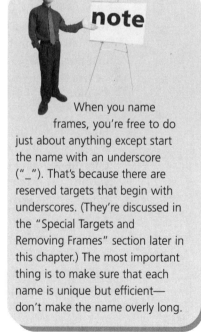

When you name frames, you're free to do just about anything except start the name with an underscore ("_"). That's because there are reserved targets that begin with underscores. (They're discussed in the "Special Targets and Removing Frames" section later in this chapter.) The most important thing is to make sure that each name is unique but efficient—don't make the name overly long.

Now, when that link is clicked on the left side, the right side will display the URL referenced in the anchor. Figure 12.5 shows an example that includes a few additional targeted links. In each case, the href URL is different, but the target is always that named frame.

FIGURE 12.5

On the left side are targeted links. On the right side is the named "viewer" frame.

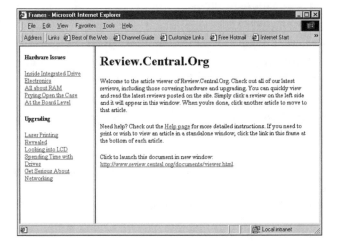

Note that the anchors can link to any URL that you'd like. For instance, you could create a link to a remote page:

```
<a href="http://www.w3.org/html/"
target="doc_viewer">Learn more about
HTML</a>
```

That page will appear in the target frame. (This is what can annoy some people about frames—they allow you to place other site's documents within your frameset, and users can't always tell where a page is coming from.)

An anchor element that's in a named frame can target its own frame if desired, although it doesn't have to. If you're viewing a document in the "doc_viewer" frame, for instance, and you click an untargeted hyperlink on that document, the resulting page will load in the same frame.

Options for `<frame>`

While the `src` attribute is the only one that you really need to worry about when creating frames, you'll find that a few other optional attributes can be handy for customizing the look of your frameset. Those attributes include the following:

- `noresize="noresize"` can be used to make it impossible for your visitors to change the size of a frame by dragging its frame border.

- `frameborder` can accept either a 1 or a 0 (as in `frameborder="1"`). A 1 means that the frame has a border, while a 0 means it does not.

- `scrolling` can accept `yes`, `no`, or `auto` as values that enable you to decide whether or not a particular frame displays scroll bars. `yes` means always, `no` means never, and `auto` means scroll bars appear only when they're needed.

- `marginwidth` and `marginheight` attributes can be used to change the margins at the left and right (`marginwidth`) and top and bottom (`marginheight`) of the frame. Each accepts a value in pixels.

- `longdesc` takes an URL as its value. This enables you to include a link to an HTML document that describes the contents of the frame, which is ideal for assistive (Braille- or speech-enabled) browsers.

Once you've worked with the frames a bit, you'll start to see the value of some of these attributes for making your frameset pages look exactly as you'd like them to.

Nesting Framesets

One issue that's bound to come up is that you may want both rows and columns on your frameset document. For instance, you might want a row along the top of the document for a banner image that displays your site's name and/or logo, and then two columns below it that are used as index and viewer. You would do this by nesting the `<frameset>` elements.

You really want two things here. First, you want two rows—a row at the top of the page and a row at the bottom of the page. Then, in that second row, you want to split it into two columns. You can accomplish that second feat by placing a second frameset within the first frameset, like so:

```
<frameset rows="100, *">
   <frame src="banner.html" scrolling="no" noresize="noresize" />
   <frameset cols="25%, 75%">
   <frame src="index.html" noresize="noresize" />
   <frame src="viewer.html" marginwidth="5" marginheight="5"/>
   </frameset>
```

```
<noframes>
<p>This site requires HTML frames support. If your
browser doesn't support frames, you can access the
<a href="/articles/index.html">article index</a>
directly.</p>
</noframes>

</frameset>
```

In this example, the second `<frameset>` element is nested within the first. In fact, it replaces the second `<frame />` element that would be required in that first frameset. That's because the nested `<frameset>` element *is* the second row of that first frameset, and it's defining that row as two columns. See Figure 12.6 for an example of how all this is coming together.

FIGURE 12.6

With nested `<frameset>` elements, you can define rows within columns and vice versa.

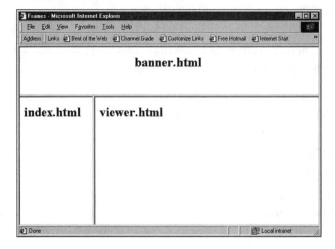

Advanced Frames

Beyond the basics of creating framesets and defining frames are some techniques that you can use to load items in different frames, or even in new windows. This section will also explore some tips and tricks for making frames a little less annoying, and for giving your visitors the option of opting out of frames. Finally, you'll take a look at the inline frame element that can be used in regular (non-frameset) HTML documents.

Special Targets and Removing Frames

I mentioned earlier that there are reserved `target` values that begin with an underscore. These values allow you to target particular frames or portions of the frameset without referring to them specifically by name. You can also use a special target to cause a Web document to appear in a new Web browser window, if desired. Here are those special targets:

- `_self`—Using this as the target value in an anchor element enables you to target the frame in which the current document appears.
- `_parent`—This value causes an anchor to attempt to target the frameset that's a parent of the current frame.
- `_top`—Using this value causes the anchor to attempt to target the current window, removing the frameset and loading the Web page referenced in href in the full browser window.
- `_blank`—This target is arguably the most fun; it allows you to open the referenced Web document in a new window.

These may seem a bit confusing. Consider the following listing, which shows a simplified version of the frameset we've been working with in previous examples and figures:

```
<frameset rows="100, *">
  <frame src="banner.html" />
  <frameset cols="25%, 75%">
  <frame src="index.html" />
  <frame src="viewer.html" name="doc_viewer" id="doc_viewer" />
  </frameset>
</frameset>
```

Now consider the following links, which could be a part of the index.html document that's loading in the second row, first column of that frameset. Here's what each of the various targets could do:

```
<!--Targets the third frame -->
<a href="newpage.html" target="doc_viewer">
<!-- Targets the frame where index.html was originally -->
<a href="newpage.html" target="_self">
<!-- Targets the first frameset, placing the page in the top row -->
<a href="newpage.html" target="_parent">
<!-- Targets the top of the page, removing the framesets -->
<a href="newpage.html" target="_top">
<!-- Opens newpage.html in a new browser window -->
<a href="newpage.html" target="_blank">
```

So, aside from all the cool possibilities for targeting frames, selves, and parents within a frameset document, we have two ways to remove the framesets altogether. `target="_top"` places the referenced page at the top of the current browser window, and `target="_blank"` creates a new page.

Offering Options to Users

Working with what you now know about frames, you may begin to see some of the options for helping visitors to your site who don't want to use the frameset interface. If you manage things correctly, you may find that it's simple to create a site that uses both frames and non-frames interfaces.

The Index Page

In many cases, one of your frames will be used to hold a document that includes a series of hyperlinks—the remote control, if you will. That's true for document-centric frames, image-centric frames, and many others. If this is the case for your page, you may find it handy to make that page available to the user directly (see Figure 12.7).

> **tip**
>
> The `target` attribute and these special target values can be used with a few other elements as well. The `<base>` element discussed in Chapter 7, "Building Hypertext Links," can accept a target, as can the `<area>` element that's discussed in Chapter 11, "Advanced Web Images and Imagemaps." And you can use `target` with the `<form>` element, which is introduced in Chapter 15, "Adding HTML Forms."

FIGURE 12.7

On the left, the original frameset. On the right, the index page in its own browser window.

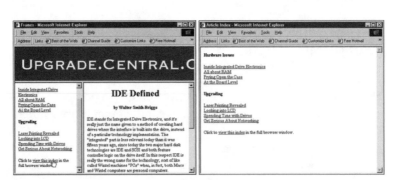

If you have a link on that page or elsewhere in your frameset, you can allow users to load that index page in a full browser window. This gives them access to the documents or images listed on that page. It'll be a little less convenient for them (they'll have to use the Back button in their browser quite a bit), but *they're* the ones who don't like frames! Here's some sample code:

```
Click to <a href="index.html" target="_top">view this index</a> in the full
browser window.
```

Self-Referential URLs

Another issue that tends to annoy detractors of frames are pages that are viewed in a frame without any reference to that page's URL. That makes it difficult to bookmark the page for later reference. It may also make that document difficult to print in some browsers.

The solution is simple. On all your pages that are destined for a frame, include their URLs as hyperlinks somewhere on the document. (The very bottom or top should suffice.) That way, the viewer knows the URL that references a particular page.

If you make a self-referential URL a hyperlink with a blank page as the target, you also make it easy for the user to print that page:

```
<p>Click to print or view
<a href="document2.html" target="_blank">
http://www.review.central.org/articles/
article2.html</a>
in its own browser window.</p>
```

Outlinks

Finally, the last major issue with frames is "framing" someone else's content. Although you may find it handy to place a document from another Web site in a frame on your site, it can be considered rude at best (or a legal matter at worst). To avoid any potential problems, it's best to use a `target="_blank"` attribute for any link on your framed site that reaches out to another server computer. That way the page appears in a blank window, just as that other Web author intended it to look.

> **note**
>
> The link could also be to a different index, which might be more attractively designed or add other non-frames elements or styles. Still, you can see how easy it is to remove the frameset and load a different page in its place.
>
> Some popular Web sites, such as About.com and Ask.com, make a habit of framing content from other sites. Both of them provide an obvious **Turn Off This Top Frame** or **Remove Frame** button, generally using a `target="_blank"` attribute. I don't know if that's enough to keep them from legal trouble or user outrage, but you can at least check out their implementations of frames if you're curious.

The `<iframe>` Element

Interestingly, this element is related to the `<frame />` element without being related to the `<frameset>` element at all. How is that? What `<iframe>` does is enable you to have an independent frame, called an *inline frame*, within a regular HTML document. The `<iframe>` container can appear inside the `<body>` element of a typical window, but it's used to display another Web page, just like a frame is within a frameset. Here's an example of how it works:

```
<iframe src="extra.html" width="300" height="300"
frameborder="1" scrolling="yes" align="right">
If you're seeing this text, then your browser
doesn't support inline frames. Click to read
<a href="extra.html">this frame's content</a>.
</iframe>
```

The `<iframe>` element supports most of the `<frame>` element's attributes, including `frameborder`, `marginwidth`, `marginheight`, and `scrolling`. It adds to those the `height` and `width` attributes that are used to set the inline frame's size in pixels. And `<iframe>` can accept an `align` attribute that can be used to make the `<iframe>` a floating element when set to `left` or `right`, just as with an `<img>` element's `align`. You'll also notice that it's a container element—the text that it contains is displayed when the browser doesn't support inline frames. Figure 12.8 shows the preceding example in a Web browser window.

FIGURE 12.8

The `<iframe>` element can be used to add markup from a different Web document in a frame within your document.

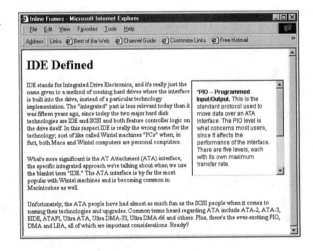

The `<iframe>` element can only be used with the transitional DTD, incidentally, because it isn't supported under strict XHTML. (A similar effect can be achieved with the `<object>` element, which is supported in strict XHTML and is discussed in Chapter 13, "Adding Multimedia and Java Content.")

Summary

In this chapter, you learned about HTML frames and how they can be used to divide a Web browser window so that multiple Web pages can be displayed on the screen at once. You also learned why some people dislike frames and that it's important to only use them when there's a strong advantage to them, and even then it's usually prudent to allow your visitors to opt out of the frames interface.

Once you've decided to work with frames, adding them is fairly easy. The `<frameset>` element is used, in place of the `<body>` element, to define the columns or rows that make up the frame-based page. You then add `<frame />` elements to define the default URL for the frame along with other attributes. One of those attributes is the `name` or `id`, which is used to identify the frame when it is to be used as a target for hyperlinks from elsewhere in the frameset.

Beyond that, you saw how to dig deeper into the `<frameset>` specification, including the nesting of framesets to create more complicated pages. You also learned how to use the special targets to launch Web pages in parent frames, without frames, and in a new browser window. Then you saw the different ways to let your visitors opt out of the frames interface. Finally, you learned about the `<iframe>` element, which can be used to create an inline frame, similar to an image, on an otherwise regular HTML document that's using the transitional DTD.

In the next chapter, you'll learn how to add multimedia content to your pages, including movies, animations, and Java applications.

13

Adding Multimedia and Java Content

Over time, the Web has become increasingly used for communicating via video and audio, as well as formatted text and images. Popular video formats such as QuickTime and Windows Media have made it possible to view movie trailers, news segments, and even home video and independent films via the Web. Meanwhile, audio has moved along as well, with the advent of technologies such as the popular MP3 format, which makes CD-quality audio available over the Internet at reasonable download speeds.

In this chapter, we'll take a look at those types of multimedia, along with some other technologies—portable documents, Flash animations, and so on—that are taking the Web experience beyond text and graphics. We'll also take a look at Java, a popular programming language and technology that many Web browsers can implement right in the browser window, making it possible for you to interact with your users programmatically. You'll see how to add Java applications to your pages and why you might do so.

Understanding Multimedia

What is multimedia? You've likely heard the term countless times, but it's still useful to define it. *Multimedia* generally refers to a computer-based presentation of data that makes use of more than one media—text *and* sound, for instance, or video *and* sound. In common usage, however, *multimedia* really suggests a medium beyond basic text and images. In other words, a soundless video stream that you view via a Web browser is still a multimedia presentation, because it's something beyond the text and images that you typically see on a Web page.

Most of the multimedia items that you encounter on the Web are composed of time-based data—video, audio, or animation that you can start, stop, and play much like a video- or audiocassette. Some of those multimedia presentations will have interactive portions—buttons to click, for instance. But for the most part, the multimedia you encounter will be similar to other forms of media you find around the house—video, audio, and so on.

Consider, for example, a video using QuickTime or Windows Media formats. Such a movie file is really a series of images, shown in rapid succession, that give the appearance of motion, somewhat like the animated GIF image discussed in Chapter 11, "Advanced Web Images and Imagemaps." Computer movie technology is a little more sophisticated than that, and movie files generally also have synchronized audio tracks, but the basics are simple—images that change over time. The same is true of audio files—thousands of sound *samples* are played per second to reproduce, at various levels of quality, a recording that has been *digitized* (turned into computer data) and saved in the form of a computer file.

Three issues are important to you as a Web author:

- First, why would you want to include multimedia elements on your Web site (and if you want to do so, should you)?

- Second, you need to know the multimedia file formats you'll be working with and how likely it is that your visitors will be able to display those types of files. The type of multimedia technology you'll be using can dictate the percentage of your users who will be able to experience the multimedia.

■ Third, and related to the second, is how you're going to add the multimedia element to your page. Will it be handled by the Web browser, or by a second application (called a *helper* application)? Or can the multimedia file be *embedded* in your page and played by a third-party *plug-in* to the Web browser? Let's look at these issues more closely.

Why Include Multimedia?

The first issue is whether or not you should include the multimedia content on your page at all. In general, the trade-off with multimedia is similar to the trade-off with images—you need to decide if the information conveyed is important enough to justify the amount of time your visitor will need to wait for the file to download and appear in the browser window. If there's a difference with multimedia files, it's that they can take tens or hundreds of times more storage space than a typical image file.

Video can require the largest files—even a one-minute movie trailer that takes up only a portion of your screen and plays for thirty seconds can require 10MB, 20MB or more of storage. Most Web users won't download such a movie over a modem-based connection. Audio files don't take as long to download, although a CD-quality song of three minutes can be up to 3.5MB in size. Animations destined for the Web tend to be a bit more optimal, but they can still be hundreds of kilobytes in size, often much larger than a typical Web image.

So, you have to decide if the multimedia item you'd like to add to your page communicates something vital. If so, you'll probably want to include it, and you may want to cause it to appear in your visitor's browser window by default. If the multimedia item isn't that important, you may want to give your visitor the choice of viewing it or skipping it. If it's only interesting because of the technology and not because of its content, you might decide not to include it at all.

Understanding Multimedia File Types

You've already seen some of the basic types of multimedia we're discussing in this chapter—video, audio, and animations. Some of the popular file types have also been mentioned—QuickTime and Windows Media for video (and/or audio, in some cases), WAV and MP3 for audio, and Macromedia Flash for interactive animations. Aside from these, there exist a number of other file formats that you may run across, as shown in Table 13.1. This table isn't exhaustive, but it does include the majority of the formats you'll encounter on the Web.

TABLE 13.1   Multimedia File Formats

File Format	Type of File	Extension
Sun Systems sound	Digital audio	`.au`
Windows sound	Digital audio	`.wav`
Audio Interchange	Digital audio	`.aiff, .aifc`
MPEG/MP3 audio	Digital audio	`.mpg, .mp3`
MIDI audio	Audio instructions	`.mid, .midi`
RealMedia	Audio/video stream	`.ra, .rm, .ram`
CompuServe GIF	Graphics	`.gif`
JPEG (compressed)	Graphics	`.jpg, .jpeg`
TIFF	Graphics	`.tif, .tiff`
Windows bitmap	Graphics	`.bmp`
Macintosh picture	Graphics	`.pict`
Fractal animations	Animation	`.fli, .flc`
MPEG video	Video	`.mpg, .mpeg`
QuickTime	Video	`.mov, .qt`
Microsoft video	Video	`.avi`
Digital video (DV format)	video	`.dv`
Macromedia Shockwave Director	Multimedia presentation	`.dcr, .dir`
Macromedia Shockwave Flash	Multimedia animation	`.swf`
ASCII text	Plain text	`.txt, .text`
Postscript	Formatted text	`.ps`
Adobe Portable Document Format	Formatted text and images	`.pdf`
Microsoft Excel documents	Spreadsheet data	`.xl, .xls`
Microsoft Word documents	Formatted text	`.doc`

One thing you'll notice about the table is that it includes the filename extension that's related to the multimedia file type. That's because filename extensions are very important for the cross-platform world of the Web. While some operating systems deemphasize or hide these extensions, it's important to get to know them if you'll be adding such files to your Web site. The filename extension is the primary mechanism that most Web browsers use to determine what a multimedia file's format is and how the file is to be dealt with.

Table 13.1 also includes some file formats you might not expect, such as the Microsoft Word and Excel file formats. While they might not be multimedia formats (arguably), they are *rich media* formats that can sometimes be downloaded and viewed over the Web, particularly using viewer applications that Microsoft has written for that purpose. Also, the ubiquity of Microsoft's applications means that most visitors will have access to Word or an application that can translate a Word document. So, allowing a user to download a Word document is one option for making formatted documents available over the Internet, particularly if, for instance, you want the visitor to be able to edit and print the document.

Finally, it's worth noting that Table 13.1 doesn't show the depth of all the formats. For instance, both QuickTime and Windows Media can be *streaming* formats, like RealMedia. *Streaming* simply means the video and/or audio is played as it's received from a server computer, instead of waiting for the entire multimedia file to arrive at the user's computer before playback. Also, QuickTime and Windows Media can be used exclusively for audio, if desired, as can RealMedia formats.

So, how does a single Web browser handle all these file formats? In most cases, it doesn't, as you'll see in the next section.

Linking Versus Embedding

Most Web browsers can deal with a limited number of file types. In general, Web browsers can display HTML documents, plain text documents, and the popular image file formats. Many Web browsers also know how to access and display information from other Internet server computers, such as File Transfer Protocol (FTP) and Usenet news servers.

On top of that, some browsers can play basic sound file formats, such as the WAV audio format. But for the most part, multimedia capabilities aren't built into Web browsers. Instead, they're the responsibility of supporting applications, either in the form of *helper applications* or Web browser *plug-ins*. A *helper application* is an application that the Web browser launches automatically to deal with a particular type of multimedia. In these cases, you're said to be linking to the multimedia file—such a link is sometimes called a *hypermedia* link.

A *plug-in* actually works with the browser application to display the multimedia file within the Web browser window, making it appear to be a part of the Web page, much like an image. In those cases, the multimedia document is said to be *embedded* on the page. Plug-ins are small files of programming code that are stored in a special folder on your hard disk—usually it's a subfolder of the Web browser's folder. When you start up your Web browser, it looks in this special folder and notes which plug-ins are installed. Then, when the browser encounters the `<embed>` or `<object>` XHTML elements, it will attempt to use one of the plug-ins to display the multimedia file in the Web browser window.

Whether you choose hyperlinking or embedding depends first of all on whether or not a plug-in is available for a particular type of multimedia file. If the plug-in doesn't exist at all, it's a moot point and you'll want to link to the multimedia file. If a plug-in does exist, there are still some other issues to consider, including how pervasive the plug-in is, how likely your visitor is to have that plug-in, and how easily the plug-in can be obtained and installed if the visitor doesn't have it already.

For instance, QuickTime movies are often embedded in Web pages. Nearly all Macintosh users have some form of QuickTime system software installed, and the QuickTime plug-in is standard with most Macintosh Web browsers (see Figure 13.1). Likewise, millions of Windows users have QuickTime installed, and it's reasonably simple to install the Web plug-in component, which is updated regularly by Apple at `http://www.apple.com/quicktime/`.

FIGURE 13.1

Here's an example of a QuickTime movie being played within the browser window.

Windows Media files are also embedded in many Web pages, for the obvious reason that the majority of computer users are running Windows and can easily view a Windows Media movie or listen to Windows Media audio.

Another of the most common plug-ins is Macromedia Flash, which enables interactive animations that you'll see often on high-dollar sites designed to sell cars or introduce new movies and television shows. A high percentage of Web users have the Flash plug-in installed, so you can often embed a Flash animation in your page without much worry. Although Macromedia Director isn't as pervasive, you can also embed Director presentations in your Web pages, as well as RealMedia presentations. Both formats offer easy-to-download plug-ins for Web users who haven't already installed them.

Some other types of files and documents are more commonly linked to, however, causing a helper application to launch. For instance, PDF documents can be embedded (there's an Adobe Acrobat plug-in that's fairly common). But more often they're linked to so that the document can be more easily saved on the user's hard disk and printed, where appropriate. MP3 files can be linked to, particularly when you want the user to be able to download the file to his hard disk and use it again later. Other sound, video, and text documents are often made available via hyperlink.

In the end, though, the decision is usually fairly simple. If you'd like your multimedia item to look like it's part of your Web page, and the element's file format is one that commonly offers a plug-in, you can consider embedding it in the page. If the multimedia item would look better or offer the user more benefits in its own window or running in its own helper application, your best plan is to create a link to it. You'll see how to do each in the following sections.

A PDF (portable document format) document is a type of application-independent document that includes font information and sometimes images embedded in the document itself. This makes it possible for the PDF document to look almost identical on different computers and computer platforms, even if those computers don't have the same fonts and internal graphics capabilities.

Adding Multimedia to Your Pages

In this section, let's take a general look at the two approaches to adding multimedia to your pages—the hyperlink and embedding. Then, we'll take a slightly closer look at some of the most popular technologies, including a discussion of streaming technologies.

Adding Hyperlinks

A hypermedia link really isn't much different from any other kind of link, except in one detail—instead of linking to another HTML document, you link to a multimedia file. The browser has to recognize the kind of file you've linked to and then load a helper application. The helper application takes over from the browser and displays the multimedia file.

Hypermedia links can look like any other hyper-link—they can be text, clickable graphics, or hot zones on imagemaps. All you have to do differently is enter an URL for a multimedia file in place of an URL to an HTML document. Hypermedia links are created like other links, too. Here's an example for a Windows sound file in MP3 format:

```
<a href="media/greeting.mp3">Greeting from
Our Fearless Leader (1.2 MB)</a>
```

When your user clicks the link, the file is downloaded to the user's computer. After that, it's up to the browser and the user's available helper applications to actually play the file. If a helper application isn't available (or isn't configured), generally the user will have the option of downloading the file to disk and storing it for later viewing or listening.

So how does this work? Every Web browser keeps a table of hypermedia file types and the helper applications associated with each type. Whenever the browser is told to link to a file that isn't an HTML document—and it's a file that the browser doesn't otherwise know how to display—it will load a helper application to display the file.

There are a number of multimedia files that the typical browser can handle:

- Graphics such as .GIF, .JPEG, and .PNG, as discussed previously
- Sound files, especially .MIDI and .WAV for background sounds
- Plain text files with a .TXT extension

Files that don't fall into these categories generally require a helper application. Figure 13.2 shows the table that Internet Explorer for Macintosh uses to determine what helper application is invoked or what other behavior takes place when a particular file is encountered in a link. You can reach this dialog box by selecting Explorer, Preference, Helpers in

note

Two recommendations:

First, you should include the approximate size of the multimedia file in the highlighted text that describes that link. That way, a visitor can get an idea of how large the file is and how long it may take to download.

Second, it's important to have permission before you link to a multimedia file on another person's or organization's site. Multimedia files can slow down Web servers while adding greatly to the total *byte count* that's transmitted by a site. With some sites, exceeding a certain transfer limit can cost money because ISPs charge for certain thresholds. For that reason, and for legal and intellectual property reasons, you should only link to multimedia files you've stored on your own server, unless you have explicit permission.

Mac OS X. Nearly all other browsers have similar preference settings. In Windows, later versions of Internet Explorer use the File Types options that are built into the OS to recognize and manage helper documents.

FIGURE 13.2

Internet Explorer's Helper preferences are used to determine how particular multimedia file formats are handled.

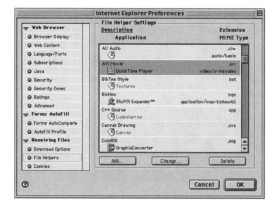

When the user clicks a link, the file format is noted and the preference table is consulted. If that user has set a special preference for this type of file—that it should be launched in a particular helper application, or immediately downloaded to disk—generally the browser will move ahead with that instruction. If the browser encounters a file for which it has no preference setting, it will probably pop up a dialog box and ask the user what to do with the file.

So, with hyperlinks, you aren't even limited to particular types of files or formats. If you'd like to make a TIFF image or a Microsoft Word document or a ZIP archive available via your Web page, you can link to it. When the link is scrutinized by the user's browser, either the file will be handled automatically by the browser or the user will be asked what he or she wants to do with the file.

Embedding Multimedia

The other approach to adding multimedia to your Web page is to embed it directly in the page itself.

note

For the record, these preferences are often set automatically. For instance, when you install some graphics applications, they'll ask if you'd like to use it as the default application for this particular file type. In some cases, that will extend to having it set as a default helper application in your Web browser. Likewise, selecting an application the first time your visitor asks for help with a new document type may automatically set the selected application as the default for that file type.

This is very similar to adding an image using the `<img />` element. In essence, embedding a multimedia file in a Web document simply defines a certain part of the Web browser window that is given over to the plug-in application, which is then responsible for displaying, playing, and otherwise controlling the multimedia element.

In general, embedding multimedia in a Web page can make the controls for the movie less accessible to special-needs users, particularly those that rely on keyboard controls instead of the mouse. If accessibility is a concern, you should consider always linking to multimedia files instead, because the standalone media players generally offer better accessibility. Likewise, embedded movies cause more problems with cross-browser compatibility than hyperlinks do. If you can sacrifice the coolness of embedding multimedia in the interest of better accessibility and features, consider a simple hyperlink to the media file.

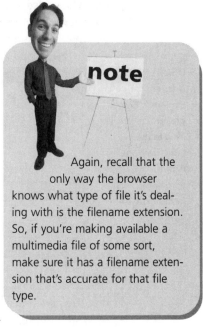

note

Again, recall that the only way the browser knows what type of file it's dealing with is the filename extension. So, if you're making available a multimedia file of some sort, make sure it has a filename extension that's accurate for that file type.

How does one accomplish this embedding magic? Actually, this gets a little interesting. The problem is that the entire plug-in approach, which is very popular with Web authors, is not XHTML-compliant. Instead, it relies on a Netscape-created element that's still in fairly wide use. That element is the `<embed>` element, and using it means you need to specify a transitional DTD for your page.

In a way, `<embed>` is sort of an `<img />` element on steroids. When you add an item via the `<embed>` element, you do so by specifying the name of the item, its URL, and, if desired, its height and width. Here's an example:

```
<embed name="Movie1" src="movie1.mov" width="240" height="120"
➥    pluginspage="http://www.apple.com/quicktime/
download/">
</embed>
```

Note that the element supports a name attribute (useful for accessing via JavaScript), as well as width and height attributes. In a way, it's very similar to an `<img />` element, with the exception of the required closing tag. That similarity can be a bit deceiving, however, because each individual browser plug-in can support additional non-XHTML attributes that will affect the playback of the multimedia (as discussed in the upcoming technology-specific sections).

In the meantime, there is an XHTML-compliant element that can be used for adding some plug-in media—the <object> container. As you'll see later in this chapter, <object> is more often used for Java applets, as well as other embedding possibilities. For instance, you can embed another HTML document within the current document, producing something that's similar to an inline frame (<iframe> is discussed in Chapter 12, "Creating Sites with HTML Frames"). The <object> element can also get a bit complicated, but you'll see some examples in the following sections.

You should consult any documentation you have for the multimedia technology you're using (QuickTime, RealMedia, and so on) to see the various ways that you can add the technology. For instance, some technologies offer both a Netscape-style plug-in and an ActiveX or Java control that makes it possible to add the multimedia item using <embed>, <object>, or both.

Embedding QuickTime

If you'd like to embed a QuickTime movie in your Web document so that it appears in the browser window, you can begin with the <embed> element:

```
<embed name="NewMovie" src="newmovie.mov"
height="320" width="240"></embed>
```

Beyond this example, however, Apple offers a slew of additional attributes that you can use to customize how the QuickTime movie and player will appear in the browser window. Some of those attributes, and their recommended values, are shown in Table 13.2.

tip

The pluginspage attribute is a handy one to include because it helps the user's browser locate the correct download page for a plug-in that isn't currently installed.

note

Internet Explorer 5.5 and higher no longer support the <embed> element, instead opting to focus entirely on the <object> element (and, more to the point, on Microsoft's own ActiveX technology). To add embedded multimedia, you'll need to use the <object> element, as discussed in the next few sections.

TABLE 13.2   Commands for a QuickTime `<embed>` Element

Command	Value	What It Does
autoplay	true	Causes movie to begin automatically
controller	false	Hides movie controls
loop	true	Loops movie over and over
playeveryframe	true	Plays every frame, even if movie is too slow
volume	0 - 256	Chooses the volume level; 256 is highest
hidden	true	Movie is hidden (useful for sound-only movies)
href	URL	Allows user to click movie to move to another URL; works only if `controller=false`

These special attributes are added to the `<embed>` element only when it's being used for a QuickTime movie. Here's a simple example:

```
<embed src="movie1.mov" autoplay="true"
height="320" width="240"></embed>
```

In this example, the movie would appear immediately in the Web browser window and begin playing as soon as the movie file was downloaded to the user's computer. The `<embed>` element is often used in a slightly different way with QuickTime movies, however, making the playing of the movie a two-step process. Here's the slightly more complicated example:

```
<embed src="post_movie.mov" autoplay="true"
➥    controller="false"
href="full_movie.mov">
</embed>
```

> **tip**
>
> Aside from the attributes in Table 13.2, you can add quite a few other attributes and options to the `<embed>` element for QuickTime. See `http://www.apple.com/quicktime/authoring/embed.html` for details and instructions.

The way this `<embed>` command is set up, the first movie loaded (`post_movie.mov`) should actually be a *poster movie*, or a movie file that only has one frame. Then, when the user clicks that poster frame, the actual movie (`full_movie.mov`) is launched, as specified in the `href` attribute. This is useful for enabling your users to verify their intent to view the movie (and therefore commit to a long download) by clicking the poster movie.

Because of the `controller="false"` attribute, the user won't be able to control the playback of the movie. Once downloaded, the QuickTime movie would begin playing all the way through without requiring any input from the user.

Apple notes that some browsers—notably Internet Explorer for Windows 5.5 and higher—don't support the <embed> element, but they do support ActiveX, a Microsoft technology for embedding programming functionality. For those browsers, you should include the <object> element along with the <embed> element, if appropriate. (Using JavaScript, which is discussed in the bonus online chapters "Introduction to JavaScript," and "JavaScript and User Input," you can determine the type of browser that you've encountered and then serve a compatible page, which might be a better solution. See the Introduction for details on where to download these and other additional chapters online.) Here's how Apple recommends that you add the <object> element:

```
<object classid="clsid:02BF25D5-8C17-4B23-BC80-D3488ABDDC6B"
➥   width="320"HEIGHT="240"
    codebase="http://www.apple.com/qtactivex/qtplugin.cab">
<param name="src" value="movie1.mov" />
<param name="autoplay" value="true" />
<param name="controller" VALUE="false" />
<embed src="movie1.mov" width="320" height="240"
➥   autoplay="true" controller="false"
➥   pluginspage="http://www.apple.com/quicktime/download/">
</embed>
</object>
```

This does a number of things. First, the <object> element will not only display the QuickTime movie in compatible browsers, but it will actually cause the ActiveX control to be downloaded to the browser automatically, if necessary. Then, with the <embed> element inside the <object> element, <embed> will be recognized by browsers that don't support ActiveX, while the QuickTime movie will play in those browsers that do require ActiveX.

Finally, it's important to note that QuickTime movies can be streaming media as well as the downloadable movie type. As mentioned earlier, *streaming* means that the movie data arrives just in time to be played back to the user. Streaming media feeds can be live events and broadcasts, or they can be regular QuickTime movies that begin playing in the Web browser more quickly than a downloaded movie.

note

For more on these instructions, see http://www.apple.com/ quicktime/products/tutorials/ activex.html.

If you're adding a streaming movie to your Web page, you'll need to make only minor tweaks to the HTML elements on your page. The real effort comes in acquiring the appropriate streaming server software, which is required to make QuickTime streaming work.

The major difference with QuickTime streaming is that you're sending a different type of URL to the end user, one that uses the realtime streaming protocol (rtsp://). You're also sending a different type of movie—if it's a downloadable movie, it needs to be saved as a Hinted QuickTime movie, which is something you can do in most QuickTime-compatible editing software. (In fact, you can do it with QuickTime Pro, which is an inexpensive upgrade to QuickTime.)

note

A *hinted* movie file is one that's saved in a special way so that streaming server software is more effective. The "hints" tell the server how the data should be put together for optimal playback.

So, for a downloadable movie file stored on a QuickTime Streaming Server computer, you'll first save the movie as a hinted movie, and then use the same `<embed>` and/or `<object>` elements to make it available. As you can see, there isn't much difference in the element, aside from the URL's protocol:

```
<embed src="rtsp://www.fakecorp.com/movies/hintedmovie.mov"
➡   width="240" height="180"
➡   pluginspage="http://www.apple.com/quicktime/download/">
```

Windows Media Movies

Windows Media offers embedding options in the form of both ActiveX controls and Netscape-style plug-ins, so you'll find that the basic elements for including a Windows media movie or a streaming media feed are about the same. In my experience, the Netscape-style plug-ins that Microsoft has created for Macintosh aren't all that effective. In many cases, your best plan for cross-platform support is to offer Windows Media movies and feeds as hyperlinks that appear in the Windows Media player.

But, if you'd like to embed a Windows Media feed in a browser window using the Netscape-style plug-in, you can use the familiar `<embed>` element:

```
<embed src="mymovie.avi" width="240" height="180" autoplay="-1">
</embed>
```

The `<embed>` element for Windows Media player embedding includes a number of parameters, discussed in Table 13.3.

TABLE 13.3 `<embed>` Parameters for Windows Media Movies

Parameter	Value	Meaning
showcontrols	0 or non-zero	0 means don't show controls; any other number means controls should be shown
autosize	0 or non-zero	0 means don't automatically size according to the movie's requirements
showstatusbar	0 or non-zero	0 means don't show the status bar
autostart	0 or non-zero	0 means don't automatically start the movie after download

As with other `<embed>` elements, you can use the `pluginspace` attribute to specify a location for the Windows Media plug-in, as well as `src` for the movie itself. Also, `type` is used with many `<embed>` element definitions to help specify which sort of media is to be expected, particularly since the Windows Media player can accept a number of different movie formats.

For the ActiveX version of the Windows Media player, you can use the `<object>` element (wrapped around the `<embed>` element, if desired):

In programming circles, `true` and `false` are sometimes represented as *non-zero* and *zero*, where 0 means false and –1 is customarily (but not necessarily) the non-zero value meaning true.

```
<object id="Player" type="application/
x-oleobject"
    classid="CLSID:6BF52A52-394A-11d3-B153-
00C04F79FAA6"
➡    standby="Loading Windows Media Player
components..."
➡    width="320" height="240"
➡    codebase="http://activex.microsoft.com/
activex/controls/
➡    mplayer/en/nsmp2inf.cab#Version=6,4,7,1112">
  <param name="autoStart" value="true">
  <param name="URL"
➡     value="http://www.fakecorp.com/movies/mymovie.avi">
  <embed src="mymovie.avi" width="320" height="240"
➡     showstatusbar="-1" showcontrols="-1" showdisplay="-1"
➡     pluginspage="http://www.microsoft.com/netshow/download/player.
htm">
```

```
    </embed>
</object>
```

Within the `<object>` definition, you can see that the `codebase` attribute is used to automatically locate and install the ActiveX component if it isn't already available. The `<embed>` element appears within the `<object>` element—just as with QuickTime, you now have both the Netscape-compatible plug-in and ActiveX scenarios covered.

The last issue with Windows Media is the case of streaming media. Using the Windows Media Encoder (`http://www.microsoft.com/windows/windowsmedia/wm7/encoder.asp`), you can encode a movie so that it streams using a Windows Media-compatible streaming server. (If you don't have such a server available, you'll need to make your movies available as regular downloadable movies instead.) You then link to the encoded file, but with one other important step in between. You first need to create what's called a *metafile* that points to the encoded file.

Generally, you feed the `.avi` file to the Windows Media Encoder, which then transforms it into an encoded Windows Media file with the extension `.wmv`. You then save that file on the Windows Media Server computer, and you create a metafile by opening a text editor and creating a new document that includes only the components that this example does, including the special `mms://` URL protocol:

```
<ASX version = "3.0">
<Entry>
    <Ref href = "mms://www.myfakeserver.com/movie/encodedmov.wmv" />
</Entry>
</ASX>
```

Save that file with a `.wvx` filename extension, which identifies it as a streaming Windows Media video file. (If you're creating an audio-only stream, you can save the metafile with a `.wax` extension.)

With that metafile created, you can store it anywhere on your regular Web server (assuming the metafile has an absolute URL to the movie file) and then access it just as if it were an AVI file. The `href` or `src` attributes of the anchor (`<a>`) element, `<embed>` element, and `<object>` element can also be pointed at that metafile, which in turn will launch the streaming media movie you've created.

RealMedia Movies

Next up is RealMedia. As a format, RealMedia doesn't give you the option to distribute downloadable multimedia—instead, it's all about streaming audio and video. So, you'll need some tools handy for encoding QuickTime or AVI movies into

RealMedia, and then you'll need a RealMedia server to use as your jumping-off point for the streamed multimedia. See `http://www.realnetworks.com/` `products/producer/index.html` for information on RealSystem Producer Basic (free) or RealSystem Producer Plus, which is Real's commercial encoding solution.

Once the movie is encoded, you'll have a file with an `.rm` extension (in most cases), which can be stored either on a Real Media server of some kind or on a standard HTTP server. In the latter case, you simply copy the `.rm` file to your server and create a link to that file:

```
<a href="rams/realmovie.rm">Click to view
the streaming file</a>
```

This approach offers limited functionality and requires a Web server that recognizes the `.rm` extension and file type, but it causes the RealMedia player to be launched for the user and the feed to be displayed.

For higher-end serving, you'll need a RealMedia server. If you've got one, you can then link or

RealNetworks, Inc. appears to make its Basic versions much more difficult to find than their Pro versions. If you can't find Producer Basic at `http://www.realnetworks.com/` `products/producer/basic.html`, try to locate an "A-to-Z" product listing at `http://www.` `realnetworks.com/` and track down a free version that you can at least test before committing to the high-dollar solution.

embed in a number of different ways—consult the Real Producer documentation for a good look at them. The most basic way is to use the `<embed>` element to access the `.rm` file that's stored on a Real Media server computer. Here's an example:

```
<embed src="http://realserver.fakecorp.com:8080/
ramgen/realmovie.rm?embed"
➡    width="320" height="240" type="audio/x-pn-realaudio-plugin"
➡    controls="ControlPanel" console="one" autostart="true">
</embed>
```

You'll notice a few differences from other types of media, including the `?embed` portion of the URL that's required to tell the RealMedia plug-in to embed the playback instead of launching the RealPlayer helper application. The `controls` and `console` attributes are also specific to the RealPlayer plug-in, enabling you to specify the look of the controls and how they interact with any other controls you embed. This example should serve you well in most cases, however—consult the documentation for other options.

Flash Controls and Movies

Macromedia Flash multimedia presentations are still often called *movies*, but generally they're a bit different from a QuickTime or Windows Media movie. Instead of a linear stream of video and audio data, a Macromedia Flash movie is often an interactive animation. In other words, you'll find yourself pointing and clicking within the Flash movie to decide what you'd like to view next.

Creating Flash movies is the subject of plenty of books, so I won't cover that in this book. But once you have a Flash movie created, you'll likely want to embed it in your Web document, which you can do using one of the two elements we've grown familiar with: <embed> or <object>. If you're using Macromedia Flash software, you may be able to generate automatic templates that give you the required HTML code. For the record, though, here's an example of both elements, used to cover all the bases for embedding Flash:

```
<object classid="clsid:D27CDB6E-AE6D-11cf-96B8-444553540000"
➥    width="100" height="100"
codebase="http://active.macromedia.com/flash5/cabs/swflash.cab#version=5,0
,0,0">
➥<param name="movie" value="flashmovie.swf" />
<param name="play" value="true" />
<param name="loop" value="true" />
<param name="quality" value="high" />
    <embed src="flashmovie.swf" width="100"
height="100"
➥    play="true" loop="false" quality="high"
➥    pluginspage="http://www.macromedia.com/
➥    shockwave/download/index.cgi?p1_prod_
version=shockwaveflash">
    </embed>
</object>
```

If you've seen the elements used for QuickTime, you'll notice that Flash's use of these elements doesn't vary much. Flash does offer a litany of additional attributes that aren't covered here, but they're for specific preferences and controls. For details on the Flash-related attributes that work with <embed> and <object>, see

http://www.macromedia.com/support/flash/ts/documents/tag_attributes.htm.

> **tip**
>
> Flash movies can also be saved as QuickTime movies, which can retain some Flash interactivity. If you feel that you'll have better compatibility by saving a Flash movie in QuickTime format, you can consider that an option for embedding your movie.

Working with Java

If you've spent much time on the Internet, you've probably heard at least a little something about Java. In a nutshell, Java is a full-fledged computer programming language that's designed to work a lot like some other popular languages—notably a programming language called C++. Many popular Macintosh and Windows applications are written in C++.

The difference is that Java is designed to run on nearly any sort of computer that might be connected to the Internet. It's popular for programmers who want to write programs for use on the Web, because once the Java program is downloaded, it can be run by nearly anyone who visits the Web site.

Java Applets

For the most part, Java programs end up being very small when they're used on Web sites, for the same reason that Web authors try to keep everything else small—it takes time to download files from the Internet. These small programs are often called *applets* because, unlike full-sized computer applications, they generally perform a specific function. That's not to take away from Java, however, as some more complex applications are written and available in that language. Figure 13.3 shows one of the Java applications that Sun makes available for free at `http://java.sun.com`.

FIGURE 13.3

Java applications tend to be a little less full-featured than applications on your hard disk, but they can still be fairly sophisticated.

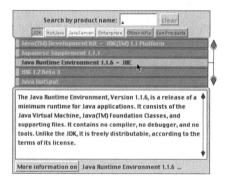

If you're not going to write Java applets yourself (or have someone else do it for you), you might want to check out what the Web has to offer in the way of freeware and shareware Java applets for your site. A good place to start is `http://www.yahoo.com/Computers_and_Internet/Programming_Languages/Java/Applets/` from Yahoo! or `http://java.sun.com/openstudio/` from Sun Microsystems, the developer of Java.

For the most part, Java applets are small games, Web communications enhancements, or ways to display data from internal databases on Web sites. It's also typical to see Java applets for presenting animated information screens, online classrooms, or even virtual meeting spaces. There are more sophisticated Java applications available online, including financial applications, business applications, and even productivity applications for word processing and similar tasks. While Java may never completely take over the Web, it's not a bad idea to understand how to work with and add Java applications to your site.

Add Applets Using `<object>`

As you've seen with other multimedia items, the `<object>` element is king in HTML 4.01, XHTML 1.0, and higher. While `<applet>` is an older element, it's still around for backward compatibility; it would require a transitional DTD. Instead, most modern browsers recognize `<object>` for Java applets, which is probably the best approach.

Here's a sample of the `<object>` element for Java:

```
<object codetype="application/java"
➡    classid="java:myapplet.class" standby="Applet Loading..."
➡    width=400 height=350>
</object>
```

In this example, the applet should be named `myapplet.class` and stored in the same directory as the document. You can also use a `codebase` attribute, if desired, to create a full URL to the applet, which would alter the element slightly:

```
<object codetype="application/java"
➡    codebase="http://www.fakecorp.com/applets/"
➡    classid="java:myapplet.class" standby="Applet Loading..."
➡    width=400 height=350>
</object>
```

That's all it takes. If the user's browser has Java enabled (not all of them will), the applet will be launched and displayed in the browser window, just as with other embedded content.

Summary

In this chapter, you learned what multimedia content is and how it relates to the Web page. You saw the different reasons for adding multimedia content to your pages, along with a few reasons to avoid it. From there, you learned how to include multimedia content by either linking to it or embedding it in the page. The chapter continued with a discussion of some specific multimedia formats—QuickTime, Windows Media, RealMedia, and Flash. Finally, it ended with a discussion of Java applets and how they, too, can be embedded in your Web pages.

In the next chapter, you'll learn a little about designing an entire Web site, including the creation of style sheets and site-wide styles that can be used to make the appearance of your Web site uniform.

14

- Building and implementing a site-wide style sheet
- Working with accessibility styles to further the goals of your style sheet
- Special international considerations, such as dealing with different languages on the page and changing the direction of text

SITE-WIDE STYLES: DESIGN, ACCESSIBILITY, AND INTERNATIONALIZATION

Chapter 10, "Get Splashy: Style Sheets, Fonts, and Special Characters," introduced you to style sheets, including a number of the Cascading Style Sheet (CSS) properties that you can use for designing individual pages. You also saw that it's possible to link to an external style sheet—either one that you create or one of the standard sheets made available by the W3C. In this chapter, let's look a little deeper into that site-wide style sheet concept. You'll also take a look at some additional style sheet properties to alter the table elements that you may have opted to use when designing your pages.

You've seen elsewhere in this book that accessibility issues and international-savvy pages are goals of the evolving HTML and XHTML specifications. As you'll see in this chapter, the CSS specification also offers a bit of help on these subjects, with special support for browsers that respond to aural (sound) style sheet entries. If your goal is to create a complete, site-wide style sheet, you may want to include accessibility styles within that sheet for the sake of completeness.

Finally, we'll discuss some of the issues that involve internationalization and language properties on your pages, including attributes that enable you to change the directions of text in tables and blocks.

The Site-Wide Style Sheet

The idea of linking to a style sheet was touched on in Chapter 10, but not fully explored. If you're designing a large Web site, particularly if you're starting from the ground up and the appearance and professionalism of the site are important to you, I fully encourage you to begin with a site-wide style sheet. Not only will this keep the text of your pages cleaner, it will also make it possible to quickly change or update the styling of nearly every page on your site. In my own experience, I can tell you that it's a pain to update all your older pages when a site goes through a redesign. If you focus your design efforts on a site-wide style sheet, however, you'll find that making changes will be much easier in the future.

And if you already have a site you're working on, you can transform it fairly easily into a site that relies on style sheets for its design. This has the added advantage of cleaning up the actual markup of the page, particularly if that page is littered with <font> elements and other elements that have been used for visual design. By removing those elements, you can make your pages easier to edit, update, and interpret when you return to the page at a later date—or, when another person goes in to update or edit the page. With a site-wide style sheet in place, the markup can look simpler because styles are defined separately for the basic block and text elements.

Once you've gone through your site and determined the styles that you'd like to use, you'll create a single style sheet document. Then, that document will be linked to all of your documents, using the <style> element, so that each page uses the same style sheet for its visual presentation.

In this section, let's take a look at how a site-wide style sheet approach can change the look and feel of a basic Web site that we'll use as a case study.

The Basic Site

We'll begin with a look at a sample basic site before redesign. Actually, this site has already existed for quite some time. For this example, it's being redesigned and updated for a site-wide style sheet approach. Until now, it has used a hodgepodge of visual elements and attributes, which means that various pages look slightly different from one another (see Figure 14.1).

FIGURE 14.1

These two pages from the same Web site have subtly different styles for headlines and text.

However, with a bit of a redesign and a style sheet, these pages can be made to look much the same with very little effort. What's more, the pages can also be designed so that a small change to the style sheet can make a big difference in how every page on the site looks—without even opening all those other pages. The changes are automatic because of the linked style sheet.

Here's a sample portion of HTML code from one of the pages on the site:

```
<head>
<title>No Styles Example</title>
</head>
```

```
<body>
<hr width="50%">

<h2><font face="arial, helvetica">From the Editor...</font></h2>

<h4><font face="times, times new roman" size="+1">Good-bye Sick
Leave</font></h4>

<blockquote>
<p><font face="times, times new roman"><b>Hello all,</b></font></p>
<p><font face="times, times new roman">How goes it in the writing world?
Things are good on this end -- especially now that I've survived my bout
with the flu currently sweeping the nation. Ouch.</font></p>
<p><font face="times, times new roman">I'm not usually one to belly ache
to strangers about being sick, but allow me some leniency this month.
Besides, my illness offers some valuable lessons for all you would-be
free-lance writers.</font></p>

<p><a href="letter.html">Editor Letter continued...</a></p>
</blockquote>

<hr width="50%">
</body>
```

As you can see, the page's markup is pretty messy, but it looks okay in a browser window, as shown in Figure 14.2. (And, in fact, I even cheated a little and put the HTML elements in lowercase—they were uppercase on the original. That was a different era of HTML...) The first thing this page can use is some cleaning up. With a style sheet, however, we should be able to change the preceding to something much simpler. First, let's consider the style sheet.

Planning the Styles

Building a site-wide style sheet will definitely take some planning, because you'll need to consider all the different elements you'll use on the page and how they should be styled. You'll also need to consider how many different styles you'll have for the same element. For instance, you might find yourself with four or five different styles that can be used with the <p> element. As you might guess, you'll probably be adding styles to your style sheet for a while as you're designing your Web site. While it's important to keep the style sheet as simple as you can, it's better to have a slightly complicated style sheet if the result is less complicated pages.

FIGURE 14.2

Here's how this small snippet looks in a Web browser.

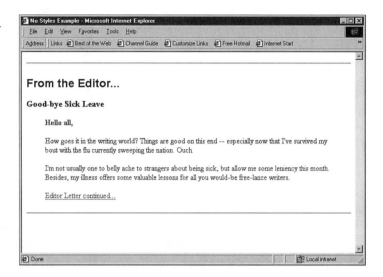

For now, let's look at that last example and see what we can come up with for style sheet entries. Here are some highlights of the process:

- If it's the "look" for the site, we can set all `<hr />` elements to 50% width with `hr {width: 50%}` instead of `<hr width="50%">`.

- Let's make all headings Arial, Helvetica, and Sans-Serif, as in `h1`, `h2`, `h3`, `h4`, `h5`, `h6 {font-family: Arial, Helvetica, Sans-Serif}`.

- In the original, `<h2>` was used for the first heading. This isn't recommended, but it was done so that the font was a little smaller. Instead, we can define a smaller `<h1>` if that makes sense for the whole site, as in `hi {font-size: 18pt}`.

- The original is using `<h4>` immediately after an `<h2>`. This isn't recommended and was only done for visual reasons, because the `<h4>` is supposed to represent a subhead. Instead, we'll define a particular type of paragraph for subheads, as in `p.subhead {font-family: Times, Times New Roman, Serif; font-size: 16pt; color: blue}`.

- We'll define a special indented paragraph style so that we don't have to use the `<blockquote>` container inappropriately, as in: `p.indent {font-family: Times, Times New Roman, Serif; font-size: 12pt; margin-left: 50px; margin-right: 50px}`.

Okay, all that effort lands us a style sheet that looks something like this:

```
hr { width: 50% }
h1, h2, h3, h4, h5, h6 { font-family: Arial, Helvetica, Sans-Serif }
h1 {font-size: 24pt }
```

```
p.subhead { font-family: Times, Times New
Roman, Serif;
font-size: 14pt; font-weight: bold }
p.indent { font-family: Times, Times New
Roman, Serif;
font-size: 12pt; margin-left: 50px;
margin-right: 50px }
```

We can even go further with this and make the style sheet a bit more efficient. Let's work from the assumption that all <p> containers will be Times, Times New Roman, and 12 point. We can define that, and then use the style sheet's assumption of *inheritance* so that we only need to change the properties that need changing for additional style sheet definitions.

Then, the style sheet would look more like this:

```
hr { width: 50% }
h1, h2, h3, h4, h5, h6 { font-family:
Arial, Helvetica, Sans-Serif }
h1 {font-size: 24pt }
p { font-family: Times, Times New Roman,
Serif; font-size: 12pt }
p.subhead { font-size: 14pt; font-weight:
bold }
p.indent { margin-left: 50px; margin-right: 50px }
```

> *note*
>
> *Inheritance* simply means that once you've defined styles for an element, any classes subsequently defined for that element will also include the new styles. If you define paragraph text as 24 points tall and define a class of paragraph text that is red, the red text will also be 24 points tall. The only exception would be if you specifically overrode the paragraph size in the red text class definition.

Notice how this makes the styles a little easier to read. The main <p> element is defined, and then the subsequent class definitions need only define the difference from the main <p> definition.

Save this style sheet as default.css, or something similar, and store it in your main Web site directory. Now the following listing should yield results that are nearly identical to Figure 14.2:

```
<head>
<title>Style Sheet Example</title>
<link rel="stylesheet" href="default.css" />
</head>

<body>
<hr>
```

```
<h1> From the Editor...</h1>

<p class="subhead"> Good-bye Sick Leave</p>

<p class="indent"><b>Hello all,</p>
<p class="indent">How goes it in the writing world?
Things are good on this end -- especially now that I've
survived my bout with the flu currently sweeping the
nation. Ouch.</p>
<p class="indent">I'm not usually one to belly ache to
strangers about being sick, but allow me some leniency
this month. Besides, my illness offers some valuable
lessons for all you would-be free-lance writers.</p>

<p class="indent"><a href="letter.html">Editor Letter
continued...</a></p>

<hr>
</body>
```

How does that look? As you can see, the markup is already quite a bit cleaner, it isn't using elements that aren't recommended (such as <h4> and <blockquote> in the wrong places), and if the page is viewed by a non-graphical browser, it won't choke on all the extra visual elements. It took a little work up front, but this will make the page markup a little more readable, and the page (and the rest of the site) will be easier to revise in the future. Plus, as you can see in Figure 14.3, it's a dead-ringer for Figure 14.2.

FIGURE 14.3

Here's the style sheet version of the page in the browser window.

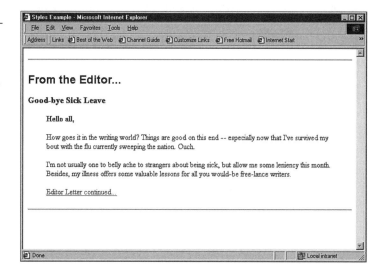

Style Sheet Power

So, you've seen some of the advantages of using style sheets. But their real strength is that you can now use this style sheet for all pages in the Web site. Once you've defined the main elements and some additional classes in the style sheet, you can generate very clean, XHTML-compliant documents that will be styled according to your defaults. Of course, you can also define more than one style sheet for your Web site and switch between them using different `<link />` elements, if desired.

And then there's my favorite advantage to style sheets—experimentation. Once you have a basic style sheet defined, you can continue to refine it as desired, experimenting to see what the overall changes would look like on your page and your site. With a few simple tweaks and additions, for instance, consider what this style sheet will do to the newly defined sample Web site:

```
a:hover { color: yellow; background-color: blue }
.indent { margin-left: 100px; margin-right: 100px;
padding-left: 10px; padding-right: 10px;
background-color: ffccff }
hr { width: 50% }
h1, h2, h3, h4, h5, h6 {font-family: Arial, Helvetica, Sans-Serif;
font-variant: small-caps}
p {font-family: Times, Times New Roman, Serif; font-size: 12pt}
p.subhead {font-family: Courier, Courier New, Monaco;

font-size: 16pt; color: blue}
```

With these changes, again saved to the same style sheet document `test.css`, I can clean up the page even more. I'll use a `<div class="indent">` (since the `indent` class has been defined without specifying an element) to cover the entire indented section of paragraphs. And I'll play with the look and feel a bit (see Figure 14.4). Here's the final version:

```
<head>
<title>Style Sheet Example</title>
<link rel="stylesheet" href="test.css" />
</head>

<body>
<hr>

<h2>From the Editor...</h2>
```

```
<div class="indent">
<p class="subhead"> Good-bye Sick Leave</p>
<p><b>Hello all,</b></p>
<p>How goes it in the writing world?
Things are good on this end -- especially now that I've
survived my bout with the flu currently sweeping the
nation. Ouch.</p>
<p>I'm not usually one to belly ache to strangers
about being sick, but allow me some leniency this month.
Besides, my illness offers some valuable lessons for
all you would-be free-lance writers.</p>
<p><a href="letter.html">Editor Letter continued...</a></p>
</div>

<hr>
</body>
```

FIGURE 14.4

Here's the page
after a little
experimenting.

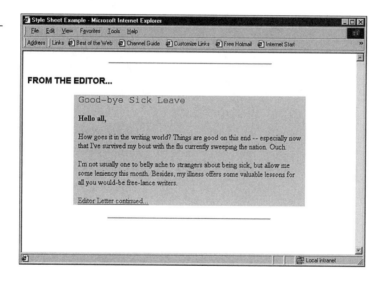

Of course, experimentation can get you in about as much trouble as it saves you. (I call this "Murphy's Law of Vertical Hold. The more you mess with something, like the knobs on a TV, the worse it looks.) But being able to change massive styling elements without digging into your page each time acts as a remote control over the design of your pages, which can be very powerful.

Accessibility Through Style Sheets

If your Web site is aimed at a sight-challenged audience, or if you'd simply like the most complete and accessible page possible, you should dig into the aural styles that the CSS2 specification makes available to you. These styles should be particularly easy to add to a site-wide style sheet that you've used to define the styling for the bulk of your elements. If you've already gone that far, adding these extras can be incredibly simple and helpful to your audience.

CSS2 offers a number of styles that are specifically designed to control the output to aural browsers that speak text aloud. Table 14.1 shows many of these properties.

note

As was mentioned in Chapter 10, CSS2 is as different from CSS1 as it is an add-on to it. Aside from aural elements, CSS2 adds styles for tables and the CSS positioning capabilities discussed in "Adding Dynamic HTML Elements," which is a bonus chapter available online. (See the Introduction of this book for details.)

TABLE 14.1   1CSS2 Aural Properties

Property	Values	Description
azimuth	left, center-left, center, center-right, right or an angle value (–360 to 360)	Enables you to specify the angle from which a sound seems to be coming
cue-after	url	Plays the sound file at the specified URL after reading the attached content
cue-before	url	Plays the specified sound file before reading the specified content
elevation	below, level, above, angle value (–90 to 90)	Enables you to specify the angle of a sound, above or below the listener
pause-after	seconds or milliseconds	Pauses for a certain number of seconds after the element is spoken
pause-before	seconds or milliseconds	Pauses for a certain number of seconds before the element is spoken
pause	seconds or milliseconds	Pauses before and after the element is spoken

Property	Values	Description
pitch	low, medium, high, number (Hertz)	Chooses the pitch, or frequency, of the spoken text
pitch-range	0, 50 or any number	The inflection of the spoken text; 0 is monotone, 50 is normal
play-during	url	Plays a sound file while the text of the element is being read
speak	none, normal, spell-out	Sets how the element's text is spoken
speak-numeral	digits, continuous	Sets whether numbers are read as digits ("1-2-3-4") or words ("one thousand," "two hundred and thirty four")
speak-punctuation	none, code	If it's code, punctuation, then it is read aloud, as in "period" and "exclamation point"
speech-rate	slow, medium, fast, number	Sets how quickly text is read; if it's a number, the number represents words per minute
voice-family	male, female, child, Zervox, Princess	Specifies the name of the voice to be used for speech (similar to font families, the voice must be installed on the user's computer)
volume	silent, soft, medium, loud	Sets the volume of the spoken text

You use these properties within a style definition the same way you'd use any other properties. For instance:

```
h1 { volume: loud; voice-family: male;
pause: 1; speak-numeral: digits }
p { volume: medium; voice-family: female;
speak-punctuation: none }
```

Most of these properties should make sense. The `voice-family` property works much like the `font-family` property, specifying voices that are installed on the user's system. The generic values—`male`, `female`, and `child`—should map to certain specific voice files on the user's computer.

The `azimuth`, `elevation`, and `pitch` properties are a bit more esoteric, but essentially they're used to fine-tune the playback of the spoken text. It's

note

Of course, you'd need an aural Web browser to test all these tags, and currently no mainstream browser supports them. It's still a young standard, though, so hopefully support is forthcoming. You can test your page for accessibility issues, however, using Bobby WorldWide at `http://www.cast.org/bobby/`.

possible to have headings, paragraphs, and other elements coming at different stereo "angles" from one another, making them easier to distinguish (or at least more entertaining).

International Issues

Another step you may want to take as you're developing a plan for your overall Web site is specifying languages for your pages. XHTML supports this with a special `lang` attribute, the `<q>` element, and some special instructions for table and text blocks.

lang and `<q>`

The `lang` attribute can work with a number of different elements to specify the language of those elements. It accepts a two-letter code to specify the language, as in

```
<p lang="es">Eso es en Espanol.</p>
```

The `lang` attribute can help the browser make decisions about how the element is rendered, including how to hyphenate words, how speech synthesizers should treat the text, and how search engines should recognize the page. By default, you specify a language as part of the XML definition of the page (as discussed in Chapter 4, "Creating Your First Page"), so generally the `lang` attribute is used to change languages mid-page.

Some of the possible language codes include ar for Arabic, de for German, es for Spanish, fr for French, he for Hebrew, hi for Hindi, it for Italian, ja for Japanese, nl for Dutch, pt for Portuguese, ru for Russian, sa for Sanskrit, ur for Urdu, and zh for Chinese.

The `lang` attribute can also be used with the `<q>` element to define quotation marks according to the attributed language. For example:

```
<p><q lang="en">I can't believe he said that,</q> Phillip said.</p>
<p><q lang="es">Si, es verdad,</q> Marcia replied.</p>
```

Table and Block Directions

Finally, it's interesting to note that you can specify the direction of text, using the `dir` attribute to most container tags. The result specifies the direction in which text flows, as in

```
<p dir="rtl">This text goes from right to left, instead of from left to right.</p>
```

The dir attribute can be assigned to <tr> or <td> elements to change the direction of text within them. While you could change the language for any block of text, this is most useful for languages that are read from right to left, such as Hebrew.

Again, this relies on implementation of the dir attribute by the browser, which isn't terribly reliable even in the latest browser versions.

Summary

This chapter gave you a closer look at creating a style sheet that can be implemented site-wide, and explained the advantages of doing so. Using a site-wide style sheet gives you a consistent-looking site, while making your XHTML code cleaner and enabling you to experiment freely with the look of the page. You also saw how this approach to style sheets can be incorporated with CSS2's aural styles to make your Web pages more accessible. And, at the end of the chapter, you saw some of the elements and attributes that enable you to specify the languages used on your pages.

In the next chapter, you'll learn about the elements used to create interactive forms on your page, including entry fields, pop-up menus, and other elements you can use to enable your users to make choices and communicate with you.

PART IV

INTERACTING WITH YOUR USERS

IN THIS CHAPTER

- The basics of HTML forms
- Adding form fields, buttons, and controls
- Using other elements to organize your forms
- Designing forms with lists, tables, and CSS

15

ADDING HTML FORMS

HTML allows you to add interface elements to your pages, such as menus, radio buttons, and text areas, that make it possible for your visitors to send you information or data. The data can be as simple as an email address sent to you for inclusion in your Web guest book. Or, the interaction can be as complex as enabling the user to make choices for an online computer application, such as those that locate doctors at HMO Web sites or that help you rent a car at a nationwide auto rental Web site.

In this chapter, let's take a look at how you can create HTML forms and make them look good. In Chapter 16, "CGIs and Data Gathering," you'll see how to create the back-end scripts that are used to process these forms.

The Basics of HTML Forms

The idea behind an HTML form and its components is simple—they enable you to ask for and accept information or answers from your users with varying levels of guidance. Users can be asked to

- Type answers, either in small boxes (such as for name or address) or in full sentences (such as for comments or complaints)

- Choose answers from a list of possibilities you create, including via a menu or check box

- Choose one answer from a number of options that you specify, using the radio buttons interface that you'll commonly find in Windows and Macintosh dialog boxes

The form is created using a series of XHTML elements that define the entry boxes, checkboxes, and other controls. Each of the form elements that you create will have a name, and that name will be used to create a variable where the user's response is stored. For instance, if you assigned the name city to an entry box and the user typed Boston, then Boston will be stored as the value for the variable city.

Those variables and their associated values are then passed on to the Web server computer, which in turn passes it along to a small computer program, called a *script*. The script is designed to interpret the data, act on the data, and (in most cases) respond with XHTML markup and text that are used to create an automatic Web page in response to the data. This page might contain the results of the data-crunching, or a simple "thank you" response.

To deal with forms data, then, you need to understand a little something about creating these scripts (which are Common Gateway Interface scripts and can be written in many different programming languages). While you probably won't learn enough from this book to produce incredibly complicated scripts, we will discuss creating them in Chapter 16. You can also use HTML form elements with JavaScript in various ways, as is discussed in the online chapters, "Introduction to JavaScript" and "JavaScript and User Input." (See the Introduction to this book for details on where to download these chapters.)

In the meantime, Figure 15.1 shows a basic form you might decide to create for your Web site. As you can see, the HTML form can appear on a page with other markup, and textual (and other) cues can appear within the form area itself. In some ways, HTML forms are very similar to HTML tables, in that they require a chunk of the page but not the whole thing. As you'll see, you can even use tables to help lay out your form, if desired.

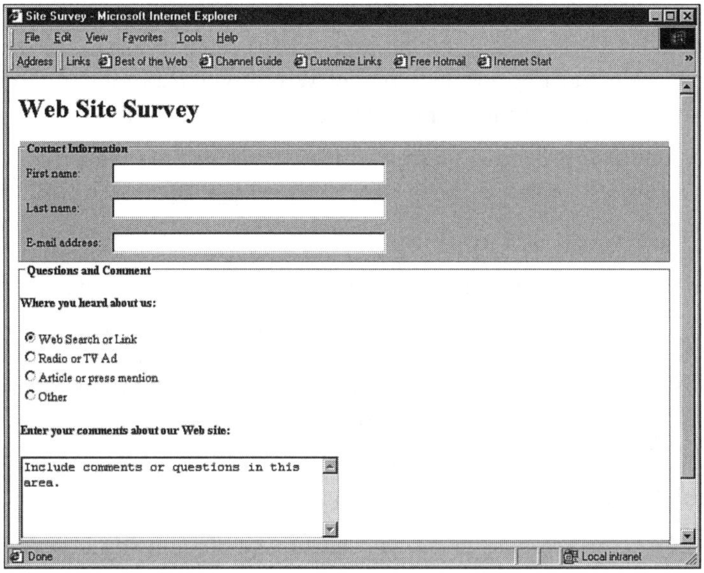

FIGURE 15.1

This form might
be used to
accept survey
results.

The <form> Element

In an HTML document, forms are created using the <form> element, which acts as a container. The form container works as follows:

```
<form method="get_or_post" ACTION="URL to data destination">
...form elements and markup...
</form>
```

The most basic <form> element has two attributes: method and action. The method attribute is used to determine how that form's data will be sent to the server. The attribute's possible values are post or get. The get method causes the data from the form to be appended to the URL for the data's destination. In most cases, it's very limited in length, often less than 100 characters. For a single form element or two, such as a quick search box or a single check box answer, get works fine. For example:

```
<form method="get" action="/cgi-bin/search">
```

If you plan to create a long form with multiple entry boxes and menus, you'll probably opt to use the post method. It sends the data separately, without any practical limit on the amount of data that can be transferred. You use a form opening tag that looks like this:

```
<form method="post" action="/cgi-bin/survey ">
```

The second attribute is `action`, which simply accepts as its value the URL for the script that will process your form's data. Most often, the script is stored in a directory called `bin/` or `cgi-bin/` located on your Web server. (Chapter 16 discusses the particulars of CGI scripts in much more detail.)

An example of the `<form>` element, then, would be the following:

```
<form method="post" action="http://www.fakecom.net/cgi-bin/survey.pl">
</form>
```

As with any HTML container element, this example of the `<form>` element has actually created a complete form (just like the `<p>` and `</p>` tags create a complete paragraph). Of course, this one doesn't do much, but it is complete. It's also worth noting that the `<form>` element can't be nested within other `<form>` elements—you need to start and end one form container before beginning another.

Other `<form>` Attributes

Aside from the two basic attributes, the `<form>` element can accept a few others. While none of these attributes are required, you may find them useful under certain circumstances. (In fact, while you're creating your first few forms, you may want to move directly to the section "Creating the Form." These attributes are a bit dense.)

The first of these is `enctype`, which accepts a MIME type entry that specifies the type of content that will be submitted. This is really only worth worrying about if you will be asking the visitor to upload a file to your server (using a special `input` element, discussed later in this chapter.) If that's the case, you should specify `enctype="multipart/form-data"`, which makes it possible to send a file (such as an image file) via an HTML form.

The `name` and `id` attributes can be used to identify the form for either scripting or for style sheets. Remember that `id` is the XHTML-compliant attribute, although `name` is sometimes still recommended for backward-compatibility. You can have both, as in `name="myform" id="myform"`.

The `<form>` element can accept a few other odd-duck attributes. The `accept` attribute can be used to specify, in a comma-separated list, the types of files that the server can handle correctly, using MIME names such as `image/jpg` and `video/quicktime`. You can view a list of MIME types at `http://www.isi.edu/in-notes/iana/assignments/media-types/media-types`. In isolated cases where

tip

By default, most Web browsers assume that the character encoding type that the page uses is the same one that any forms would accept. So if the page is set to Spanish already, the browser will most likely assume that Spanish-language characters are acceptable.

you're asking the visitor to upload a file, the browser can check the `accept` attribute to make sure that the visitor is uploading a file type that's on the specified list. If the user is trying to upload a file of a type that isn't in the `accept` attribute, the browser can opt to deny the upload and display an error message.

The `accept-charset` attribute is similar. What it does is allow you to specify the character encodings that the server is prepared to accept when processing the form's data. For instance, if you wanted to be able to process characters that are specific to Spanish, you might need to include `accept-charset="es"` as part of your `<form>` element. Character set values can be found at `http://www.iana.org/assignments/character-sets` on the Web.

Creating the Form

Now that you've seen how to begin and end a `<form>` element, you're probably just about ready to start adding some substance to it. You can add all sorts of elements to your forms, including areas for entering text, menus for selections, check boxes, and radio buttons for options. You'll also need to add at least a few buttons, including the special buttons that enable your visitors to submit the form's data to your Web server computer.

Text Fields and Attributes

One of the more common uses for forms is to accept multiple lines of text from a user, perhaps for feedback, bug reports, or other uses. To do this, use the `<textarea>` element within your form. You can set this element to control the number of rows and columns it displays, although it will accept as many characters as the user desires to enter. It takes the following form:

```
<textarea name="name" rows="number" cols="number">
default text
</textarea>
```

The `<textarea>` element is a container element. What's contained between the tags is the *default text*, which is text that you can use to tell your users what you'd like them to type in. For instance:

```
<form method="post" action="/cgi-bin/form1.pl">
<textarea name="comments" rows="4" cols="40">
Enter your comments about our Web site.
Include your e-mail address if you'd like a response.
</textarea>
</form>
```

The default text appears in the text box just as typed. In Figure 15.2, notice that text inside the `<textarea>` element is formatted as if it were inside a `<pre>` container. Any returns or spaces you add to the text are displayed in the browser window.

FIGURE 15.2

The `<textarea>` element in action.

The `name` attribute is used to assign a unique identifier to the text area. When the data is passed on to the processing script, the name is used as a label for the data associated with that text area. You'll need to include instructions in the processing script itself for processing this data, but at least you'll have a name to go by.

The `rows` and `cols` attributes can accept different numbers to change the size of the `<textarea>` box, but you should make sure that the majority of browsers can see the entire box onscreen. Handheld browsers and some text-based browsers only display 40 or 60 characters in width.

Among some of the other attributes that `<textarea>` can accept is `readonly` (which should be added as `readonly="readonly"` for XHTML compliance). This attribute prevents the text area from being edited and makes it so the text between the two `<textarea>` tags is sent as the data associated with the text area.

The `<input>` Element

The `<textarea>` form element is a fairly basic data entry tool, allowing your users to type whatever text they feel is appropriate, within a certain number of characters. Often, however, you'll find it useful to limit the responses that your users can give. The `<input>` element lets you be a bit pickier about the type of input you're going to accept from the user. It enables you to create a number of different types of controls, including

- **Text boxes**—(type="text") Users can type shorter entries, such as name and address information.

- **Passwords**—(type="password") In these special text boxes, what is typed by the user isn't shown onscreen.

- **Check boxes**—(type="checkbox") With these controls, you let the user select or deselect a particular item.

- **Radio buttons**—(type="radio") With these controls, the user can select one, and only one, of a series of options.

- **Hidden fields**—(type="hidden") This special type of input element is simply a field that can be sent with the form using a prespecified value.

- **Control buttons**—(type="reset" or type="submit" or type="button") Finally, the <input> element enables you to create a number of different types of buttons that are used for submitting the form, resetting the form, and other tasks you designate.

The <input> element follows this format:

```
<input type="type_of_input control" NAME="name" size="number"
maxlength="number" />
```

The only required attributes are type and name. Some other types of the <input> element will also accept the attribute value, which is used to set the value or values that the individual can select. The <input> element can also accept a variety of other attributes, but they come up when you're creating different types of controls, so we'll cover them in turn.

Text Boxes

The first possible value for the type attribute is text, which creates a single-line text box of a length you choose. Notice that the length of the box and the maximum length entered by the user can be set separately. It's possible to have a box that's longer (or, more often, shorter) than the maximum number of characters you allow to be entered. Here's an example of a text box:

```
Last name: <input type="text" name="last_name" size="40" maxlength="40" />
```

When entered in a proper <form> container, this <input> element yields a box similar to the one shown in Figure 15.3. If desired, the attribute value can be used to give the text box a default value, as in the following example:

```
City: <input type="text" name="city" size="50" maxlength="50" value="New
York" />
```

FIGURE 15.3

Using the text option with the type attribute.

Password Entry Boxes

Setting type="password" is nearly identical to setting type="text", except that using the password entry box usually causes the Web browser to respond to typed letters by displaying bullet points, asterisks, or similar characters to keep the words from being read over the user's shoulder. Here's an example:

```
Enter User Name: <input type="text" name="username" size="25"
maxlength="25" />
Enter Password: <input type="password" name="password1" size="10"
maxlength="10" />
```

When characters are typed in to this text box, they are displayed on the screen as shown in Figure 15.4.

FIGURE 15.4

When you specify a password entry box, typed characters are hidden from view.

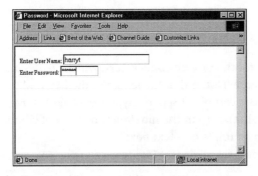

It's important to note, however, that the only *security* that is really provided is the bullets or asterisks. The password itself is passed on by the browser in *clear text*—it is not encrypted or masked in any particular way.

Check Boxes

Setting type="checkbox" in the <input> element
enables you to offer a check box "on/off" or
Boolean control for your forms. This is best
used when there are two possible values for a
given choice—and no other values. You can
also decide ahead of time whether or not a
check box will be checked already (so that it
must be unchecked by the user if desired) by
using the attribute checked="checked". Here's
an example of adding check boxes to a form:

```
Where you heard about us:<br />
<input type="checkbox" name="web"
checked="checked" />Web Search or Link
<input type="checkbox" name="advert"
/>Radio or TV Ad
<input type="checkbox" name="press"
/>Article or press mention
<br />
Check here to join our mailing list: <input type="checkbox" name="mailing"
/>
```

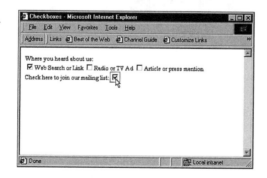

tip

For better security, you
should use a secure HTTP
(shttp) connection that
encrypts transmissions so
that they can't be inter-
cepted. Secure servers are
discussed briefly in the
online chapter, "Web Publishing
Tools." (See the Introduction to
this book for details on where to
download the bonus chapters for
this book.)

In this example, each of the values is *standalone* in the sense that more than one of
these boxes can be checked at once. In the case of the first three, all three options
could be selected. That may or may not be the desired result. The fourth check box is
also evaluated separately from the first three, so it doesn't really matter that it
appears on its own line and has a different label.

FIGURE 15.5

Each check box
is evaluated sep-
arately; note the
prechecked
option below the
other three.

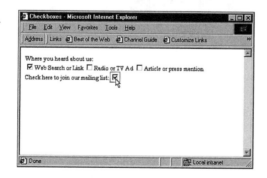

Radio Buttons

Like `checkbox`, `radio` is designed to offer your user a choice from predetermined options. The difference is that `radio` also forces the user to select only one response from among options. Whereas `checkbox` is Boolean or true/false, `radio` is multiple choice.

While `radio` is similar to `checkbox`, you'll notice one major difference—it uses the same `name` attribute value for each of the elements in the same grouping. In other words, among the multiple options from which the user will select only one value, all of them must have the same `name` value so that the browser knows that they're grouped.

The `radio` input type also requires you to use the `value` attribute, and each `value` attribute must have a unique value that can be assigned (to the variable created by `name`) if selected. For instance, look at the following example:

```
Where you heard about us:<br />
<input type="radio" name="where" value="web" checked="checked">Web Search
or Link
<input type="radio" name="where" value="advert">Radio or TV Ad
<input type="radio" name="where" value="press">Article or press mention
<input type="radio" name="where" value="other">Other
```

This example is shown in Figure 15.6. With `radio`, it's important to assign a default value because the user may simply skip the entry altogether. While the user can't check more than one, he or she might not check any of them. So, choose the value that you think makes sense as the default and set it as `checked="checked"`, just so the form-processing script doesn't have trouble.

FIGURE 15.6

Radio buttons limit the user to one choice among many.

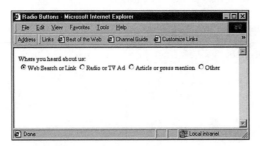

Hidden Fields

This `input` type really isn't "input" at all. Rather, it's designed to allow you, the form designer, to pass along a preset value to the Web server or the script that will be processing the form. This is generally done when you're using the same script for a number of different forms or pages and you'd like the script to know which form is accessing it. The `<input type="hidden" />` element can accept the attributes `name` and `value`, as in

```
<input type="hidden" name="identify"
value="form2" />
```

The Reset Button

Aside from entry boxes, checkboxes, and hidden fields, you can also use `<input>` to create buttons. Using the `reset` type of the `<input>` element, you can automatically add a button to your form that clears all other elements of entered data when clicked. When the user clicks this reset button, it resets all the entries and selections that the user has made to that point. For example:

```
<input type="reset" value="Reset the Form" />
```

The `value` attribute isn't required, but it's used to give the button a unique name. If you don't include it, the button will simply say Reset.

The Submit Button

The `<input>` element also has a type that creates a button to enable the user to submit the data that's been entered into the HTML form. This is how the user signals that he or she is done with data entry and ready to send it to the server. The `submit` type accepts only the attribute `value`, which can be used to rename the button. Otherwise, the only purpose of the **Submit** button is to send off all the other form information that's been entered by your user. See the following two examples:

```
<input type="submit" />
<input type="submit" value="Send it in!" />
```

You can use just about anything you want for the `value`, although it's best to remember that really small words such as "OK" don't look great as buttons. To make a button larger, you can create a `value` with spaces on either end, like in the following:

```
<input type="submit" value="    Submit    " />
```

The form already knows how and where to submit the data, thanks to the form's own `method` and `action` attributes. So, the **Submit** button itself is rather simple.

The Image Submit Button

If you'd like to use an image for your **Submit** button, you can use `type="image"` with the `<input>` element. The element also needs an URL to the image file and alternate text for non-graphical browsers, so it ends up looking like this:

```
<input type="image" src="images/buttons/submit.gif" alt="Submit Form" />
```

That's easy enough. But you should know that there are other ways to add custom buttons that are more highly recommended, so I'll focus on those.

Other Buttons

HTML 4.01 and higher offers another element for creating form buttons, the `<button>` element. It offers three `type` values: `reset`, `submit`, and `image`. What's different about the `<button>` element is that it's actually a container, and it enables you to use markup within the button itself. For example:

```
<button name="submit" type="submit">
<span style="font-family: Courier; font-variant: small-caps; font-size:
14pt">
➥Send</span></button>


<button name="reset" type="reset">
<img src="reset.gif" alt="Reset" />
</button>
```

The `<button>` element can accept `name`, `type`, and `value` attributes, although `type` is the only one required for **Reset** and **Submit** buttons. However, for the best coding, you should at least include a `name` attribute. Figure 15.7 shows these enhanced buttons.

FIGURE 15.7

These customized buttons use the `<button>` element and include markup and style information.

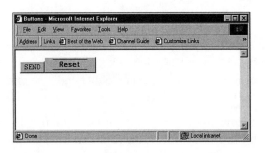

Creating Menus

Another type of input control that you can offer to users revolves around the `<select>` element, which can be used to create different types of pop-up menus and scrolling menus. This is another control designed specifically for allowing users to make a choice—they can't enter their own text. The `<select>` element requires a `name` attribute and allows you to decide how many options to display at once with the `size` attribute.

Also notice that `<select>` is a container. Options (using the `<option>` element) are placed between `<select>` and `</select>`, each with a particular value. When one of those options is chosen, its value gets assigned to the name that's specified in the opening `<select>` tag.

The attribute `selected="selected"` sets the default value in a given list. An example of all this might be

```
Select how often you visit this site:
<select name="frequency">
<option selected="selected" value="first">First Time</option>
<option value="monthly">Monthly</option>
<option value="weekly">Weekly</option>
<option value="daily">Daily</option>
</select>
```

You can also use the `size` attribute to display the menu in its entirety. Simply change the first line of the example to the following:

```
<select name="frequency" size="4">
```

Both examples are shown in Figure 15.8.

FIGURE 15.8

A pop-up select menu and a scrolling list, thanks to the size attribute.

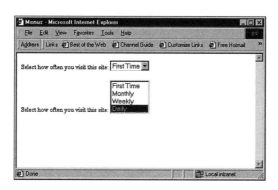

In the first example, selecting the menu item with the mouse causes the menu to pop up on the page. The user can then select from the choices. In the second example, it's necessary to click the desired item.

But what if you want to allow users to select more than one option at a time? Another attribute for the `<select>` element allows the user to select more than one option from the menu. Using the `multiple="multiple"` attribute forces the menu to be displayed as a scrolling list, regardless of the existence of a `size` attribute. (You should still use `size` to specify the number of items that appear at once in the list.) An example might be the following:

```
<p>What topics do you enjoy reading about
online (pick all that apply):</p>
<select name="topics" multiple="multiple">
<option value="upgrade">Upgrading
computers</option>
<option value="repair">Repairing
computers</option>
<option value="apps">Application How-
Tos</option>
<option value="tricks">Tips and
Tricks</option>
<option value="news">Industry news</option>
<option value="rumor">New Product
rumors</option>
<option value="none"
selected="selected">None</option>
</select>
```

note

Different browsers can auto-select options in different ways—some will submit `<select>` results that have no value, while others will select the first value in the menu as the default. So, it's best to create your own default using `selected="selected"`, particularly if you want to avoid inaccuracies when your scripts are processing form data.

In this case, the user can select multiple options, or none.

Before we get away from `<select>` controls, there's one other element that you can toss into the mix: `<optgroup>`. This element enables you to group disparate options within the same `<select>` control. Consider this example:

```
<p>Where did you hear about us (pick all that apply):</p>
<select name="refer" multiple="multiple">
<option value="npr">Public Radio</option>
<option value="netrad">Network Radio News</option>
```

```
<option value="satrad">Satellite Radio</option>
<option value="travel">Travel TV</option>
<option value="food">The Food Channel</option>
<option value="pbs">Public Broadcasting</option>
<option value="times">The Times</option>
<option value="news">The News-Hearld</option>
<option value="none" selected="selected">None</option>
</select>
```

There's nothing particularly wrong with this list, except that we might be mixing apples and oranges a bit. As it gets longer and longer, it becomes more unwieldy. The solution is to use `<optgroup>`, which accepts a `label` attribute that can be used to label groups within the list:

```
<p>Where did you hear about us (pick all that apply):</p>
<select name="refer" size="15" multiple="multiple">
<option value="none" selected="selected">None</option>
<optgroup label="Radio">
<option value="npr">Public Radio</option>
<option value="netrad">Network Radio News</option>
<option value="satrad">Satellite Radio</option>
</optgroup>
<optgroup label="TV">
<option value="travel">Travel TV</option>
<option value="food">The Food Channel</option>
<option value="pbs">Public Broadcasting</option>
</optgroup>
<optgroup label="Newspapers">
<option value="times">The Times</option>
<option value="news">The News-Hearld</option>
</optgroup>
</select>
```

If your user's Web browser is compatible, it should display the list in a slightly different layout, which should make it easier to make selections (see Figure 15.9). Note that not every browser recognizes `<optgroup>`. When it doesn't, you're not any worse off than with a full list.

FIGURE 15.9

Here's a list organized by <optgroup> elements.

Sample Feedback Form

At this point, let's take the bulk of what's been discussed and toss it all together into a sample form. We'll be putting together a feedback survey form, using the elements that have been discussed so far:

```
<form method="post" action="mailto:surveys@fakecorp.com">

First name: <input type="text" name="first_name" size="40" maxlength="40"
/><br />

E-mail address: <input type="text" name="e-mail" size="40" maxlength="40"
/><br />

Where you heard about us:<br />

<input type="radio" name="where" value="web" checked="checked">Web Search
or Link</input><br />

<input type="radio" name="where" value="advert">Radio or TV Ad</input><br
/>

<input type="radio" name="where" value="press">Article or press
mention</input><br />

<input type="radio" name="where" value="other">Other</input><br />

<p>Enter your comments about our Web site.<br />

<textarea name="comments" rows="10" cols="40">

Include comments or questions in this area.

</textarea>

</p>

Check here to join our mailing list: <input type="checkbox" name="mailing"
/><br />

<button name="submit" type="submit">

<span style="font-family: Courier; font-variant: small-caps; font-size:
14pt">Submit Survey</span>
```

```
</button>
<button name="reset" type="reset">
<span style="font-family: Courier; font-
variant: small-caps; font-size: 14pt">Clear
Page</span>
</button>
</form>
```

You can see how this looks in Figure 15.10. Overall, the form still doesn't look all that great as far as alignment and design. We'll cover those topics in the rest of this chapter.

You may also have noticed that the `<form>` element itself uses an interesting `action` attribute—it includes a mailto: style URL. This makes it possible for the form's data to be mailed to a given email address instead of being processed by a script. You may find this useful if you want to go through the forms by hand, or if you have an email-based processing solution. (See Chapter 16 for more discussion of email processing.)

tip

A lot of users like to move through HTML forms using the Tab key. If you'd like to specify which direction a press of the Tab key will take a person, you can add the `tabindex` attribute to any form element, using any number between 0 and 32767 as a value. (For the item that should be first, set `tabindex="1"`, for the second item, set `tabindex="2"`, and so on.) Once you've added those numbers, elements will be reached in the order specified by the `tabindex` attribute when the Tab key is pressed.

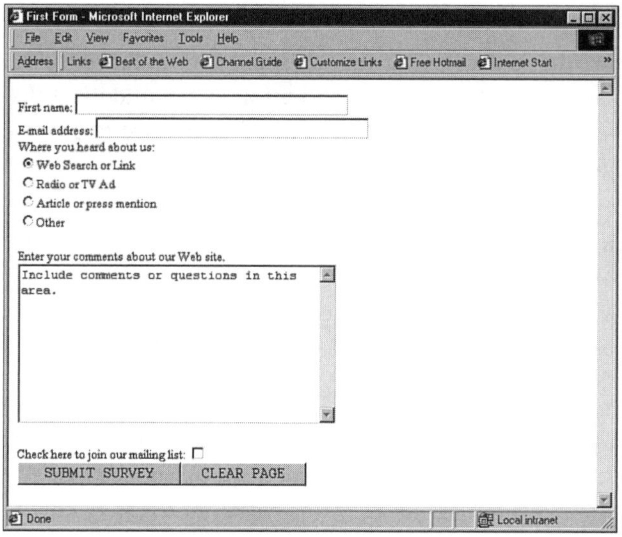

FIGURE 15.10

Here's the sample form, functional if not pretty.

Designing Forms Well

You've seen how to create forms, but we haven't covered how to make those forms attractive. It takes a little thought and quite a bit of XHTML markup to make the form elements look good, logical, and interesting to your users—interesting enough that they dive in and use the form. In this section, let's take a look at some approaches to designing useful forms.

Form Design Issues

Central to the idea of form design is making the form easy for users to understand so that they follow through and fill it out. The less incentive you give them to fill out the form, the less likely they are to try. A short, clean form is more likely to entice users than a long, confusing one.

Here are some guidelines you should consider when building your forms so that they're easier to use and more effective:

- **Use other XHTML elements to make things clear**—You can use `<br />`, `<hr />`, and paragraph tags to set apart different chunks of your form, while emphasis (`<em>`, `<strong>`) can be used to make labels and other parts of the form easier to read.

- **Keep your forms short**—This isn't always possible, but even when your forms are long, it's important to at least use `<hr />` and similar elements to break them up a bit. Splitting up forms into smaller sections makes them easier on the eye.

- **Use intuitive design**—Common sense is sometimes the key to a good form. For instance, putting the Submit button in the middle of the form will keep people from filling out the rest of it. Often it's best to use `<select>`, radio buttons, and check boxes to keep your users from guessing at the type of data you want them to enter.

- **Warn users of unsecured transactions**—You should tell your users if your Web server is secure—and how they can make sure that the connection is current. If you ask for credit card numbers or similar personal information over an unsecured connection, let them know that, too.

Finally, you can use style sheets just as effectively with forms as with other elements. In some cases, you might find them even more useful, particularly for breaking up parts of the form into chunks. And, as you'll see in this section, HTML offers some accessibility elements to help make forms easier for assistive browsers.

Line Breaks, Paragraphs, and Horizontal Lines

Unlike text-oriented XHTML, your best friend in form design is not really the paragraph element as much as it is the `<br />` element. This is because you want to directly affect the layout of the forms, instead of leaving it up to the browser. Therefore, you've got to be a little more proactive. You'll end up with a lot of line break elements before your form is through.

Consider the following example:

```
<form>
Enter your name and phone number:
First Name: <input type="text" name="first" size="30">
Last Name: <input type="text" name="last" size="40">
Phone: <input type="text" name="phone" size="12">
</form>
```

To get each of those text boxes on a separate line, and thus make them more pleasing to the eye, you need to add a few instances of `<br />`:

```
<form>
Enter your name and phone number:<br />
First Name: <input type="text" name="first"
size="30"><br />
Last Name: <input type="text" name="last"
size="40"><br />
Phone: <input type="text" name="phone"
size="12"><br />
</form>
```

> **tip**
>
> Notice the use of instructional text for these text boxes. Most of your forms will need instructions throughout, just as any paper-based form does. It's a good idea to standardize your instructions. You may also want to use bold, italic, or other emphasis to make the instructions or labels stand out from your other text.

Adding the `<br />` element forces each subsequent text box to the next line. This is a more attractive form, and the `<br />` elements make it a little easier for the user to understand, as shown on the bottom half in Figure 15.11.

Horizontal Lines

By placing `<hr />` elements in your form, you make it clear that new instructions are coming up, or that the form has reached the next logical chunk of entry. The `<hr />` element simply makes the form easier to look at as it guides the user through the different parts of the form. In the following, I've added `<hr />` at the logical breaks:

```
<form method="post" action="/cgi-bin/form1.pl">
```

FIGURE 15.11

Simply adding

 makes
the form a little
easier to look at
and use.

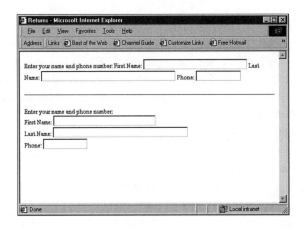

```
First name: <input type="text" name="first_name" size="40" maxlength="40"
/><br />

Last name: <input type="text" name="last_name" size="40" maxlength="40"
/><br />

E-mail address: <input type="text" name="e-mail" size="40" maxlength="40"
/><br />


<hr />

Where you heard about us:<br />

<input type="radio" name="where" value="web" checked="checked">Web Search
or Link</input><br />

<input type="radio" name="where" value="advert">Radio or TV Ad</input><br
/>

<input type="radio" name="where" value="press">Article or press
mention</input><br />

<input type="radio" name="where" value="other">Other</input><br />

<hr />

<p>Enter your comments about our Web site.<br />

<textarea name="comments" rows="5" cols="40">

Include comments or questions in this area.

</textarea>

</p>

Check here to join our mailing list: <input type="checkbox" name="mailing"
/><br />

Check here if you'd like a sales call: <input type="checkbox" name="call"
/><br />

Check here if you'd like a print catalog: <input type="checkbox"
name="catalog" /><br />

<hr />
```

```
<button name="submit" type="submit">
<span style="font-family: Courier; font-variant: small-caps; font-size:
14pt">Submit Survey</span>
</button>
<button name="reset" type="reset">
<span style="font-family: Courier; font-variant: small-caps; font-size:
14pt">Clear Page</span>
</button>
</form>
```

The `<hr />` elements make the form a little longer, as shown in Figure 15.12. But you haven't sacrificed the approachability by adding `<hr />` elements. Increasing the white space and organization in a form is nearly as important as keeping it short enough so it isn't intimidating to users.

FIGURE 15.12

Adding a few horizontal lines makes the form a bit more logical.

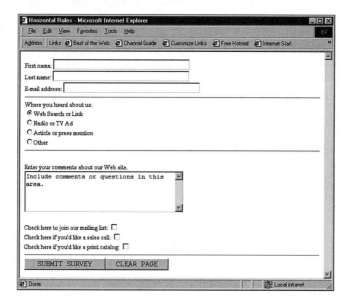

Using Paragraphs

Paragraph containers are good for keeping form data together in smaller chunks. As always, a paragraph element will add space on each side of the text that it encloses. This makes it possible to create visual chunks without the full break that a `<hr />` suggests. The extra spacing also makes the page a bit less cluttered and easier to follow. Figure 15.13 shows how the following `<p>` additions change the page for the better:

```
<form method="post" action="/cgi-bin/form1.pl">
<p>
First name: <input type="text" name="first_name" size="40" maxlength="40"
/><br />
Last name: <input type="text" name="last_name" size="40" maxlength="40"
/><br />
E-mail address: <input type="text" name="e-mail" size="40" maxlength="40"
/><br />

</p>
<p>
Where you heard about us:<br />
<input type="radio" name="where" value="web" checked="checked">Web Search
or Link</input><br />
<input type="radio" name="where" value="advert">Radio or TV Ad</input><br
/>
<input type="radio" name="where" value="press">Article or press
mention</input><br />
<input type="radio" name="where" value="other">Other</input><br />
</p>
<p>
Enter your comments about our Web site.<br />
<textarea name="comments" rows="5" cols="40">
Include comments or questions in this area.
</textarea>
</p>
<p>
Check here to join our mailing list: <input type="checkbox" name="mailing"
/><br />
Check here if you'd like a sales call: <input type="checkbox" name="call"
/><br />
Check here if you'd like a print catalog: <input type="checkbox"
name="catalog" /><br />
</p>
<hr />
<button name="submit" type="submit">
<span style="font-family: Courier; font-variant: small-caps; font-size:
14pt">Submit Survey</span>
</button>
<button name="reset" type="reset">
<span style="font-family: Courier; font-variant: small-caps; font-size:
```

```
14pt">Clear Page</span>
</button>
</form>
```

FIGURE 15.13
Use paragraph
elements to
break up the
page with more
white space.

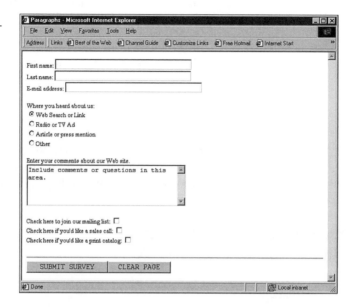

Other Elements for Form Formatting

One of the most annoying parts of setting up a form so far has been the inability to line up text box fields as they go down the page. For instance, whenever the **Name:** and **Address:** fields have been used in examples, they've always looked a little ragged.

One solution is the <pre> element. Because anything between the two <pre> tags uses the same spacing and returns, this element does two things. First, it allows you to line up your text boxes. Second, it eliminates the need for <br /> elements at the end of <input> elements, because the browser will recognize your returns. The following is a ragged-looking example:

```
<p>
First name: <input type="text" name="first_name" size="40" maxlength="40"
/><br />
Last name: <input type="text" name="last_name" size="40" maxlength="40"
/><br />
E-mail address: <input type="text" name="e-mail" size="40" maxlength="40"
/><br />

</p>
```

To improve this situation, you can put form elements inside a `<pre>` container and format them yourself:

```
<pre>
First name:      <input type="text" name="first_name" size="40"
maxlength="40" /><br />
Last name:       <input type="text" name="last_name" size="40"
maxlength="40" /><br />
E-mail address:  <input type="text" name="e-mail" size="40" maxlength="40"
/><br />


</pre>
```

Remember that you need to use the spacebar, not the Tab key, to create the space between the name of the box and the text box itself. As before, you may need to play with the formatting a little to get things lined up like they are on the bottom of Figure 15.14.

FIGURE 15.14

Use the `<pre>` container to align elements of your form, as shown in the bottom three rows.

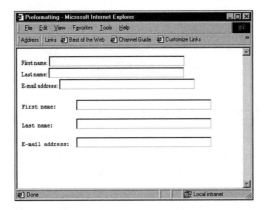

Using Lists for Forms

Another form design trick involves using the list tags to create organization for your forms. Nearly any form element can be part of a list, and there are often good reasons to use them. Consider the following example:

```
Where you heard about us:<br />
<dl>
<dd><input type="radio" name="where" value="web" checked="checked">Web
Search or Link</input></dd>
<dd><input type="radio" name="where" value="advert">Radio or TV
Ad</input></dd>
<dd><input type="radio" name="where" value="press">Article or press
```

```
mention</input></dd>
<dd><input type="radio" name="where"
value="other">Other</input></dd>
</dl>
```

You've used lists in this way before, to create indented lists or outline formats that help you communicate a little better. In this case, it also makes the form look better.

Using Tables for Forms

You may also find it useful to align and manage your form elements with table cells. They can give you some fine control over the placement of text and form controls. For example

```
<form>
<table>
<tr>
<td>First Name</td> <td><input type="text" name="first_name"></td>
</tr>
<tr>
<td>E-mail Address</td> <td><input type="text" name="e_mail"></td>
</tr>
</table>
</form>
```

This basic approach can be improved upon in any way you see fit, including removing borders (so that the organization appears to be created without table cells), cell padding, row or column spanning, and so on.

Form Structure

Later iterations of the HTML standard have added two elements, <fieldset> and <legend>, that can be used for creating structure within a longer form. As it turns out, they're also handy for assistive browsers and can be used with style sheet properties.

The <fieldset> element is used simply to create groupings of form elements and markup. In many browsers, you'll see border lines drawn around the defined field-sets. In our example form, one <fieldset> might be the personal information at the top, while another might be the questions section. The `<fieldset>` element, because it's similar to a `<div>` element, is also very useful for style sheet properties.

The `<legend>` element is used to label a particular fieldset or otherwise add a textual label to the underlying structure of the form. `<legend>` will not only appear in a browser window, but can be read aloud or otherwise rendered by assistive browsers as well. Listing 15.1 shows an example that includes these elements, along with many of the others discussed in this section. Note that this example is the XHTML used to generate the survey page shown in Figure 15.1.

Listing 15.1   A Full Survey Page

```
<!DOCTYPE html PUBLIC "-//W3C//DTD XHTML 1.0 Strict//EN"
"http://www.w3.org/TR/xhtml1/DTD/strict.dtd">
<html xmlns="http://www.w3.org/1999/xhtml">
<head>
<title>Site Survey</title>
</head>

<body>
<form method="post" action="/cgi-bin/form1.pl">

<h1>Web Site Survey</h1>

<fieldset style="background-color: #CCCCCC">
<legend><b>Contact Information</b></legend>

<table cellpadding="5">
<tr>
<td>First name:</td> <td><input type="text" name="first_name"
➥size="40" maxlength="40" /></td>
</tr>
<tr>
<td>Last name:</td> <td><input type="text" name="last_name"
➥size="40" maxlength="40" /></td>
</tr>
<tr>
<td>E-mail address:</td> <td><input type="text" name="e-mail"
➥size="40" maxlength="40" /></td>
</tr>
```

Listing 15.1 (continued)

```
</table>
</fieldset>

<fieldset style="background-color: #FFFFFF">
<legend><b>Questions and Comment</b></legend>

<p>
<b>Where you heard about us:</b></p>
<input type="radio" name="where" value="web" checked="checked">Web Search
➥or Link</input><br />
<input type="radio" name="where" value="advert">Radio or TV Ad</input><br />
<input type="radio" name="where" value="press">Article or press mention</input><br />
<input type="radio" name="where" value="other">Other</input><br />
</p>

<p><b>Enter your comments about our Web site:</b></p>
<p>
<textarea name="comments" rows="5" cols="40">
Include comments or questions in this area.
</textarea>
</p>
</fieldset>

<fieldset style="background-color: #CCCCCC">

<button name="submit" type="submit">
<span style="font-family: Arial, Helvetica; font-variant:
➥small-caps; font-size: 12pt">Submit Survey</span>
</button>
<button name="reset" type="reset">
<span style="font-family: Arial, Helvetica; font-variant:
➥small-caps; font-size: 12pt">Clear Page</span>
</button>
</fieldset>
</form>
</body>
</html>
```

Accessibility: Labels and Access Keys

Recent iterations of HTML and XHTML have added an element and an attribute to help with accessibility issues. The `<label>` element is used to create a relationship between a `form` element and the text that precedes it. It also requires the use of an `id` attribute to the form element itself. The `<label>` container surrounds the text that labels the form element. It has a `for` attribute, which references the `id` of that form element. For example:

```
<label for="first">First Name:</label><input type="text" name="first_name"
id="first">
```

This element specifically indicates the text that is a label for a particular form element. This is considered assistive because it can tell speech synthesizers how to render the labels in a particular way. It's also useful because it specifies which text is a label for which form element, even when lists or tables are being used to format the form.

You can also label a form element *implicitly* by surrounding it with the `<label>` element, as in

```
<label>
First name:
<input type="text" name="first_name">
</label>
```

This makes it possible to specify the label text without using the `for` and `id` attributes.

Along with `<label>`, the entire repertoire of form elements can be used along with the `accesskey` attribute to enable form elements to be selected with a single keypress. For instance:

```
First name: <input type="text" name="first_name" accesskey="f">
```

This example will enable some browsers to move the user directly to the **First Name** entry box when the **F** key is pressed on the keyboard, usually in combination with another key. (On Microsoft Windows computers, generally it's the **Ctrl** key; on Macs, it's often the **command** key.)

Summary

In this chapter, you learned how to add HTML forms and form elements to your pages. The chapter began with an overview of how forms work and which items need to be present in the `<form>` element itself. You learned how to add text areas, text entry boxes, radio buttons, check boxes, password fields, hidden fields, and menus to your HTML form. From there, the discussion turned to creating attractive, easy-to-understand forms through certain layout and labeling techniques. This included some methods that can be used to better organize your form and make it more accessible to assistive browsers.

In the next chapter, you'll see how Common Gateway Interface scripts work, and how to use scripts to work with HTML form data.

16

CGIs AND DATA GATHERING

In Chapter 15, "Adding HTML Forms," you got an in-depth look at creating and formatting HTML forms. In this chapter, you'll see the other side of HTML forms—gathering the data and reporting back to the user. This is accomplished using *scripts*, small programs that are stored on the Web server computer. Form data is sent to these scripts, as specified in the action attribute to the <form> element. Once the script receives the form data from the Web server, it should look through that data, compute what it needs to compute, and reply to the user. In this chapter, we look at the components that make up this back-end system, and you'll get a taste of the scripting that's required to make this all work.

What Is CGI?

Fill-in forms for your Web pages don't do anything by themselves. Your readers can fill them in, but when they click the **Submit** button, the data won't go anywhere unless you've written a special script to process the data. (As you can see in the online chapters "Introduction to JavaScript" and "JavaScript and User Input," you can also use JavaScript and client-side scripting to process some types of data. See the Introduction to this book for details on where to download these chapters.)

So how do you get data from the HTML form to the script? That's where the Common Gateway Interface (CGI) comes in. By developing CGI scripts, you can make your forms interactive.

CGI scripts bring your static Web pages to life—returning requested data, responding to user input, and making a record of how many people access your site. In this way, the script interacts with your user, responding to what they enter in forms instead of simply displaying static Web pages.

In practice, a link to a CGI script works the same way a link to an HTML page works. But under the hood, a CGI script is much more than a normal Web page. When a typical Web page's URL is requested via hyperlink, a file is read, interpreted, and displayed by the browser. When an URL to a CGI program is requested, it causes a program to be executed on the server, and that program can do just about anything you want it to: scan databases, sort names, or send email. CGI scripts allow for complex back-end processing. In the case of an HTML form, generally the CGI will receive the values in that form, process them, and then reply to the user.

CGI changes the definition of what a Web page is. While normal pages are static and unchanging, CGI programs enable a page to react to the user's input, making them dynamic.

CGI Languages

You do not write CGI scripts in HTML, CSS, or even JavaScript, which are all languages that can be used in Web documents. CGI scripts are written in other computer languages, such as Unix shell scripting, Perl, C, AppleScript, and Visual Basic, so you need knowledge of at least one of these languages. You then store the script separately, in its own file, on your Web server computer. Here's a look at some of the languages you can use for CGI scripting:

- Unix shell scripts (or the similar Windows batch files) are a good choice for small or temporary CGI programs. They are easy to write and you can see results immediately, but they aren't designed for high-volume use by multiple users, as might occur with a shopping-cart application on a busy commercial Web site. A shell script often has a filename with a .sh suffix.

- Perl is a good choice for medium-complexity programs, and most platforms support it. It's fast, easy to program, and *interpreted*, meaning that it doesn't need to be *compiled* into a fixed, formal application as with the C programming language. Also, Perl libraries exist that automatically translate any data sent to your CGI program into a usable form. Information on Perl itself is available all over the Web, including at `http://dir.yahoo.com/ Computers_and_Internet/Programming_ and_Development/Languages/Perl/` and `http://www.yahoo.com/Computers_and_ Internet/Internet/World_Wide_Web/ Programming/Perl_Scripts`.

- For very complex data manipulation, it's best to use a full-fledged compiled language, such as C. It will give you the fastest response and let you work with your information in the most flexible way. C libraries also exist for using Web data. Other C variants, such as Objective C and C++, are popular on some platforms.

> **note**
>
> *Interpreted languages* are those that don't require that a script or program be translated into *machine code* before it's executed. The script stays exactly as written until it's executed. Only when the script is put into action does the interpreter quickly change its typed commands into machine language that the server computer can recognize. This extra step makes interpreted scripts a little slower, but they're also easier to edit and tweak when necessary.

- Macintosh Web servers are popular alternatives to Windows and Unix/Linux, and easy-to-create hooks exist between the Web server applications and Mac scripting languages such as AppleScript. You might start with the AppleScript-focused `http://www.scriptweb.com/`.

A Simple CGI Script

Although CGI programs can become extremely complex, they can also be quite simple. One of the simplest is the Unix shell script shown here:

```
#!/bin/sh
echo "Content-type: text/html"
echo ""
echo "<html><head><title>CGI Generated Page</title></head>"
echo "<body>This page was generated by a <em>simple</em> CGI
script.</body></html>"
```

Even if you aren't familiar with Unix, you may be able to see what this simple script is doing. The first line of this script (`#!/bin/sh`) tells Unix which shell this program is written for. If the program were a Windows NT batch file, the line could be excluded. (For our purposes, you can ignore that first line if you aren't familiar with shell scripting at all, and move on to the next line.)

The second line (`echo "Content-type: text/html"`) uses the `echo` command to tell the Web server what type of information is to follow in *MIME (Multipurpose Internet Mail Extension)* format. (The `echo` command is a common way for batch and shell scripts to "type" text as if a person were at the keyboard.) MIME is a method of delivering complex binary data using only ASCII text characters. There are hundreds of standard MIME formats now registered, but the two most common for CGI applications are text/html (for HTML/XHTML output) and text/plain (for plain ASCII output).

The third line (`echo ""`) is simply an empty space to tell the server that what follows is the data described by the "Content-type."

Finally, the fourth and fifth lines are the actual HTML data. These are sent through the server to the browser and interpreted just the same as instructions would be if they'd been read from an HTML file.

In other words, this simple script begins by telling the Web server to expect some HTML, and then it sends the server a few lines worth of text and HTML markup. Whenever this script is executed, these lines are sent to the remote browser, where they'll be interpreted and displayed just like any other Web document.

Referencing CGIs

Although conventions differ between servers, most require CGI programs to be installed in a special CGI directory. This is a subdirectory of the main directory on the Web server's hard drive, and it's usually called cgi-bin. If you aren't allowed to install your program in that directory (or if you're not sure), talk to your system administrator or your ISP.

You may also need to ask your administrator or ISP how to install the script itself, which is usually

note

Not all ISPs require that you have a special CGI-BIN directory; one of the servers I use on a regular basis allows CGI scripts to be launched from anywhere within my assigned directory space. When that's the case, however, you'll often find that you need the script to have an accurate filename extension, such as `.pl` for Perl scripts, `.sh` for shell scripts, and `.exe` for executable programs (such as compiled C language programs). Often a script stored in the CGI-BIN directory doesn't require a filename extension.

a matter of copying it from your own computer to the appropriate directory of the main Web server. The cgi-bin directory may not be called exactly that, and it may be located in an odd place on your Web server. (For instance, on many MacOs X servers, which are Unix-like at their core, CGI scripts are stored in the /Library/WebServer/CGI-Executables/ folder even though they're referenced using a standard call to the cgi-bin directory in an URL.)

After your CGI script is in place, you can reference it from a browser like any other URL. For example, if you installed a program called script.sh in the cgi-bin directory, its URL would be as follows:

```
http://www.fakecorp.com/cgi-bin/myscript
```

These URLs can be used like any others, including as href URLs in anchor elements or as src URLs for images.

How Scripts Work

Although creating detailed CGI scripts can get complicated, the basic theory behind what's going on isn't that tough to understand. Scripts are designed to accept data and/or generate HTML documents in response. It all begins when the script is called, via an URL, often as the action of a <form> element. When the server notes this call, it locates the script in the cgi-bin directory and tells that script to execute. The script then checks the method used to send the data (if any) and then retrieves that data. The script begins to cull through that data looking for important information. When it finds what it's looking for, it computes, stores, or does whatever else it needs to with that data. Then, in most cases, it returns an HTML document to the user's browser, with the results of the computation, a thank-you page, or something similar.

Scripts can also be called directly, without a <form> acting as the intermediary. Instead, the script might be part of a hyperlink, or it might even be the URL in an <img> element. When that happens, it's often designed to either launch a very simple script or a complex one. A fairly simple script might be one that returns a "quote of the day," a random number, or a page counter. A very complex script might be responsible for an entire Web application, such as those used to take online merchandise orders or manage travel reservations.

In either case, eventually the script will need to check for data from the user and evaluate that data using some set methods. Let's take a look at how that works from the point of view of the script, as well as what the script will see when data is submitted to it.

Receiving Form Data

You may recall from Chapter 15 that there are two different methods to pass data to your CGI script. These two methods, get and post, cause data to be sent in different ways.

The method used to send the data is stored in an *environment variable* called REQUEST_METHOD on the Web server. (Environment variables are those that the Web server stores so that their values can be accessed by scripts.) The get method simply appends your form data to the URL and sends it to the server. Most servers will then store these appended data elements in another environment variable called QUERY_STRING. This *string* is generally limited to less than one kilobyte of data (approximately 1,000 characters), which explains why the get method is less popular.

Using the post method causes the length of the data string to be stored in a variable called CON-TENT_LENGTH, while the data itself is redirected to stdin ("standard in"). In effect, the data is made to appear to your script or program as if it was typed in to the server using a keyboard. Your script must then be designed to *parse* that input.

There are actually two steps to receiving the input: decoding and parsing. Data sent from your Web browser is encoded to avoid data loss—essentially, by turning spaces into plus signs (+) and non-text characters (such as an exclamation point) into a percent sign (%) and a hexadecimal code. For instance, ! is turned into %21.

> **note**
>
> The term *string* is used in programming to suggest a single series of characters, generally accessible using a *variable name*. In this case, it's the environment variable QUERY_STRING. So, a script can be written to check the QUERY_STRING variable for relevant data and then act on that data.
>
> In English, *parsing* means to explain the grammatical form or function of a word. In computerese, *parsing* means something more like breaking up unreadable computer data into something that people (or at least programs written by people) can work with.

Once you've worked through the decoding process, you're left with a text input that follows this format (where the ampersand simply separates each pairing of name and value) :

```
NAME1=VALUE1&NAME2=VALUE2&...
```

An example of this might be

```
address=1234 Elm Ave&city=Atlanta&state=GA
```

And so on. You might notice that these entries actually pair up nicely with the names you specified in your HTML form for each of the elements used to receive input. For instance, let's say you have the following form snippet:

```
<p>
Last name: <input type="text"
name="last_name" size="40" maxlength="40" />
<br />
City: <input type="text" name="city"
size="50" maxlength="50" value="New York" />
</p>
<p>
Where you heard about us:<br />
<input type="radio" name="where" value="web"
checked="checked">Web Search or Link
<input type="radio" name="where"
value="advert">Radio or TV Ad
<input type="radio" name="where"
value="press">Article or press mention
<input type="radio" name="where"
value="other">Other
</p>
```

The values parsed from the data stream might be something like this:

```
last_name=Smith&city=Denver&where=advert
```

Or something similar, according to the choice made by your user. Those are really the basics of how to use form data in scripts.

The `mailto:` Option

This section may seem like something of an aside, but it makes sense in this context. Chapter 15 mentioned the possibility of using a `mailto:` URL in your `action` attribute instead of referencing a CGI script directly. What happens then is simple—the unparsed, undecoded form data is sent directly

tip

There are programs designed specifically for decoding Web data. cgi-bin.pl is the Perl library for this on Windows and Linux servers. Mac Web servers might use Parse CGI for AppleScript CGI scripts.

note

If you're not using a parsing program or library (which, ideally, would allow you to easily reassign the values in this file to variables in your script), your script will need to accept this data stream, strip the ampersands, and reassign the values to appropriate variables. That's a tougher requirement, and it's beyond the scope of this text. To learn more about how to write CGI script that parse input, try to find a book that covers CGI specifically or that covers a scripting language frequently used with CGI, such as Perl. You can also find several tutorials online.

to the specified email address (assuming the user's Web browser is equipped to send mailto: messages). Here's an example of a mailto: URL in a `<form>` element:

`<form action="mailto:surveys@fakecorp.com" method="post">`

When your user clicks the Submit button, the results of the form are now forwarded to the specified email address instead of being sent to a CGI script. And that's great if you don't have access to your Web server's CGI directory. The only downside is figuring out what exactly you should do with the email message once you receive it. Most likely, it isn't yet ready for easy reading.

The first problem is that the email message is still encoded in the post format that forms use to send messages to scripts. Figure 6.1 shows an example of a typical received message—it's not a very pretty sight.

FIGURE 16.1

Here's what an email message looks like when it's sent from an HTML form.

```
first_name=Rich&last_name=Guy&e-
mail=richguy%40fakeisp.net&where=web&comments=L
ove+the+site%21+I%27ll+bookmark+it.&submit=Subm
it+Query
```

The second problem is an extension of the first: You're either going to have to process all these emails by hand or write a program that interacts with your email program to handle these messages. Either approach is probably fine for the small-business or home Web designer; at least you get the form data from users without requiring you to implement a CGI script. In some cases, there may be an easy solution—many modern email programs can interact with scripting languages such as Visual Basic Scripting or AppleScript. Those scripts then parse the output and do something automatically (such as make a computation based on the data and respond to the user via email).

You might also notice one last problem—once the user clicks Submit and data is sent by email, the page just sits there because there isn't a CGI script that can respond to the form page with an acknowledgment page. Instead, you'll need to

note

Interestingly, some versions of Internet Explorer will send form data in a decoded format when IE recognizes a mailto: URL. Unfortunately, you can't count on all your users to have IE when they're accessing your form, so you'll still likely have to deal with this encoded data sometimes.

include a Back button or hyperlink on the page to let users move back to a previous page. Add a clickable image, for instance, that says something like "Click after submitting," and then hyperlink that button to another page.

Another solution is a little more automatic: You can use JavaScript to respond to the user's click, launching a new page at the same time. (See "JavaScript and User Input" online for details. To learn where to find it and several other additional chapters on the Web, see the Introduction to this book.)

Your Script's Output

Creating output with a script is probably the easiest part. Because stdout ("standard out") is redirected to the HTML browser, you simply need to use print (Perl and other languages), echo (Unix shell and Windows batch scripts) lprint (C language), or similar commands that print directly to the screen, terminal, or console. You use the print command to output HTML codes, just as if you were using your text editor.

note

If you have access to the cgi-bin directory but you aren't much of a programmer, you can install a generic forms-to-email gateway, like the one available at http://www. worldwidemart.com/scripts/for mmail.shtml. This solution is a bit more elegant because it will redirect the user to a new page after the form has been submitted. Plus, you'll receive the form data fully parsed and ready to read.

Here's a short snippet of a Perl script to do just that:

```
print "Content-type: text\html\n\n";
print "<html>\n<head><title>Submission - Thank You!</title></head>\n"
print "<body>\n<h1>Success</h1>\n<p>Thank you for your submission<\p>\n"
print "<p>Click to go back to the <a href="index.html">main page</a>. <\p>
\n</body></html>"
```

Remember that all this "standard in" and "standard out" stuff is so your script seems as if it's typing something into the server computer. In this case, when sending to standard out, it's as if an HTML document is being typed and sent to the Web browser, which will then interpret the text and markup as it would any HTML document.

In a number of programming languages, \n is the *newline* character, which simply feeds a return to standard out, as if you had pressed the Return or Enter key while typing. Otherwise, this should look rather familiar; it's basic HTML.

Whatever the programming language's "print" command is, as long as it's designed to print to stdout, you should be able to create automatic Web pages in this way. In fact, you can use the same approach, along with variables you define and use within your script, to print out pages that include information about the user's computer, information from the form that was submitted, or information that has been calculated in response to items that were submitted on the form. For instance, Figure 16.2 is the output generated from a call to a sample CGI script called printenv that's included with many different operating systems. It's used to print the environment variables that a given Web server makes available to you for scripting purposes.

FIGURE 16.2

The output of the printenv script shows you how variables can be used in output, as well as how many variables there are for your scripts to use.

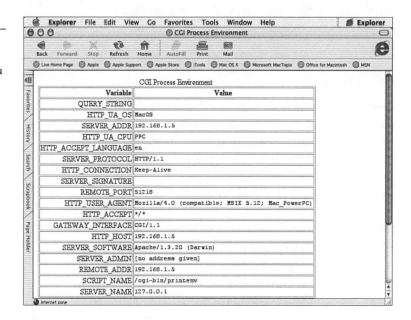

Finding and Using Scripts

While a tutorial on any particular scripting language is outside the scope of this book, we can take a quick look at some other resources you might want to consider when it comes to CGIs. In fact, if you're lucky at all, you may come across scripts that don't require much or any programming. If they're reasonably well documented, you can sometimes even edit publicly available scripts a bit to get them to work with your site.

In this section, you'll see some of the Web sites you can visit to learn more about scripting and to get scripts you can use on your own server. You'll also see a few sample scripts and resources that will give you a sense of how all this scripting stuff works and, frankly, if it's the sort of thing you're interested in pursuing for your site.

In some cases, you may find it easier to use just download and use prebuilt CGI scripts with your site. You may also want to explore JavaScript or similar options that are discussed in "Introduction to JavaScript," which is a bonus chapter available online.

Working with Other's Scripts

As with any programming endeavor, there are people who love to create scripts and people who, well, could do without it. Regardless of the category you fall into, you may find it helpful to visit some sites on the Web that focus on CGI scripting, including those that make sample scripts available for download. In some cases, scripts are available for free and can be freely altered, so that you can turn a given script into something you find more useful. In other cases, you may come across commercial solutions that enable you to purchase and use a script on your site or server.

One great place to start is the CGI Resource Index at `http://cgi.resourceindex.com`. This site includes links to thousands of different CGI scripts—both freebies and commercial scripts—that you can use to alter your site. They run the gamut from Web counter scripts to full-fledged site management applications. For instance, you can use a downloadable script for processing an HTML form. Some scripts will work with a backend database, for instance, while others can be used simply to parse the form data and send it to you in email. One such script is Form Processor from FreeScripts.com (`http://www.freescripts.com/scripts/`).

Installing the Script

Once you've downloaded a script you'd like to use, such as Form Processor, it needs to be installed in your cgi-bin directory. (Most scripts available on the Web work on Unix-based servers, but you'll find scripts designed for Windows- or Mac-based servers as well.)

note

Not all Web servers require you to place CGI scripts in a cgi-bin directory. Some will execute the CGI script wherever you store it on the Web server. You may still need to set permissions for the script, however. For Unix-based servers, you'll probably set the permissions to *read*, *write*, and *execute* for the owner, and *read* and *execute* for others (group and world). (This means, in the interest of security, you're giving yourself permission to alter the script, but nobody else can.) Again, consult your administrator or ISP for specific instructions regarding your particular Web server, as permissions are sometimes set differently on different servers.

When installing the script in your cgi-bin directory, you may need to set permissions so that the script can be properly accessed and executed by the Web server. For Unix-based servers, this is generally done using the `chmod 755 scriptname.pl` command at a command-line prompt or in a terminal window. (If that last sentence doesn't make much sense to you, consult your system administrator or ISP.) You may also find that your FTP application will allow you to change permissions for scripts.

Once installed, the script will likely require some special configuration. In many cases, you'll edit a text-based configuration file that's stored somewhere on your server computer. This file will be used to set options, choose default directories, and determine other behaviors. In the case of Form Processor, the script mentioned earlier, a few simple configuration options are built into the script, including options that determine whether an email with the form data is sent or whether a text file is saved. Other options enable you to append data to a contact file or to send a confirmation email to users when they submit the form.

Along with this configuration, Form Processor also uses a series of hidden fields to choose preferences such as to whom the processed form data should be emailed:

```
<input type="hidden" name="admin" value="admin@fakecorp.com">
<input type="hidden" name="subject" value="Web Order">
<input type="hidden" name="redirect"
value="http://www.fakecorp.com/orders/confirm.html">
```

Along with these hidden fields, the script uses a system of codes for the `name` attributes within the forms. Those codes make it possible to set the order of the fields that are reported to the user. And, using particular name entries (such as user_email) enables the script to recognize the email address for use with the auto-generated reply.

If there's one issue you'll occasionally encounter when using other's scripts, it's some level of incompatibility. If you're installing Perl scripts, you may need to know the version of Perl (such as Perl 5) that's installed on your server computer, and occasionally you may need to ask your administrator or ISP to turn on a particular preference or enable some secondary level of support, such as a particular library or directory path. For the most part, though, you'll find that installing somebody else's scripts is fairly painless, and you'll soon get used to the configuration files and preferences, particularly if you read any included documentation carefully.

Using a Hosted Script

Another approach to using outside scripts is something called a *hosted script*, which simply means the script remains on the host's server computer. Because a form `method` statement or the `src` attribute for any sort of link can point to a remote URL, you can actually have your forms processed (or other CGI scripts invoked) on another server. This is particularly useful if you don't have access to the cgi-bin directory on your server and/or you are limited in the number or types of CGI scripts that you can run from your server. (Such limits aren't completely uncommon, particularly on free or inexpensive servers.) In that case, the best solution might be a hosted script of some sort.

The CGI Resource site includes a page that links to various hosted options at `http://cgi.resourceindex.com/Remotely_Hosted/`. Again, the types of CGIs vary greatly, from counters to bulletin boards to online chats. As you might expect, a number of them exist for processing forms. For basic form processing, a service such as Form Buddy at `http://www.formbuddy.com/` might do the trick. You create a form and use Form Buddy's CGI script URL as the method of your form. Then, when the user submits the form, the data can be emailed to you, or it can be stored on the server and you can access it later. Also, the CGI can send an acknowledgment email message to the user who submits the form (assuming that user also submits a valid email address). Of course, the site is ad-supported, but that may be a small price to pay if you can't otherwise install CGI scripts on your server.

Hosted CGIs can get more complex, too. For instance, Formsite.com can be used to create a variety of different forms using templates as a guide. Depending on the level of service (in some cases, you'll have to pay), you can either create a form and link to Formsite.com for the CGI processing, or host the entire form (or forms) on its site. Formsite.com's templates range from guest books and password protection to order-taking e-commerce pages.

> **tip**
>
> You'll find other third-party scripts discussed in Chapter 17, "Forums, Chats, and Other Add-Ons," which covers a number of different community-building scripts and applications for creating bulletin boards, chat rooms, and so on.

Creating Your Own Scripts

If you plan to create your own scripts, you'll need to start by learning a compatible language (if you don't already know one). Far and away the most popular language is Perl, although many Mac users opt for AppleScript, and simple CGIs are often written as Unix shell scripts. To learn more about Perl, check out *Perl 5 by Example*, ISBN: 0-7897-0866-3, also published by Que.

When you're creating Perl scripts, you'll often do so in standard text editors, such as Emacs or Pico. If you aren't developing in Unix, programming text editors for

Windows or Macintosh will work just as well. Perl is an *interpreted* language. This means that scripts don't need to be compiled ahead of time, so you won't need development environments or compilers such as those required for C or similar programming. You will need to test your scripts, however. The easiest way to do that is probably to run a local, Perl-capable Web server on your computer (or over your local network). Enable CGIs on that Web server, install them in the appropriate directories, and begin your testing.

Although Perl is designed for a command-line Unix environment (which is broad enough to include any Linux-variant FreeBSD versions and their progeny, such as MacOs X), it's available for other platforms as well. The Classic MacOs (MacOs 9.x and earlier) has MacPerl (`http://www.macperl.com/`), which can be used for slightly modified Perl scripting and Mac-based CGIs. For Windows, Indigo Perl (`http://www.indigostar.com/indigoperl.htm`) is a freeware solution that includes a built-in Apache server that enables you to test your Perl scripts. Another popular option for Windows is ActivePerl (`http://www.ActiveState.com/Products/ActivePerl/`).

If you're testing your scripts on your home or office computer instead of on a remote server, you should consider shutting down your Internet connection while your Web server software is active. Even if you're only playing around with a Web server and scripts, others could access that server over the Internet and gain access to your personal data. It's not a huge risk, but to be safe, a computer that's used for testing Web servers and scripts should be isolated from the Internet to avoid remote tampering.

For more on Perl programming, you may want to visit Perl.com. There you'll find articles, discussions, How-To's, and tools. Other resources include the Perl Mongers (`http://www.perl.org/`) and the Perl Monks (`http://www.perlmonks.org/`), two different groups of Perl programmers and aficionados banding together to share information, code snippets, and other resources. For even more, check out Yahoo!'s Perl pages at `http://dir.yahoo.com/Computers_and_Internet/Programming_and_Development/Languages/Perl/`.

For other CGI programming, generally you need to choose a language that your Web servers (both your testing server and your target, final Web server) are comfortable dealing with. If that's Unix, you can use many of the aforementioned languages—Perl, C, or shell scripts. For Windows, you might opt for Visual Basic or a language supported by the particular server application—that may also be Perl or C. For Macintosh, use AppleScript, MacPerl, or a similar scripting environment, such as Frontier technologies (`http://www.userland.com/`), which is also available for Windows.

Summary

This chapter continued the discussion from Chapter 15, focusing on the Common Gateway Interface scripts and programs that are required to process HTML form data. You learned what CGI scripts are and how they work. You learned how form data is submitted to the script, parsed into useful data, and stored in variables. You also saw how such form data can be sent, if desired, via email.

The second part of the chapter focused on getting and installing CGI scripts, including a discussion of some online resources and some representative scripts for form processing. There was also a brief discussion of what's in store for you if you opt to learn a scripting language and attempt to write your own scripts.

In the next chapter, you'll be introduced to how to create and host forums on your site, add live-chat capability, counters, and other third-party solutions to your site, and make sense of the statistics generated at your site.

17

Forums, Chats, and Other Add-Ons

In Chapters 15 and 16, you saw two different approaches you can take to interacting with your users—HTML forms and CGI scripts. But what if you're not interested in programming, scripting, or any sort of hassle like that? Then you're my kind of Web developer!

Fortunately, many different options enable you to add interactive elements to your Web site without requiring much—or any—programming knowledge. In some cases, you can download and install software on your Web server that's been written by someone else. In other cases, you may not have to download anything at all—instead, you might link to a *hosted* service, where the application resides on someone else's Web server.

What sort of applications are we talking about? You'll find tons of downloadable and hosted Web solutions, including *forums* (sometimes called *bulletin boards*) for message-based discussions and *chat* applications for real-time discussions. You'll also come across solutions for counting your page visitors, tracking Web statistics, and much more.

Creating and Hosting Forums

Before the Internet became popular, many of the people who wanted to meet in "cyberspace" did so via online services such as America Online or dial-up bulletin board systems (BBS), most of which were locally run using a computer, a modem, and a phone line or two. The bulletin board software would answer the phone, log in the user, show some news about the BBS, and allow the user to post messages in various forum areas to participate in ongoing discussions.

While the phone-based BBS isn't quite the cutting-edge tool that it once was, much of its functionality has been moved to the Internet in the form of Web-based forums and bulletin board applications. Forums exist on all sorts of topics—computer support, politics, music, and so on.

If you want to interact with your visitors, answer questions, or try to strike up lively discussions—in other words, build up a community of repeat visitors—you'll probably want to consider a bulletin board system of some sort. Corporate or organizational sites can benefit from forums as well, if only because users will often answer each other's questions (or can find the previous answers you've supplied).

Forum Types and Technologies

As with many Web applications, there are two major types of forums—server-based and hosted. A *server-based* forum application will need to be installed on your Web server, generally as a series of CGI scripts, and will need to be maintained on that server. That may include backups, database maintenance, and occasionally reinstallation.

Server-based forums come in a vast range of technologies and capabilities, ranging from ASP (Active Server Pages) applications to CGI scripts written in Perl and C. Some will require your Web server to offer certain database capabilities, such as an ODBC (Open DataBase Connectivity) database. Others may require PHP (a server-side scripting language) or any variety of other scripting solutions that are available for different Web-hosting server platforms.

Hosted solutions are actually stored on someone else's server—usually a company devoted to that purpose. You sign up for a forum that you'd like to host, in some cases paying for the privilege. You're then given a username, password, and URL. You access the forum, set up the topics, and publicize it. You'll likely link to it from your own site, and you may be able to make it look somewhat as if it's actually part of your site. But the URL is different (because it's not on your server), and you may not have access to the actual files in which messages are stored.

Hosted forums are easy to use, but the downside is a certain lack of control. Your forums will likely have to comply with the host's terms of service, and may be subject to editing or censorship. Also, you may not be able to back up and/or transfer the messages easily if you change your mind and opt for a different solution. While many people are turning to a variety of hosted applications on the Web these days, generally the convenience comes at the expense of turning over a little power to the hosting company.

Choosing a Server-Side Forum

There's a great deal of forum software for the various Web server platforms you'll encounter on the Internet, so the first consideration in forum shopping is what sort of server you're using for your Web site. You'll need to ask the system administrator or your Web-hosting company these questions:

- Is the server based on Unix, Windows, or Macintosh?
- What access do I have to the server—can I install in the `cgi-bin` directory, or should I install somewhere else?
- What scripting technologies, CGI languages, and/or database technologies are available?
- What are the version numbers of the particular languages or scripting environments that are available?

You'll find that most ISPs (if that's who you're dealing with) are familiar with these questions and can tell you their do's and don'ts regarding Web applications. Likewise, if you're planning to implement server-side applications for your company Web site, your IT department or system administrator should be able to answer these questions.

Once you're familiar with the options and limitations of your Web server, you can start researching compatible forum software. A great place to start is the Conferencing on the Web guide (`http://thinkofit.com/webconf/`), where you'll find links to most of the Web forum packages available.

The main decision you'll likely need to make is whether or not you want to pay for the forum software. There's a fair amount of freeware available for your forums, but few of those options give you the flexibility and professional look-and-feel of the more expensive commercial software. Commercial software can vary in price, from tens to hundreds of dollars, but in many cases the price can be worth it.

Aside from the look of the software, the differences tend to be in the following areas:

- **Customization features**—Can you make the forums look like they're a part of your Web site? Can you change colors, fonts, and so on?

- **Management features**—How do you manage users and messages? Does the software offer sophisticated support for registered and non-registered users, or is everyone lumped into a single category? Can you send email messages to all of your registered users? Can you block certain users or add users as moderators or forum managers?

- **User interface features**—Can visitors use HTML markup, images, emoticons, and other widgets to make their discussions a little more personal and fun?

Here are a few of the more famous and notable server-side Web forum software packages:

- **WWWBoard** (http://worldwidemart.com/scripts/wwwboard.shtml)—This one isn't the prettiest bulletin board system available, and it can get unwieldy if it sees a lot of action. But it's freeware and it's been around a long time, so it's popular. It's written in Perl, requiring Perl 4 or higher, and has ports to Windows and Macintosh.

- **WebBBS** (http://www.extropia.com/applications/web_bbs.html)—This is another popular, simple discussion system, similar to WWWBoard, with very little in the way of user interface options and user-management features. It requires Perl 5.

- **IkonBoard** (http://www.ikonboard.com)—Another freeware solution, this one is popular because it looks a bit like Ultimate BB (discussed below), which defines the look-and-feel standard for bulletin boards. Surprisingly, it's free, but you may need to do some tweaking and regular maintenance to get it running and stay on top of the updates. The software requires Perl 5.004.

- **YABB** (http://yabb.xnull.com/)—The name stands for Yet Another Bulletin Board, but this one is a great option considering it's freeware (probably thanks to the fact that it's an open source project). With the look-and-feel of a good Ultimate BB clone, YABB also offers a lot of the customization and management features of higher-end software. This requires Perl 5 and works with Unix and Windows NT.

■ **Discus** (http://www.discusware.com/)—Discusware offers two versions of its software, a freeware offering and a commercial one. Both are good competitors in their respective markets—the freeware version is very popular, and the commercial version is reasonably inexpensive ($149). In fact, many users like the no-nonsense tree-based interface, which isn't as graphical as Ultimate and its clones but is still very well thought-out. It requires Perl 5.005 running on a Windows or Unix server.

■ **Ultimate Bulletin Board** (http://www.infopop.com/)—This one has been the standard-bearer for a long time, particularly when it used to have a freeware version. Now you can download a trial version that has a limited number of uses, and the license for the full version is $199. Ultimate BB looks great, and it offers customization, email options, HTML, searching, personal profiles, and much more. It uses Perl; a PHP version called UBBThreads is also available.

■ **vBulletin** (http://www.vbulletin.com/)—Another Ultimate BB clone, vBulletin gets higher marks from some users than the original. It's a little less expensive ($85 a year or $160 to own it) and uses PHP and MySQL for a faster interface than most Perl solutions. PHP 3.0.9 and MySQL 3.22 are the minimum requirements. The company offers vBulletin Lite, which can be used for testing or for smaller sites (it's feature-limited, but it works). Figure 17.1 shows vBulletin's support forum, which itself uses the vBulletin software.

FIGURE 17.1

The vBulletin software offers a reasonably inexpensive commercial solution that's graphically appealing.

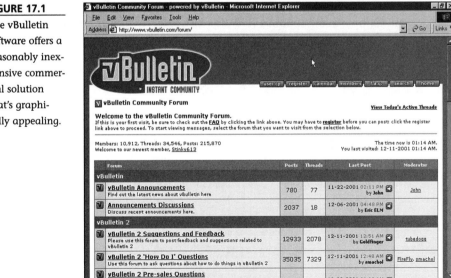

Installing a Server-Side Forum

So what does it take to install a server-side forum? Each one is a little different, and some of them can require some tedious configuration—particularly the free ones. Generally, the process goes something like this:

1. Download the software package and decompress its archive to reveal all the files.

2. Copy (or upload) files to various directories on your Web server, mostly the `cgi-bin` directory. You may also need to copy or upload images and other ancillary files, such as help files, to other directories on your server, according to the software's instructions.

> Changing Web server permissions settings can be a bit unsettling because making a mistake can sometimes create a security hole. You should read the instructions for the forum software carefully, and consult with your ISP or system administrator if you're not familiar with setting file and folder permissions.

3. Set permissions for the forum scripts, so that the scripts can be executed by the Web server software when requested by a browser. (Generally this will be done either using your FTP software or at the Unix command line, if your Web server supports a command-line login.)

4. Set any options and preferences, including an administrative account, the original forum topics or questions, the look-and-feel, and so on. Sometimes these configuration options are done via an HTML document, and sometimes they're done by hand-editing a configuration text file (see Figure 17.2).

FIGURE 17.2

Here's a sample configuration file for YABB.

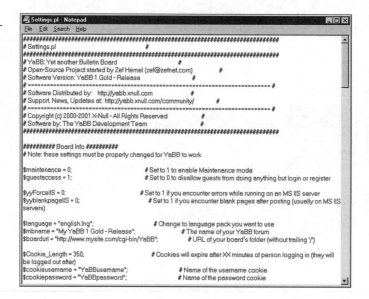

Once the system is set up, generally you access it using a straightforward CGI URL, such as `http://www.fakecorp.com/cgi-bin/forum.pl`. Then the forum application takes over and the users can begin reading and posting. The application will also likely have administrative features, which you should be able to access using the administrative account you've created.

Hosted Forum Solutions

If you're not keen on digging into configuration files, uploading files to your server, or changing permissions and doing other admin-level things, a hosted solution might be better for you. With a hosted bulletin board, you create an account, log in, and create the bulletin board. Then, your users will be able to access the bulletin board via a special URL that points to the host's server. The software doesn't run from your server, so you have a little less control over it. A good hosted bulletin board will be run by professionals who know what they're doing, though, so hopefully it will be fairly bulletproof and convenient.

Remember that using a CGI application, particularly a sophisticated one that involves this much user interaction, could pose a security risk to your server. You should read the documentation for your Web forum software closely for security issues, including creating a unique administrator account and password. Likewise, because you're managing the software yourself, make sure you keep up with the updates and new versions, particularly if they fix security issues.

Ultimately, the decision may come down to how much control you want over the forum software. If your pursuit is commercial, back-ups are critical, and you can't stand the idea of another company controlling some of your content, you should probably skip a hosted solution. If you still don't want the hassle of running a board but you want more guarantees, you can go with a higher-end commercial hosting company, which may be willing to write a specific contract giving you as much control as you want.

If you're an individual, hobbyist, or non-profit, you may find that a hosting solution is the best way to quickly get your discussion groups up and running. For informal discussions, Q&As, and other less-than-critical solutions, a hosted forum might be the way to go. Figure 17.3 shows one of my hosted forums in action.

FIGURE 17.3

Here's my forum on Mac upgrades hosted by EZBoard. Although it's not on my server, it still matches the design of my Web site.

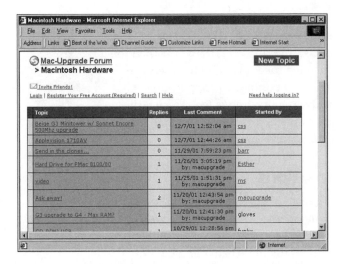

Hosted solutions range from ad-supported free-bies to expensive commercial applications. Here's a look at some of the available hosted discussion group applications:

- **EZBoard** (http://www.ezboard.com/)—Discussion boards can be created for free, if you don't mind banner and pop-up ads. For a minimal fee, a discussion community can remove the ads. EZBoard even includes a donation mechanism you can use to get the money from your users. The look-and-feel is similar to Ultimate BB, and the customization options are pretty good, including backups for paid boards.

> **tip**
>
> Read any user agreements and privacy agreements carefully when you're creating or using a hosted message board. They're ripe for email address gathering, generally for the purposes of spam or unsolicited advertising.

- **BoardHost** (http://www.boardhost.com/)—The bulletin board software is very basic, but some folks like it this way—threaded discussions without all the subject and topic pages. Setting up a basic board is free, with premium service options that get rid of the ads.

- **TimTyler Solutions** (http://www.timtyler.com/siteForums/)—This is a basic forum application that's a bit pricey compared to some other services. With a sign-up fee and monthly fee, the major advantage appears to be personal customer service.

- **MSN Communities** (http://communities.msn.com/)—Would Microsoft allow itself to be left out? Here you can create an ad-driven community for free. It includes more than bulletin boards, offering support for users to post photos, calendars, and chat. It's full-featured, but you can't make the forums look like an extension of your own Web site.

- **World Crossings** (http://worldcrossing.com/)—This is the hosted version of Web Crossings software, from the same company. The forums aren't graphical UBB clones, but they're functional, with "conversation" and "threaded" options for different types of boards. It's free because it's banner-ad supported, but it's a great choice if you'd like the simple, less-busy approach to useful forums.

- **InfoPop** (http://www.infopop.com/)—The company that makes UltimateBB will host UBB-based forums for you, for a price. Intended for corporate clients (it would appear), the cheapest price for this service is $299 a month.

Add Live Chat to Your Site

For years, one of the strengths of the big-name online services such as America Online was their ability to host live chats—text-based discussion groups where all participants are active at the same time. You type a comment, others respond, and so on.

For the most part, this sort of interaction is beyond the capabilities of an HTTP server or even many CGI applications, because Web technologies rely on the static approach—click a link, load a page—that HTTP offers. While that works for forums and bulletin boards, live chat requires a different technology. In the case of Web-based chat, this is usually a Java applet, although other options also abound.

You'll find that most consumer-oriented chat options are hosted by their respective companies and tend to be ad-driven. If you're looking for institutional or corporate use, some full-featured alternatives are available for a price.

Remember, too, that chatting doesn't even have to be all that specific to your Web site. Several of the Internet chat options that are popular for one-to-one communication also enable you to create your own chat groups and link to them from your Web documents:

- MSN Messenger—http://messenger.msn.com/
- Yahoo! Messenger—http://messenger.yahoo.com/
- AOL Instant Messenger—http://www.aim.com/

You have two ways to add a Java-based chat room to your Web site. The first way is to simply create a hyperlink to a hosted chat room that's configured and served on another server. The other way is to download chat server software and run it from your Web server. Unless you have physical access to your Web server, a hosted chat room is probably your best option. Even access to the CGI directory may not help you with something as sophisticated as a Java chat server.

If you want to place a Java server on your site, however, you do have a few options:

- **DigiChat** (http://www.digichat.com/)—With this server installed on your Web server computer, you can offer Java-based chat rooms to any compatible client. Features include moderated chats, content filtering, and a high level of customization. Licenses for the server start at $595 and go up depending on the number of users. You can also have the chats hosted for $25 per month and up.

- **ChatBlazer** (http://www.chatblazer.com/)—Prices start at $395 for the Gold server and go up for the Enterprise edition, which is priced depending on the number of Web sites it supports and can go as high as $9,995. Works on any server that supports Java, and supports embedding on your Web pages for a more integrated design.

- **iChat** (http://www.ichat.com/)—Focusing on the corporate customer, iChat offers service licenses starting at $495. The software includes "auditorium" modes for a moderated chat that many people can listen to, but only the people "onstage" and selected others can participate in.

- **VolanoChat** (http://www.volano.com/)—Another pricey option starting at $495, VolanoChat offers you many of the same features that the others do— moderated chats, banner ads, membership, and chat room transcripts. The company offers a free, fully operational demo limited to five users.

Beyond the big guys, you'll find a number of services that enable you to create your own hosted chat rooms for free, or nearly free. These chat services give you less control over the configuration and user management, and many are ad-based or are basic offerings that attempt to entice you into subscribing to a pay service. But they might work well for a small or growing site. Here are a few examples:

- **ChatPod** (http://www.chatpod.com/)—This ad-based service offers free Java chat rooms that you can link to from your site. ChatPod is a service of the same company that makes DigiChat software, so you can upgrade to one of their hosted solutions if desired.

- **Multicity** (http://www.multicity.com/)—Offers tiered pricing for chat rooms— a basic room supporting 25 people is free, the 50-user level is $30 a month, and a 100-people room with other pro-level features is $50 a month. It offers both Java and HTML clients so that non-Java browsers can still participate. Multicity also offers message boards, instant messaging, Web polls, and even hosted auction sites.

- **Talkcity** (`http://www.talkcity.com/`)—This very popular destination offers free chat rooms that you can create and use on the service, or ownership of a chat room for $3 a month. The service requires users to sign in and offers safer (content-regulated) chatting options. They'll also list your premium site to millions of users or make it completely private.

- **GroupBoard** (`http://www.groupboard.com/`)—Not only can you chat on this site, but you can use a whiteboard to draw pictures for the entire group to see. That might be useful for meetings or teaching, but mainly it's just fun.

- **Bravenet** (`http://www.bravenet.com/`)—Offers basic, hosted, ad-driven Java chat rooms, along with many other such services for improving Web sites.

Counters and Web Statistics

Most Web authors like to know how well their sites are doing—how many people visit, which pages they look at, and what about the site seems to be succeeding. That's the whole point of Web statistics, which is what we'll talk about in this section.

Most Web server applications keep fairly detailed statistics about the activities on the site, including which pages have been visited, how often, by which IP addresses, and sometimes which page the user came from most recently (the "referrer" page). If you're interested in those things, you'll need to dig into your Web server's statistics log files.

Not all Web authors have access to these log files. If you don't, or if you simply want a more visual approach to page tracking, you can add a *counter* to your pages. Most counters act a little like a car's odometer, counting up one tick every time that particular page is visited. Some are more sophisticated, only counting unique visitors, giving you more detailed statistics, and so on.

Accessing Your Web Statistics

If you run your own Web server, you probably have some idea where your Web statistics are stored—most likely you have a log file that's auto-generated by the Web server software and stored somewhere on the server computer. (Unix-compatible computers generally place a log file in the /var/log/httpd/ directory, for instance.) If you have an ISP-based Web site, the ISP probably still makes a log file available to you somewhere in your Web space, with which you can download and work.

This log file is filled with an entry for every access request, whether it's for a Web page, an image, or some other resource on your Web site. Generally speaking, just looking at such a log page will tell you next to nothing about your Web site. Instead, you'll need a program of some kind that can take that log file (or, more appropriately, a copy of that log file), analyze it, and report its findings to you.

Perhaps the most popular application for doing that is Analog (http://www.statslab.cam.ac.uk/~sret1/analog/), which is available for nearly any computer operating system. It's not much of an application in its own right—that is, you don't do much clicking or choosing while it's running. Instead, you launch the application and point it to the log file. (Often this simply means having the log file in the same directory as the application.) It analyzes the log and generates an HTML document that gives you an idea of how well your Web site is performing (see Figure 17.4).

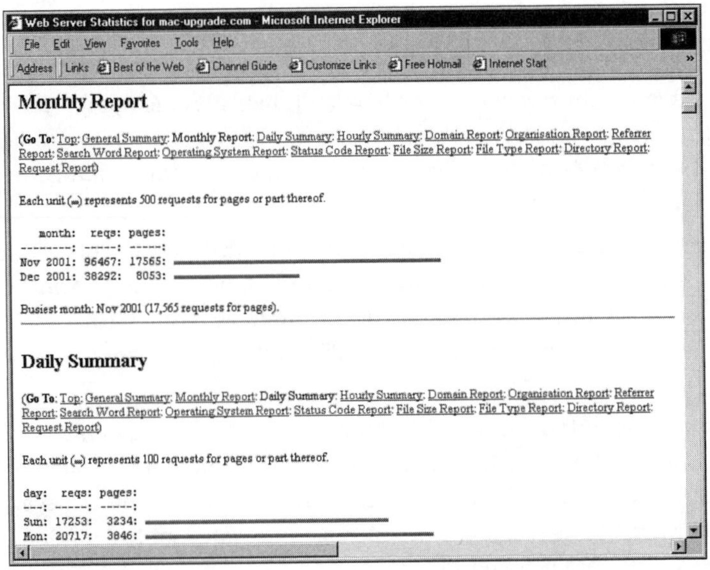

FIGURE 17.4

Analog's output is a fairly uniform HTML document that shows you what's going on with your site.

Analog (and other analysis programs) will tell you the total requests and the total *page views*. For most applications, the number of page views that your site receives is the most interesting because requests can include images, multimedia, and other items that don't really account for additional visitors. You'll also find that Analog offers interesting averages, such as the average number of page views per day, and other tidbits, such as which days of the week seem to have the most traffic.

tip

Some ISPs offer automatic analog output posted somewhere in your own Web space. Others offer proprietary Web-based interfaces for checking statistics.

Adding a Web Counter

Even if you do have access to your Web statistics, many Web authors like to post Web counters to provide a quick indication of how many people have loaded a particular page. While a counter will only give you the basics about how many people visit your site, it can be handy and entertaining.

The easiest way to add a counter is as a *server-side include (SSI)*, which is discussed later in this chapter. But if your Web server or ISP doesn't support SSI, or if you'd like more flexibility for your counter—such as graphics—you might opt for either a CGI-based counter or a Java-based counter.

A CGI counter is best if you don't want to rely on the Web browser, as you do with a Java counter. Instead, a CGI counter relies on your own server, so you know the count is always working. CGI counters can be very basic, offering only text-based results, or they can be fairly ornate, with numbers, banner advertisements, and all sorts of add-ons.

If you have access to your cgi-bin folder, you can install a CGI-based counter yourself, or your ISP may offer such a counter. CGI counters can be found online at a number of places, including Matt's Script Archive (`http://www.worldwidemart.com/scripts/`), CGIAdmin.com (`http://www.cgiadmin.com/freescripts/`), FreeCode (`http://www.freecode.com/index/`), CGIExtremes (`http://www.cgiextremes.com/`), and anywhere else fine CGIs are downloadable.

If you don't want to install a CGI, a fair number of Web counters are external, hosted services—and a number of them are free. Here's a look at a few different options:

- **Digits.com** (http://www.digits.com/)—This popular graphical counter is free as long as you include the Digits.com graphic and a link to the site.

- **Web-Stat** (http://www.web-stat.com/)—More than a counter, Web-Stat can do quite a bit of the traffic analysis that can be done with Analog and similar applications, although it doesn't require access to the log file. Instead, you place code on your page and the Web-Stat server tracks users. Web-Stat costs $5 a month.

- **CyberCount** (http://www.cybercount.com/)—Similar to Web-Stat, CyberCount offers a graphical counter and Web statistics tracking. It's free if you also run their banner ad on your pages, or $5 a month ad-free.

- **FastCounter** (http://www.bcentral.com/products/fc/default.asp)—Another popular option from Microsoft's bCentral, it's free to registered bCentral members. (bCentral is a "small business solutions" site that focuses on generating Web traffic for its members via Web rings, search engine submission, and similar options.)

These counters are simple to add—you'll be given a selection of HTML code to paste into your Web document. When you put the Web document on your server and access it via a Web browser, the counter is activated, the remote server is queried, and the statistics are tracked.

Server-Side Includes

Server-side includes, or SSIs, were among the earliest add-ons to Web servers. SSIs are used to include certain text files or server variables in your Web documents. For instance, if you store a text document (even a snippet of XHTML code) that includes the header you use for multiple pages on your Web site, you can use an SSI command to include that code on the relevant pages. Then, the server pieces the document together and sends it to the requesting browser as if it were all one file stored on the server.

Along with text files, SSIs can be used to include certain environment variables. SSIs depend entirely on your Web server software—there's no official standard, and SSIs can be implemented in any way that the server desires. Generally, these commands are fairly simple, but they can be effective. For instance, SSIs can be used to include the current date, the current URL, information about the user's browser, and other environment variables. In addition, many servers implement Web counters using SSI, and you can often execute a small CGI script and put the results on your page.

You'll find that SSI support isn't offered by every ISP, and they may be turned off by your system administrator for security or server-load reasons. If you do have access to SSIs, you'll likely need to discuss their implementation with your system administrator. The exact commands and syntax at your disposal may vary depending upon the actual Web server software in use.

As a general template, you'll need to take a few steps to use SSIs on your site:

tip

The environment variables were discussed in Chapter 16, "CGIs and Data Gathering." You should be able to access those same variables from your SSI commands.

1. Confirm with your ISP or system administrator that your Web server is capable of using SSIs and that they're turned on.

2. Save your pages with a `.shtml` or `.shtm` filename extension. That's how the server knows to expect SSIs on the page.

3. Add the SSI commands to your page. Generally, they're added using the HTML comment tag with the SSI command inside the brackets:

```
<!-- #include file="banner.txt" -->
```

Aside from the `#include` command, SSI implementations usually have an `#echo` command, which causes the Web server to add something to your page:

```
<!-- #echo var="DATE_LOCAL" -->
```

Using that command, you could add the current date to your page. Remember that SSIs work by replacing the text within your Web document *before* it's sent to the Web browser. So, you can even place the commands inside XHTML containers, if desired:

```
<p>Document was last modified: <b><!-- #echo var="LAST_MODIFIED" --
></b></p>
```

When this page reaches the Web browser, it will no longer have the `<!-- -->` command in it because the entire bracket is replaced with the value of the `echo` command. That's how SSIs work. Once the server has parsed the page, the comment brackets are completely replaced with the SSI's value. Even if the user used the `View Source` command in a Web browser, the SSI command wouldn't appear there.

Here's how a counter, banner, or rotating "Saying of the Day" often works—using the `exec` command. This actually launches a script, with the result of that script being included at the place where the script call is on the page. So, if you have a script that calls a counter, and the script `counter.pl` is in the same directory as the page you're authoring, you could include its results like this:

```
<p>This page has had <!-- #exec cmd="./counter.pl" --> visitors since
March 1.</p>
```

You may have seen a line similar to this on many Web pages. What the SSI is doing is executing the script, plugging the result into the page, and thus replacing the SSI command with a number.

One thing that's interesting about the `exec` command is that it tends to only work for scripts that are in the same directory as the Web page you're authoring. And, for security reasons, many Web servers won't allow you to place executable scripts in a regular HTML directory. Instead, you'd need to access the `cgi-bin` directory. You can do that using the `virtual` command instead:

```
<!-- #include virtual="/cgi-bin/counter.cgi"
-->
```

The `virtual` command actually works by building its relative URL based on the "virtual server" that it's dealing with—that is, the local domain name and server address. In this example, the virtual command will go to the root of the Web server's drive, locate the `cgi-bin` directory, and execute the script from there.

note

As with any CGI script, this script would need to be executable. On Unix and Windows servers, you'd need to set the appropriate permissions, or the script would need to be an executable application. Again, check with your ISP or administrator if you aren't sure how to set permissions.

Summary

In this chapter you saw some of the add-on products, both freeware and commercial, that you can use to make your Web site more community-focused, more automated, or just a bit more fun. For instance, adding discussion groups is a great way to foster community and participation among your users, which generally means a more active Web site. Likewise, chats are a good way to get together in real-time with your visitors and share information or simply have a good time.

This chapter also discussed the fine art of counting pages, including special counter programs you can add to your site, as well as programs you can download and use on your own computer to analyze your site's log files.

tip

If your Web site uses Apache server software, visit `http://httpd.apache.org/docs/howto/ssi.html` for more on its implementation. You'll notice that you can get even more advanced with SSI, including creating variables and performing some conditional expressions!

Along with CGI and Java-based solutions, this chapter discussed hosted solutions for chat, messages, and counters that are run from the hosting company's server instead of your own. The advantages are that you don't have to set up the programs and configure them to keep them running, while the disadvantage is a certain lack of control. Still, hosting is one way to add high-end applications to your site without too much trouble.

Finally, the chapter ended with a quick look at SSI technology, which lets you include files, CGI results, and other scripted solutions on your page, thanks to server-side processing.

Index

C

C, CGI (common gateway interface) script language, 305

calling CGI (common gateway interface) scripts (URLs), 307

camcorders, DV-compatible, 48

<caption> element, 132-134

captions (hyperlinks, tables, tags), 134

cascading style sheets. See CSS

cascading style sheets 1 (CSS1), font properties, 192

cascading style sheets 2. See CSS2

catalog sites, images, 30

cellpadding attribute, 140, 143

cells in tables, 131-132, 136
 aligning, 135
 blank, 133
 color, 139
 content, formatting, 152
 data, aligning, 137
 fixed widths, 150
 padding, column width, 150
 ranges, 137
 spacing, 143, 150
 spanning, 138

cellspacing attribute, 140, 143

<center> element, 179

centering tables, 142

CGI (common gateway interface)
 Resource Index Web site, 313
 Resource Web site, 315
 scripts
  calling (URLs), 307
  compatibility, 314
  configuring, 314
  creating, 315-316
  example, 305-306
  form data, receiving, 308
  hosted, 314
  HTML (Hypertext Markup Language) forms, 274
  installing, 306, 313-314
  languages, 304-305
  links, 304
  mailto: option, 309-311
  MIME (Multipurpose Internet Mail Extension) format, 306
  output, creating, 311-312
  permissions, 314
  preferences, 314
  referencing, 306
  server-side forums, 320
  storing, 313
  testing, 316
  user interaction, 304
  Web server software, 51
  working with, 313-315
 URLs (uniform resource locators), accessing server-side forums, 325
 Web counters, 331

cgi-bin directory, installing scripts, 313

CGIAdmin.com Web site, 331

characteristics of columns, 159

characters
 newline (/n), 311
 special, 200-201

charts, images (Web pages), 30

ChatBlazer, Java server option, 328

ChatPod, chat service, 328

chatting
 adding, 327-329
 Java servers, 328
 server software, adding chat, 328

check boxes
 creating, 279-281
 Keep Proportions, 106
 standalone values, 281

circle shape, hot zones, 214

cite attribute, 91

classes
 elements
  adding, 184
  defining, 180
 pseudo, 196-197
 <span> element, 185
 special, 183-184

classifieds, images, 30

clear property (block appearance), 194-195

client-pull, 129

Format menu, JPEG/JFIF, 206

Image menu

Crop, 103

Image Information, 112

Resize, 103, 205

#include, 333

Picture menu

Colors, 205

Resolution, 206

Show Information, 112

Size, Scale, 106

Save As Type menu, JPEG-JFIF Compliant, 206

Set menu

Play Animation, 211

Settings, 211

Speed, 211

View menu, Animation, 210

View Source, 333

virtual, 334

comment elements, 63, 147

common gateway interface. See CGI

communication, Web (HTTP), 11

compatibility

browsers

HTML (Hypertext Markup Language) trends/issues, 40

tables, 137

CGI (common gateway interface) scripts, 314

images, file formats, 99

modes (HTML editors), 45

components

ActiveX, 252

email addresses, 124

compression of images, 206

Compression Factor slider (Options dialog box), 206

computer addresses, 10

Conferencing on the Web (Web site), 321

configuring CGI (common gateway interface) scripts, 314

connecting computers (Internet), 10

connections

HTTP (Hypertext Transfer Protocol), security, 281

TCP/IP (Transmission Control Protocol/Internet Protocol), 10

Web servers, 49

consistency, Web page design planning, 38

consoles attribute, 253

containers

elements

<area>, 213

<body> element, 67

caption, 134

<head> element, 64

<map>, 212-213

<table>, 132-133

non-empty elements (HTML or XHTML), 19

content

attribute, 129

cells, formatting, 152

control buttons, creating, 279

controller attribute, 248

controls attribute, 253

coordinates, hot zones, 212

coords attribute, 213

copying images, 99

copyrights

comment elements, 63

images, 99

Web pages, adding, 67

counters

hit, 52

Web counters, adding, 331-332

creating

forums, 322-323, 327

hot zones, 213

hyperlinks, 121

Crop

command (Image menu), 103

tool, 102

cropping images

GraphicConverter, 105

Paint Shop Pro, 102

CSE HTML Validator Lite, validating Web pages, 73

CSS (cascading style sheets)

alignment properties, 193-196

background properties, 192-193

block appearance properties, 193-196

browsers, 178

color properties, 192-193

:first-letter pseudo class, 197

:first-line pseudo class, 197

How can we make this index more useful? Email us at indexes@quepublishing.com

Media. *See* **Windows Media**

menus

creating, 285-287

displaying (HTML forms), 285

options, grouping or selecting (HTML forms), 286

messages, email (encoded), 310

<meta> element, 66-67, 129

meta elements, attributes, 66

metadata, adding, 66

metafiles (Windows Media), 252

methods

attribute, 275

get or post, receiving form data (CGI scripts), 308

reduction (color), 205

<span> element, 184

Microsoft Windows. *See* **Windows**

MIME (Multipurpose Internet Mail Extension) formats (CGI scripts), 306

modes

backward-compatibility, browsers, 62

compatibility, HTML (Hypertext Markup Language) editors, 45

modifying

frames, 221

image size, 112

Web pages (site-wide style sheets), 258-259

Movie Maker (Windows), 48

movies

accessibility, embedded multimedia, 246

encoding, Windows Media Encoder, 252

Hinted QuickTime movies, 250

poster movies, 248

QuickTime movies, embedding, 242

Windows Media movies, <embed> parameters, 251

moving text, 104

MP3

documents, linking, 243

multimedia file format, 239

MSN Communities, hosted forum solution, 327

MSN Messenger, chat, 327

Multicity, chat service, 328

multimedia

adding, 243-254

documents 244-245

downloading, 239

embedding, 241-249

file formats, 239-241

Gopher sites, 127

hyperlinks, 121

linking, 241-243

plug-ins, 241

time-based data, 238

tools, 47

viewing, 30

Web pages, organizing, 28-31

Multipurpose Internet Mail Extension (MIME) formats (CGI scripts), 306

N

/n (newline character), 311

Name entry box, 107

named anchors, referencing, 122

names

accounts, 124

attribute, 121, 227, 246, 276-279

domain, 50-51, 124

family names, fonts, 191

filenames

images, 105, 108

Web server space, 52

machine, 124

values, radio buttons, 282

Web pages, adding, 67

namespaces (XML), 61

naming

documents, Web document organization, 55-56

frames, 227-228

images (GraphicConverter), 106

Web pages, 65

navigating

HTML (Hypertext Markup Language) forms, 289

Web sites, 31

navigation toolbar, inserting tables, 148

Nearest Color (reduction method), 205

nesting

frames, 229

hyperlinks, 121

lists, 93

tables, 149-154

How can we make this index more useful? Email us at indexes@quepublishing.com

How can we make this index more useful? Email us at indexes@quepublishing.com

X-Y-Z